World Wide Web

J O U R N A L

The Web After Five Years

THE WORLD WIDE WEB JOURNAL   *Volume 1, Issue 3, Summer 1996*

SUBSCRIPTION PRICES (subject to change without notice)

Price	Country
USA	$75.00
Canada & Mexico	$81.00
Europe, Africa, Central & South America	$105.00
Asia, Australia, & New Zealand	$110.00

Shipping is included in subscription prices, and is via US Postal Service Second Class in the USA, and Air Mail to all foreign addresses

Single copies of the World Wide Web Journal are available to North American customers from O'Reilly & Associates, Inc., or from your local bookseller. Customers outside the U.S. and Canada, please inquire at your local bookseller or contact one of our Overseas Distributors listed at the back of this journal.

Payment may be made by check or credit card. Checks should be made out to O'Reilly & Associates, Inc., and must be in U.S. dollars, drawn on a U.S. bank. Foreign customers may call to arrange payment by wire.

CORRESPONDENCE

Address subscription orders, changes of address, and business correspondence to:

The World Wide Web Journal
O'Reilly & Associates, Inc.
103 Morris Street, Suite A
Sebastopol, CA 95472
800-998-9938 USA/Canada * 707-829-0515 Overseas or Local * 707-829-0104 FAX

For online information about submitting articles see *http://www.w3.org/pub/WWW/Journal/cfp*.
Letters, technical correspondence, and submissions should be addressed to:

The World Wide Web Journal
Rohit Khare, Editor
World Wide Web Consortium
MIT Laboratory of Computer Science
545 Technology Square
Cambridge, MA 02139
email: *khare@w3.org*

The World Wide Web Journal (ISSN 1085-2301) is published quarterly by O'Reilly & Associates, Inc. Second-class mail permit is pending. POSTMASTER: Send address changes to O'Reilly & Associates, Inc. 103A Morris Street, Sebastopol, CA 95472

Printed on
Recycled
Paper

World Wide Web

J O U R N A L

The Web After Five Years

O'REILLY™

WORLD WIDE WEB JOURNAL
THE WEB AFTER FIVE YEARS   Volume 1, Issue 3, Summer 1996

Editor: Rohit Khare

Special Section Editor: Roger Hurwitz

Managing Editor: Donna Woonteiler

News Editors: D.C. Denison, Kirstin Alexander

Production Editor: Nancy Crumpton

Technical Illustrators: Chris Reilley, Michelle Willey

Software Tools Specialist: Mike Sierra

Freelance Coordinator: Clairemarie Fisher O'Leary

Cover Design: Hanna Dyer

Text Design: Nancy Priest, Marcia Ciro

 This book is printed on acid-free paper with 85% recycled content, 15% post-consumer waste. O'Reilly & Associates is committed to using paper with the highest recycled content available consistent with high quality.

ISSN: 1085-2301

ISBN: 1-56592-210-7   7/1/96

W3C Administration

Albert Vezza
  W3C Chairman and Associate
  Director of the MIT Laboratory
  for Computer Science
  av@w3.org

Jean-François Abramatic
  Director for Development
  of INRIA
  jfa@w3.org

Tim Berners-Lee
  Director of the W3C
  timbl@w3.org

Vincent Quint
  Deputy Director for Europe
  Vincent.Quint@w3.org

User Interface

Vincent Quint
  Area Coordinator
  Vincent.Quint@w3.org

Bert Bos
  bert@w3.org

Thilo Horstmann
  horstmann@w3.org

Jose Kahan
  Jose.Kahan@w3.org

Yves Lafon
  lafon@w3.org

Hakon Lie
  howcome@w3.org

Chris Lilley
  chris@w3.org

Dave Raggett
  dsr@w3.org

Irene Vatton
  Irene.Vatton@w3.org

Daniel Veillard
  Daniel.Veillard@w3.org

Technology and Society

Jim Miller
  Area Coordinator
  jmiller@w3.org

Rohit Khare
  khare@w3.org

Architecture

Dan Connolly
  Area Coordinator
  connolly@w3.org

Anselm Baird-Smith
  abaird@w3.org

Jim Gettys
  jg@w3.org

Philipp Hoschka
  Philipp.Hoschka@w3.org

Henrik Frystyk Nielsen
  frystyk@w3.org

Cross Areas and Technical Support

Stephane Boyera
  Stephane.Boyera@w3.org

Tom Greene
  tjg@w3.org

Sally Khudairi
  khudairi@w3.org

Yves Peynaud
  Yves.Peynaud@inria.fr

Arthur Secret
  secret@w3.org

Jay Sekora
  js@w3.org

Administrative Support

Beth Curran
  beth@w3.org

Susan Hardy
  susan@w3.org

Josiane Roberts
  Josiane.Roberts@inria.fr

ALCATEL NV

AT&T

Adobe Systems Incorporated

Apple Computer, Inc.

Airospatiale

AGF Group

Alis Technologies, Inc

America Online

American International Group Data Center, Inc. (AIG)

American Internet Corporation

Architecture Projects Management Ltd.

Belgacom

Bellcore

Bitstream, Inc.

British Telecommunications Laboratories

Bull S.A.

Centre National de la Recherche Scientifique (CNRS/UREC)

CEA (Commissariat ` l'Energie Atomique)

CMG Information Systems

CWI (Centre for Mathematics and Computer Science)

CIRAD

Cap Gemini Sogeti

Compuserve Computer Answer Line Consiglio Nazionale delle Richerche

CyberCash

Cygnus Support

Dassault Aviation

Data Research Associates, Inc.

Delphi Internet

Deutsche Telekom

Digital Equipment Corporation

EEIG/ERCIM (European Research Consortium for Informatics and Mathematics)

ENEL

ENSIMAG

ETNOTEAM

Eastman Kodak Company

Electriciti de France

Electronic Book Technologies

Enterprise Integration Technologies Ericcson Telecom

FORTH (Foundation for Research and Technology - Hellas) / ICS (Institute of Computer Science)

FTP Software, Inc.

First Floor, Inc.

First Virtual Holding

Folio Corporation

France Telecom

Fujitsu Ltd.

GC Tech S.A.

GMD

GRIF, S.A.

General Magic, Inc.

Groupe ESC Grenoble

Grenoble Network Initiative

HAVAS

Harlequin Incorporated

Hewlett Packard

Hitachi, Ltd.

Hummingbird Communications Ltd.

IBM

ILOG, S.A.

INRETS

Iberdrola

Incontext Corporation

Industrial Technology Research Institute

Infopartners S.A.

Institut Franco-Russe A.M. Liapunov d'informatique et de mathematiques appliques

Internet Profiles Corporation

Joint Information Systems Committee

Justsystem Corporation

Kumamoto Institute of Computer Software, Inc.

Los Alamos National Laboratory

Lotus Development Corporation

Metrowerks Corporation

MCI Telecommunications

The MITRE Corporation

Matra Hachette

Michelin

Microsoft Corporation

Mitsubishi Electric Corporation

MTA SZTAKI

NCSA / Univ. of Illinois

NEC Corporation

NTT Data Communications

NYNEX Science & Technology

National HPCC Software Exchange

The NetMarket Company

Netscape Communications Corp.

Network Computing Devices

NeXT Computer Inc.

Nippon Telegraph and Telephone Corporation (NTT)

Nokia

Novell, Inc.

O2 Technology

Object Management Group, Inc. (OMG)

Omron Corporation

Open Market

Open Software Foundation Research Institute

Oracle Corporation

O'Reilly & Associates, Inc.

PIPEX Public IP Exchange Ltd

Pacifitech Corporation

PointCast Incorporated

Process Software Corp.

Prodigy Services Company

Reed-Elsevier

R.I.S. Technologies

The Royal Hong Kong Jockey Club

Council for the Central Laboratory of the Research Councils (Rutherford Appleton Laboratory)

SICS (Swedish Institute of Computer Science)

SISU (Swedish Institute for Systems Development)

STET

SURFnet bv

Sema Group

Siemens Nixdorf

Silicon Graphics, Inc.

Sligos

Softquad

Software 2000

Sony Corporation

Spry, Inc.

Spyglass Inc.

Sun Microsystems

Tandem Computers Inc.

Teknema, Inc.

Telequip Corporation

Terisa Systems

Thomson-CSF

UKERNA (United Kingdom Research and Education Networking Association)

U.S. Web Corporation

Verity Inc.

Vermeer Technologies

VTT Information Technology

WWW - KR

Wolfram Research, Inc.

The Wollongong Group

C O N T E N T S

*This issue's cover
image Copyright ©
1995 PhotoDisc, Inc.*

C O N T E N T S

C O N T E N T S

EDITORIAL

WELCOME TO THE "NEW" *WORLD Wide Web Journal*—this issue inaugurates an expanded structure that will be the foundation of issues to come. As the incoming Editor, I am committed to making the *World Wide Web Journal* an effective forum for researchers, developers, and policymakers interested in working with the W3C and the wider Web community.

About Our Editorial Structure

There are three parts to the *Web Journal*: news and features from W3C and the Web community, technical reports and proposals forwarded by the W3C Director, and novel, independently refereed papers and correspondence from academic and industrial Web researchers.

In the first section, you'll find profiles of W3C's people and projects as well as feature interviews and/or round-table discussions with prominent Web figures. In addition, the *Timeline* provides a comprehensive, chronological record of the myriad W3C activities: products, meetings, workshops, press releases, conferences, and more.

The second section, *W3C Reports*, is the official technical record of the W3C. Each submission is approved by the Director, Tim Berners-Lee, and bears the "W3C" logo. These will primarily be Working Drafts, recommendations, and documents from W3C workshops and related venues.

The third section, *Technical Papers*, is a refereed forum for contributors from the wider Web community. Each selected paper will bear a "W3J" logo to reflect this status, in addition to any conference logo. We have very high hopes for this section, and it will be launched carefully. Through Issue 3, technical papers have been refereed by program committees of Web conferences and workshops. We are currently in the process of establishing an independent Editorial Board and referee system to solicit and select papers across the gamut of Web-related research. This structure will be in place for the Fall 1996 issue.

At first blush it may seem paradoxical to posit a paper journal about the Web. If the medium is truly the message, are we saying that physical publication maintains a certain primacy over electronic communication? Well, print is a finite medium, in time, space, and scope. A print journal can only capture the ideas in the air at a single instant, from only a few authors, on only a few topics. The limits of print "subvert" the traditional virtues of electronic publishing—immediacy, expansiveness, casual access, customization—in order to provide a shared experience for our readers and a solid foundation for our community.

Of course, as part of our commitment to making the Journal an interactive forum, the complete contents of each issue will be available at W3C's Web site 90 days after print publication.

The Web After Five Years

Has it really been more than five years since HTTP and HTML were invented? On one hand, we're still striving to recapture the interactivity and intimacy of Tim Berners-Lee's original Web vision. Measured in Web-years, though, we're entering wholly uncharted territory as the Web and the Internet explode into a mass, commercial medium. This issue tries to look forward by examining both aspects of the Web: intercreativity by small groups as well as the technical, economic, and ethical challenges of tracking and measuring mass Web usage.

As a computer scientist and economist, I have been fascinated by the coming information economy revolution. Ideas some have seen as long-range possibilities, such as advertiser-supported Internet services, microtransactions, and so on, became very real business plans by the second half of 1995. The vibrant growth of Web-based advertising prompted the W3C to track the Demographics area late that year.

Simultaneously, we began learning about different cultural attitudes and regulatory policies regarding privacy and the protection of demographic data around the world. W3C's Technology and Society Group is interested not only in what's "on the wire" (i.e., Web protocols and tools), but how these technologies intersect with moral and legislative issues. Our goal is to develop the mechanisms that will allow consumers and regulators to set their own policies.

To investigate further, we joined forces with several other academic departments at MIT and organized the *Workshop on Internet Survey Methodology and Web Demographics*, held in January, 1996. Selected research reports presented at that workshop are published in this issue, along with commerce- and measurement-related papers from the *Fifth International World Wide Web Conference*, held in May, 1996, in Paris.

Welcome to Your Web Journal

This is a fledgling publication, but it is your publication. I look forward to working with you to help "reach the full potential of the *Web Journal*." We need your contributions to keep the Journal lively—send us your letters, technical correspondence, and submissions. Please feel free to contact me and visit our Web pages at *http://www.w3.org/pub/WWW/ Journal.*

Finally, my sincere thanks go to Donna Woonteiler and the entire O'Reilly & Associates staff, and to Roger Hurwitz of the MIT Artificial Intelligence Lab. The volume in your hands is truly a testament to their commitment and vision. ■

Rohit Khare
khare@w3.org
June 1996, Cambridge, Massachusetts

INTERVIEW
TIM BERNERS-LEE
On Simplicity, Standards, and "Intercreativity"

There's not much white space left on the white board in Tim Berners-Lee's office. Berners-Lee, the creator of the World Wide Web and the director of W3C, has spent most of the previous afternoon fine-tuning Consortium priorities. Yet when Rohit Khare and D.C. Denison arrive for a morning interview, it's not entirely clear from the tangle of arrows and circles what areas have won out: HTML development or security; content labeling or demographics. So the conversation naturally begins with the topic on the wall: priorities.

Q: *How do you go about setting priorities for the W3C?*

A: With great difficulty. We do a certain amount of putting out fires and a certain amount of growing—nursing little trees. We've found that different technical areas, different political and social areas—each one has to be treated on its merits, because the timing con-

straints and existing situation tend to be different. In the final analysis, we are guided by our own perceptions of where we're going, and by feedback from the advisory committee. We put a lot of conflicts in front of the members. After all, our members do represent those people who are seriously interested and involved in the growth of the Web. They are the people best positioned to help us answer those questions.

Q: *The Consortium's content-labeling project, PICS, has recently been at the top of W3C's agenda. Why?*

A: The famous *Time* magazine "cyberporn" cover story (July 3, 1995). That topic was already on the back burner for us, because one of our members had flagged it as an area that we should start thinking about. So we had already started looking into it. Which was fortunate, because suddenly there was great public awareness of that issue.

Q: *And even though the* Time *story was quickly discredited, W3C had to get involved?*

A: Yes. Because when the article broke, not only did justice have to be done, it had to appear to be done. So we gave it an extremely high priority. Sometimes things get thrown into the limelight. There are always fancy new features going into HTML. But of course we also get involved with issues that we think are important, where there is no public pressure.

Q: *What's an example of that kind of issue?*

A: Internationalization is one. The pressure for that in the United States is not so strong, but we feel it's important for the world that internationalization should be solved, so we have to put some effort in ourselves. Also things like architectural changes which will relieve the pressure on the Internet. No one person seems to have an incentive to do it, so in that case we have to put in the push ourselves.

Q: *It's interesting that during the last five years, some issues have gone up and down in priority. Security, for example.*

A: Security has gone down a bit. That was a very big issue when the Consortium was first formed. That's what the press was talking about at the time. Now people have realized two things: 1) They've got some basic security for their credit cards, and 2) There are a lot of pieces to the security system, and there's going to be a lot of development over the next few years. The whole world will not change its way of working in the next two months. So the press fever has died down. That doesn't mean that the amount of work to be done has died down.

Q: *Let's go back five years to the summer of 1991. You've just released the "WWW Program" on the Internet. Who are the first people to use it?*

A: There were three groups. I tried to spread it through the high-energy physics community, because that's what I needed to justify my spending time on it, of course; it spread through the hypertext community, because I put it on the *alt.hypertext* newsgroup; and it spread through the NeXT community, because those were the people who could actually run the software.

Q: *What did people use it for?*

A: I've always known that the route to adoption of technology can take very strange directions—in order to get from A to B, you have to find a downhill path, where each step is downhill for whoever is going to take it. The path can wander around a lot, and it did wander around a lot. Of course there was the initial problem of bootstrapping the snowballing of clients (if you can bootstrap a snowball). We did that by making the first server a regular file server, but the second server was a server for the CERN phone book, which was a gateway into the relational database. That's probably interesting to the people who are saying that the new wave of servers will be gateways into relational databases. Anyway the phone book was a crucial problem that needed solving, so the Web justified its existence by solving that crucial problem. It allowed information which was only on the mainframe to be accessed from other platforms. But it left a lot of community people at CERN thinking that the World Wide Web was a rather strange phone book program.

> *"That was a surprise to me—that people were prepared to painstakingly write HTML."*

Q: *Any surprises at the way people started using the Web?*

A: I was surprised that people were prepared to write HTML. In my initial requirements for this thing, I had assumed, as an absolute precondition, that nobody would have to do HTML or deal with URLs. If you use the original World Wide Web program, you never see a URL or have to deal with HTML. You're presented with the raw information. You then input more information. So you are linking information to information—like using a word processor. That was a surprise to me—that people were prepared to painstakingly write HTML.

Q: *If people didn't have to write HTML, the Web would be different, wouldn't it?*

A: Yes. There'd be more gray material, more material on the fringes of publicizable material. Whereas at the moment, it's still a lot of trouble to publish something. It's not just a

question of hitting the *save* button. Because of that threshold, the only information that's published on the Web is information that's of sufficient value to a large number of people. So World Wide Web sites have tended to be corporate sites, corporations talking to consumers, rather than groups wondering what they're going to have for lunch.

Q: *So, the bi-directionality is missing, because people are writing HTML.*

A: Yes. Writing HTML is like a programming task; it is not a way of expressing your reaction to something you've just read. The result, from the process point of view, is that it's remarkably similar to the paper publishing process, with a great big sequence—from the idea, to the writer, to the code, to the publisher—going through the bottleneck of the person who runs the server.

The original idea, however, was that it should be totally bottleneck-free, something between people and information.

Q: *Five years into the development of the Web, are you worried about the so-called second system effect?*

A: The second system effect, if I remember it correctly, is that when you design the second system, you fix all the problems of the first and fall into all the problems that the first system avoided. So yes, we are in a position to have the second system effect; for example, we are in a position to make something that is inherently more complex, that has no clean architecture. That's a danger. If we produce something that's too complex, for which there are no simple, underlying rules, then we will be in a mess. I believe W3C has a mandate to keep an eye on architectural integrity and simplicity.

Q: *Are you frustrated at the pace that the Web proceeds?*

A: Not really. People are generally amazed by the way the Web has spread, not by how long it took to get here. Most people only got on board in 1992–93.

Q: *90 percent of the people who currently use the Web have only been using it a year or so.*

A: Right, so to them it's a 12-month phenomenon. People are not worried that it's taking a long time. During the last five and half years there are a lot of things that have not changed, and that's okay. From the invention of the steam locomotive to the very latest automobiles, wheels are still around, there are still four in most cases. It is not that we expect that rockets will have won out, or that now we should be moving onto twenty wheels. So it's quite reasonable that there are databases, and hypertext use of databases, and maybe we shouldn't feel that we need to go beyond that as we spread into a larger community.

Q: *From the start of the Web, you've been promoting interactivity as the ideal. Do you feel that we're any closer to that? If not, what's it going to take to make the Web more interactive, more collaborative?*

A: The word "interactive" is terrible in a way, because people mean different things by it. To really be able to work at a distance, to use a knowledge space, you need all of it. So when some people say "interactive," they mean taking real-time audio and video and integrating it with the Web so you can create a meeting document and talk to people in it. Another form of interactivity is to be able to make a comment on somebody's paper, to put a yellow sticky on it and say, "This is really important," with a link to why it is. Yet the real-time video problems and the annotation problems are totally different, and they're both big problems.

Q: *How do you sort them out?*

A: Well, I've recently started using the term "intercreativity" instead of interactivity. By this I mean something like building things together, which is more than filling out a form and hitting "submit." Imagine, for example, a heap of objects—a compass, a magnet, and some iron filings. You come across them in a 3D virtual world, and you can use them to learn something about magnetic fields. Suppose you can take these magnets and their properties to another virtual world and with them create a little tower of magnets and discuss it with your friends. Suppose you can build with other people within the virtual space. That will be much more satisfying and more productive than any of the current forms of interactivity. Yet that sort of thing will also need a lot of engineering; you will have to roll in a lot of things.

Q: *So how would you define "intercreativity" succinctly?*

A: Building together, being creative together.

Q: *Are we getting any closer to that ideal?*

A: As usual, interface technologies are always further ahead on the viewing than on the creation. Intercreativity happens when you are able to build, make something, express yourself while you are in the same mode as when you are reading, absorbing, surfing. In other words there's no difference. When you have something that you need to express, the threshold is so low that you can move it out into the communal space.

Q: *There's a democratic ideal in there, isn't there?*

A: Yes. I believe in democracy, in people governing themselves. My belief is that for society to work, every individual has to be involved on a number of different scales. Each individual has to look after themselves, typically their family, their work group, their town, their county—there are a number of different groups. Sometimes these nest, which tends to make life easier, sometimes they're disparate, clashing. Also every individual has to have a lookout for the planet. People need a balance so society can work out. I believe this is programmed into people, that people feel fundamentally uncomfortable unless they have a balance. The Web has to be sufficiently flexible for that, so this variety of interconnectivity can happen. That's why a Web that's specifically aimed at the inter-corporate or the intra-corporate or family use is not going to work. You have to have a Web which allows the family photograph album to link up to the group picnic to link to the corporate home

page if necessary. The hive is only one scale—a large one.

Q: *How about the Web as a cultural phenomenon? How does that strike you, to drive down the highway and see URLs on billboards?*

A: That's very difficult. For a lot of people the URLs appearing on buildings has suddenly happened. They've heard about the Web one moment on CNN, and then suddenly it seems to be everywhere. But the Web started off as a hard push for the first couple of years, and it slowly gathered momentum. For me there's been no one point where suddenly the Web seemed to explode, where I sat back and thought "Wow, how amazing!" Although every now and then something has struck me as being kind of strange.

Q: *But none of them have been milestones?*

A: None of them have been a milestone. You see your first URL on a building; your first URL on television; your first URL on a t-shirt, on a bar of soap. We had a pair of boxer shorts in the office with URLs. But I didn't regard them as a milestone. Actually, I'll tell you one milestone: when Frans van Hoesel put up the hypertext of the Vatican Renaissance exhibit that the Library of Congress was hosting. At that point he took some really good, high-quality material and used hypertext to produce a beautiful way of browsing around it. That showed a whole lot of people that you could put really gripping quality onto the Web. That was a milestone. The Xerox PARC map project was another early milestone. It was crude, but it demonstrated to people that URLs didn't have to be just a file name; hyperspace was infinite in as many dimensions as you choose to pick.

Q: *How about the first baby pictures on the Web, or the lists of music CDs, or the confessional aspects of the Web. Surely you didn't see that coming?*

A: No, but in all the initial talks we gave about the Web, we explained that you would have your own private Web, and that still hasn't come yet.

Q: *The idea of the "home page" evolved in a different direction.*

A: Yes. With all respect, the personal home page is not a private expression; it's a public billboard that people work on to say what they're interested in. That's not as interesting to me as people using it in their private lives. It's exhibitionism, if you like. Or self-expression. It's openness, and it's great in a way, it's people letting the community into their homes. But it's not really their home. They may call it a home page, but it's more like the gnome in somebody's front yard than the home itself. People don't have the tools for using the Web for their homes, or for organizing their private lives; they don't really put their scrapbooks on the Web. They don't have family Webs. There are many distributed families nowadays, especially in the high-tech fields, so it would be quite reasonable to do that, yet I don't know of any. One reason is that most people don't have the ability to publish with restricted access.

Q: *You've said that the traditional browsers will eventually go away—*

A: What I said was that this idea of a *separate* browser should go away, the entire user interface should be integrated. Clearly some of the browser companies worried that I was suggesting the browser *companies* would go away—that wasn't at all the suggestion. But the desktop metaphor and the browser metaphor have got to become one. Whether the browser software swallows the desktop software, or the desktop software swallows the browser software—that's up to the marketplace to decide. But there's no reason why both sides shouldn't have a shot at it. When you turn on your computer what you should see is information, what you should deal with is information. You should be able to create it, to absorb it; you should be able to exchange it freely in the informational space. The computer should just be your portal into the space, in my view.

Q: *Do you see a difference between information and knowledge?*

A: If we're looking at the engineering of an organization, we're talking about knowledge: the value of the organization, the knowledge of the people in it. You need to take that knowledge and share it, you need to make the organization be able to think. That means you have to make that knowledge exist, rather than having the individual knowledge of individual people. So, yes, I make the distinction between information and knowledge when I discuss this in regard to companies.

Q: *So far technology talks about information.*

A: Technology moves information around in order to share knowledge. In the abstract space, one sees information as a representation of the knowledge of the organization.

Q: *What kind of developments do you see five years down the road? Do you think the Web will still be around in recognizable form?*

A: If we stick to its definition as universal information, we know the Web will still be there, by definition. But the question of what sort of information will be out there, and how people will be using it—I think could change very dramatically.

Q: *In what way?*

A: When people are able to interact with the Web, you'll see it change the way very rapidly. For example, Java and downloadable code will make it possible to dramatically decrease the time costs for changing what software you have on your machine. One of the analogies I sometimes draw is that before the Internet it would take a few days to get software. You'd have to have it shipped, you'd probably get a tape and you'd ask the systems manager to put it on the minicomputer for you. With the Internet, you only had to spend the afternoon, the tape had been replaced with an FTP transfer, but you were still left with the installation. With the Web all you have to do is browse around and click. If you have a browser you can install another browser in about three clicks. That's a fairly short time cost for the market to be able to change. When you have agents on your machine, then the time cost

will be even smaller because the agents will download the software onto your machine to prepare for your next day without you having to do anything. When that happens we're going to see technological revolutions happen extremely rapidly.

Q: *That's a little scary. An Internet year is short enough.*

A: What is a Web year now, about three months? And when people can browse around, discover new things, and download them fast, when we all have agents—then

---

"If you have a browser you can install another browser in about three clicks. That's a fairly short time..."

Web years could slip by before human beings can notice.

Q: *These racing Web years could take a physical toll on those of us who work on the Web.*

True. But the plus point is that we will be able to live for three or four hundred Web years, which will be very exciting.

Q: *You often speak of the need for the Web to be open, free from exploitation by one dominant commercial player. How can we keep the Web interoperable with such rapid growth?*

A: It's always going to be hard. As long as there's the Web and it's this exciting, there's going to be innovation. When there's innovation, there's competition; there will always be competition for markets. But so long as there is more that you can do building on top of the Web than you can by meddling with what's inside, it will be a win-win situation for companies getting together to agree that when they can both do something, they should do it

---

> *"There have been programs like PICS which have gone from zero to basically global acceptance in a very short period of time."*

---

in the same way. There is a danger of fragmentation, but there is also a tremendous incentive for companies to make sure that the Web does not fragment. There is always an incentive for one company to try to move standards, to change standards and leave other companies inoperable, but there's a tremendous incentive for the community as a whole to prevent that.

Q: *Do you often feel as if W3C is behind the train laying down track?*

A: In some cases, it looks like that, because necessarily with HTML if a company comes out with a way of making text diagonal, you can bet they'll generate a lot of press coverage out of it, in order to gain market share. Then within the next two weeks another company finds it's no big deal to make sloping text, and they come out with sloping text. For a while there will be sloping and diagonal text. That

may last for a few weeks but then there is no interest from the marketing point of view in competing on whether sloping or diagonal is a more impressive way of describing text. There is a serious technical reason for having just one tag. There are serious motivations for sitting around a table to decide, "Okay, let's work on a single standard here. In other cases, such as PICS, we're way ahead of the train."

Q: *So you're feeling more confident that W3C can counter this raging marketplace and keep the Web open?*

A: I think a lot of the progress we've made has given us a lot of confidence in the model that we have. I think we will always be worried about the future. The day we aren't, we'll pack up shop. It will never be clear, never obvious; you will never take it for granted. Yet we've made a lot of progress. There have been programs like PICS which have gone from zero to basically global acceptance in a very short period of time. The fact that HTML converges at each stage even though there's a lot of froth on the top of the wave—that's been very satisfying for the community. The froth is divergent, but the body tends to be convergent. But nobody can ever take this process for granted. The future will always be difficult to predict. We will always have to be extremely flexible in how we deal with new events, and the ways in which we try to bring our own agenda—architectural cleanliness for the long term—into the marketplace. ■

WORK IN PROGRESS
People & Projects at W3C

JIM MILLER
PROMOTING THE PICS FIX

His days start with early morning breakfast meetings. He fields more than a hundred email messages a day, plus a fistful of phone messages. And when he's not touring around Europe promoting his latest project, he's in Washington, D.C., doing the same.

Jim Miller is in high demand.

A W3C research scientist, Miller is one of the core players in the development of PICS, the Platform for Internet Content Selection. Today he's working to further its success, gaining the support of the Internet community, as well as private companies, to adopt the PICS rating system.

PICS offers a bright alternative to government regulation: an independent rating system that allows people with different concerns and tolerance levels to set their own standards. By including "labels" in Internet documents, authors and even private companies (or "labeling bureaus") can "rate" a Web page or site depending on the content. Labeling filters then do the rest of the work for the reader.

In an ironic twist, Miller says PICS actually came about because of the Communications Decency Act originally passed by the U.S. Senate last year. "The Communications Decency Act itself is a legislative response to an important issue," he says. "Basically, there was no reasonable means of regulating the Internet short of censorship. At the time, it may have been the best that could have been done.

"I think PICS is a better approach, but it wasn't available at the time. It's fair to say the legislature caused PICS to be developed." The original idea blossomed in August and was officially released early this year. Now, he says, "We have the technology."

The technology was almost the easy part. Now comes the time for promoting PICS, getting other countries involved in using the system, and enticing private for-profit companies to become "labeling bureaus" on a non-profit basis. This spring, Miller spent two weeks touring Europe to introduce the press, government officials, and industry leaders to PICS.

"It's still going to take a little bit of time. All major providers will have support for it by the end of the year. Our hope is that by the end of the year there will also be bureaus available for people to do third-party rating," says Miller. "There's more and more support coming for the system in Europe and elsewhere."

The PICS system is especially well adapted for global use, where countries with different concerns can use it to filter material. A country like Germany even has conflicting standards within its borders, as some states are more tightly controlled than others.

"Each of the countries has a different set of issues they're worried about . . . and a different relationship with the government." While the U.K. is concerned mainly about the advocacy of violence on the Net, countries like France and Germany are worried about neo-Nazi literature online. Not only is this material

offensive to most residents—it's also illegal to distribute.

You might think someone this involved with computers and technology has been programming software since birth. But Miller actually received his first degree from MIT in what he calls "metallurgy"—materials science and engineering. While still a student, he worked part-time at Bolt, Beranek, and Newman. "I knew I wanted to be in computer science. I was working at a computer science company while I was in college, but I didn't think a computer science degree would be the best route."

After getting his master's in engineering management in Alaska, he returned to MIT in 1981 to work in the Artificial Intelligence Lab. "I actually went there on the condition that I not be a graduate student." However, he enjoyed teaching so much while he was there, he decided to complete the credentials required to teach college and received his Ph.D. in 1986. He then spent several years apiece teaching at Brandeis University and working at Digital Equipment and the Software Research Institute. Just one year ago, he returned to MIT once again—this time to head up the "Technology and Society" project.

"My interest has always been to make the computer a useful tool. I try to design systems that are easy to use and fulfill a useful need," says Miller. This often requires maintaining a delicate balance between those on the creative, conceptual side and those on the technical end who must actually put the idea into practice.

"It's a listening role," he says. "I work with people who are primarily interested in what the user will see—and those primarily interested in how hard it is to program. I absorb the input from both sides and I make the decision. If there's an argument, it comes back to me."

Besides playing the middleman at work, Miller also has some not-so-hidden talents. He speaks French fluently (something that came in handy on his last visit to Paris during a surprise presentation in French). He plays classical flute and sings opera around the house with Barbara, his wife of 17 years. And if you happen to be at Sanders Theatre in Cambridge next Christmas, be sure to catch him singing and dancing with the Revels (he's a tenor).

Miller's already got several new projects on his plate. He recently attended a meeting in Washington, D.C., on the Joint Electronic Payments Initiative (JEPI) to develop a protocol for payment recognition. "That's the stuff that happens after you shop and before you purchase. We're working on a protocol that lets you do that on the Web." He's also working on the "Digital Signature Initiative," which will embed code within documents to verify their source (such as a signature on the bottom of a page, or for public documents), giving the reader confidence in their authenticity. And next semester, he hopes to return to teaching "Structure and Interpretation of Computer Programs" at MIT, a course he helped develop.

Beyond that Miller expects to continue doing exactly what he's doing now, working on W3C projects from a variety of angles, adding to his collection of adapter cables for his portable computer—one set for each country.

"I'd like to continue doing these types of projects," he says. "It draws on both technical and people skills. I just love it."

– Kimberly Amaral

DAVE RAGGETT
THE WORKING DRAFT

This document describes the career of Dr. David Raggett, who has shown an uncanny ability to be there at the beginning of crucial Internet developments, including the World Wide Web, HTML, and virtual reality. Regularly employed by Hewlett Packard Labs in Bristol, England, he has been a Visiting Scientist with the W3C in Cambridge, Massachusetts, since May 1995. He lives nearby with his wife and two children. Other functions include his position as co-chair of the IETF working group for HTTP, which he set up in December 1994. His current projects cover authentication and micropayments, HTML style sheets, Java, and fonts. He is referred to as "the father of HTML" by VRML innovator Mark Pesce.

Introduction

Dave Raggett, 40, has been a major player on the World Wide Web development scene since its earliest days. Hypertext and the Web seem a natural form of expression for the tall, slender Briton, whose thought patterns and ideas move quickly, as complex and interlinked as the Web itself. Although he has not received the media attention accorded others involved with the inception of the Web, Dave Raggett doesn't seem to mind. He's too busy working on what's next.

Associations

With a degree in physics and a doctorate in astrophysics from the University of Oxford, Raggett has been immersed in hypertext development since the late 1980s. He started with a project at Hewlett Packard Labs in Bristol, England, that combined hypertext and expert systems to allow salespeople to easily put together quotes for workstations, including pictures of custom configurations. Since then, he has pursued his ideas on the distributed maintenance of such a knowledge system, working with individuals and companies from around the world to bring the World Wide Web to fruition.

A Walk Through Raggett's Involvement with the Web

Raggett has been heavily involved in developing standards for the Web, including authoring HTML+, HTML 3.0, HTML 3.2, and 3.5 specifications. These specifications gave browser authors common feature sets to support, helping to move the Web into the big time. "I get a kick out of seeing URLs everywhere," he admits when asked about his reaction to the increasing growth and ubiquity of the Web.

Currently a visiting scientist with the World Wide Web Consortium (W3C), Raggett is pushing the boundaries of the Web even

more. Easy-going, friendly, and with credentials of gold, Raggett is a natural choice to be a W3C facilitator. The job entails working with leaders in academia and industry to help design and define the future of the World Wide Web. Through these negotiations, Raggett aspires to develop HTML to the point where it is a competent format for publishing on the Web as well as printing on paper, for a wide range of applications.

Previous Work

Raggett's involvement with the Web began humbly enough. In 1991, Raggett sent off a proposal to the *alt.hypertext* newsgroup in which he suggested a new "skunkworks" project—engineering slang for an underground and underfunded, but often highly efficient, "just get the job done" kind of project. The goal was to invent a simple global hypertext system analogous to Microsoft Windows Help, but one that worked across the Internet. Previous systems had required a degree of compilation; unhappy with this, he wanted something that was directly interpreted. Some of the responses to his proposal mentioned work that Tim Berners-Lee was doing at CERN, including a simplified form of SGML. Through the rest of 1991 and 1992, Raggett teamed up with Berners-Lee and other members of the www-talk mailing list on developing the Web's formative technologies, including X-based browsers, as well as refining Berners-Lee's simple original version of HTTP.

In March of 1993, Lynx 2.0a was released, followed in April by the release of NCSA Mosaic for X 1.0—with ports to the Apple Macintosh and Microsoft Windows available by August. Raggett regarded the efforts made by the NCSA team in porting Mosaic—releasing easily runnable binaries for a variety of platforms, as—"brilliant." With easily usable Web browsers beginning to find a market with the masses, Raggett began to collaborate with Marc Andreessen and Eric Bina, both with NCSA at the time, on defining the basic tags to be used with forms. The results grew to become HTML+, later proposed as an Internet Draft.

With no formal planning, Raggett continued working with the ad hoc development of HTML, including meeting with members of the SGML and hypertext communities to bring the Text Encoding Initiative and the Web together.

Definitions

At the First International World Wide Web Conference in May 1994, Dave Raggett presented the HTML 2.0 specification, which was a "sanitized version" of HTML as it stood at the time. It incorporated the model for forms, nested lists, the <IMG> tag, and the <HEAD> and <BODY> containers.

Clarifications to the HTML spec progressed, including work on tables, math, and style sheets. Raggett incorporated much of it into the specification for HTML 3.0, which he released as an Internet Draft in March 1995. Unfortunately, it was rejected by the IETF, and fragmentation of HTML and what came to be called "tag abuse" continued.

In the Fall of 1995, Raggett was able to facilitate a meeting with representatives of Netscape, Microsoft, Sun, Spyglass, and Path-finder, along with Tim Berners-Lee and Dan Connolly, in an effort to come together on standardizing HTML. Agreements reached at the meeting, in addition to contributions by the HTML Working Group, have led to the recent release of HTML 3.2, which represents a baseline level of HTML for browser vendors to support.

Raggett is also involved in the next version of HTML, dubbed Cougar, which is slated to include extended support for math, the first phase of extensions to the form tags, captions for figures, style sheets, and frames support based on an extension to style sheets.

On the HTTP end, Raggett pushed to take Tim Berners-Lee's original version of HTTP—a simple "give me this file . . . here it is" protocol, with the browser left to guess the file format—to the next level. Along with Berners-Lee and Dan Connolly, who was adapting MIME for use with HTTP, Raggett helped rationalize and formalize a specification for HTTP. Co-chairing the IETF working group for HTTP, Raggett has collaborated with many other contributors in designing and testing HTTPng, an improved version of the protocol that supports more efficient connections to servers and the multiplexing of multiple messages over a single connection.

The VRML Element

Ever the Renaissance man, Raggett has interests that extend beyond hypertext into virtual reality, and he is one of the pioneers in the movement to bring virtual reality on-line. Virtual Reality on the Web took flight during a critical Birds-of-a-Feather workshop on virtual reality and the Web that Raggett ran with Tim Berners-Lee at the first World Wide Web Conference in Geneva in May 1994. At the Internet Society conference, held in Prague the next month, Dave Raggett presented a paper entitled "Extending WWW to Support Platform Independent Virtual Reality." It was during this period that Raggett coined the acronym VRML, for Virtual Reality Markup Language (which was subsequently changed from Markup to Modeling).

Raggett originally envisioned VRML as object oriented, based on the concepts of indoor and outdoor scenes. He also saw the need for a scripting language that would be independent of VRML. His original research into virtual reality was done in the context of video teleconferencing, combining model-based coding techniques with a virtual reality model of a scene, like cameras mapping points on a face. Raggett feels that VRML has not yet lived up to the ideas he set out in his paper—"something more than pixels and polygons"—and would like to make it more scalable. He notes, "After HTML, making cyberspace 'real' is going to be a big avenue."

Activity List

These days, Dave Raggett is helping to map the future of the Web with other members of the Consortium. Following up on his work creating the Arena reference browser, he is developing a Web browser written in Java, for use in demonstrating extensions and improvements to HTML.

Raggett is amazed that the Web has continued to grow along an exponential curve, though he points out that in some ways it has moved quite slowly because there are a lot of ideas that have yet to be implemented. Calling the Web a "bit of a hacker's phenomenon," he would have liked to have seen the growth of the Web better harness the power of skunkworks projects and public domain software. And as he watches the Web grow increasingly complex, Dave Raggett hopes that those of us involved in this growth will remember that "simplicity is very important."

— David Belson

SALLY KHUDAIRI
<TITLE>WEBMASTER
</TITLE>

Problem: What do you do with the original Web site—W3C—once it has grown to proportions no one wants to guess at, has more contributors than the United Way, and needs to be more scrupulous than the United Nations?

Solution: Hire a new webmaster.

Enter Sally Khudairi "with the mop in one hand, the iron and starch in the other . . ."

Whoa, what have we here? A webmaster or a cleaning woman for the Augean stables? Or both?

How about both and then some? How about someone trained as an architect and visual designer (Northeastern, Boston Architectural Center, Harvard, and Tulane), someone who teethed on one of the original Apples brought home by her parents?

How about someone who brings a diverse set of skills and bounces from place to place solving problems, imposing ordered process on apparent chaos, and along the way adding to an already broad understanding of computers, design, and communications?

That's what W3C has in its new webmaster. When you look at where she's been, what she's done, and who she's done it for you can't help but be impressed. Her clients include Ziff Davis Interactive, Yahoo! Computing, Lycos, Houghton Mifflin Company, Sky-Media, Central Artery/Tunnel Project, Automobiles Citroen, PowerEgypt, and Coopers & Lybrand.

And by the way—it is "webmaster" not "webmistress."

"I love the term—it implies you're a master at your profession."

Now if someone could only define that profession!

"I've had a bizarre background," she says, "flipping back and forth between design and project management." And it's all been heavily flavored with computing, of course.

Khudairi is aware of the task in front of her, and while she's respectful, she doesn't seem to be so much awed as just plain excited. "I've been sucked into the Web and I can't get out—I don't want to get out."

She's a designer who knows that design is "a way of life" and that Web design is "not a matter of putting lines on paper—you have to be able to understand it as more than a two-dimensional entity."

She also knows that anyone tackling this job has to have many dimensions to her life. She's not a computer geek, but she is comfortable with geek-speak. And while she may not pry under the hood herself very often (no, she doesn't know CGI scripting or Java), she knows what is under the hood and she understands the constraints the technology puts on designers.

Khudairi is not one of the original people who looked over the shoulder of Tim Berners-Lee at CERN six years ago and said, "Hey, great idea, Tim." But she has been with the Web long enough to see it grow from a tool to something that looks more like an entertainment medium. In other words, she appears to have a respect for the past without being too heavily invested in it.

So what is she going to do with the W3C site?

The conventional wisdom, of course, is for the site designer to first determine the audience and what its wants and needs are. But with W3C that doesn't do much good. The audience is incredibly broad and diverse—"more than 256 colors," quips Khudairi. "They are developers and technologists, marketing people, corporate leaders wanting to learn more about what we do, or people who have just heard about the Web and assume this is the place to start surfing."

But if you can't really zero in on an audience, then what?

In a word: structure. Create a structure that will help people find their way around. If the Web is the information superhighway, one thing you notice about the W3C site right away is there's no map. As you prowl around, you can't tell at any given moment whether you're on a dirt lane, a state highway, or the Interstate. The only signs point to other roads that are rarely identifiable in terms of their relationship to a whole, or a subset, or they point to "home." And while the home page has lots of links embedded in short pieces of text, it really doesn't help much in grasping the site's overall content and design.

Working with colleagues at W3C, Khudairi is now trying to sift through the site and determine a logical way to structure it that will be useful for a diverse audience.

So will this be a team effort?

"Absolutely," she declares. "What's interesting is that you can really tell when a site is maintained and administered by one person because it's very flat . . . ideas come from everywhere. Innovation is in front of you and you just have to grab it and go."

How about some hints of what to expect on a future W3C site? Khudairi agrees.

Structure

Three major divisions: User Interface, Technology and Society, and Architecture.

- User Interface deals with: HTML, Graphics + 3D, Internationalization, Fonts, Style, SGML, Amaya (the W3C-developed browser/editor)

- Technology and Society deals with: Demographics and Privacy, Intellectual Property Rights, Payments, PICS, Security

- Architecture deals with: Addressing, Protocols, HTTP-NG, Mobile Code, OOP, Repli-

cation, Resource Discovery, Jigsaw, Daemon, WWWLibrary

"Structure needs to exist," Khudairi says, "but it has to be a structure you can work in more than one direction."

Images

"Users have become a lot more sophisticated and they're expecting more," Khudairi says. "Yes, we'll incorporate new graphics, our organization will change to reflect the changes in the Web."

Does that mean dancing bears?

"I'd love to have Shockwave or Java on a home page that I've designed," Khudairi says. "But does everyone have access to Shockwave? Access is the issue. You don't have Shockwave or Java on your site just for the sake that it's there."

Access to All Browsers?

Hardly. "You can't please everybody all the time, you just can't." Having said that, Khudairi knows that she has to reconcile this reality with another one that's just as real and demanding—the point of W3C is to not exclude anyone.

Shorter Pages?

"We've got a lot of long pages on the site; people are scrolling and scrolling. Personally I'd like to see our pages a little shorter, structurally I understand why they're not."

In other words there will continue to be a lot of contributors building the site in their own way. But she does see a way to impose some order to these contributions beyond the overall structure.

Style Sheets!

"One thing that I am salivating over is Cascading Style Sheets," she says. "We will definitely have style sheets incorporated into our site."

Not sure what style sheets are? Check out the latest thinking about them on the W3C site. You should find it easier to discover everything you need to know, about style sheets and other things Web.

From chaos to structure while the whole world watches. . . . Hey, all Hercules had to do to clean those stables was divert a couple of rivers!

– Greg Stone

Consortium Announces Active Object Agreement

DECEMBER 11, 1995, *Cambridge, Massachusetts*
W3C successfully convenes a neutral forum for Consortium members IBM, Microsoft, Netscape, Spyglass, and Sun to agree on developing a common way of inserting active objects into the Web's hypertext documents. This will allow for different browsers to recognize the same "live" objects, which can move, dance, calculate, and otherwise jazz up a page. *The resulting consensus proposal for OBJECT can be found in this issue.*

4th International World Wide Web Conference

DECEMBER 11-14, 1995, *Boston, Massachusetts*
An overflow crowd from industry and academia meets for four days of meetings, workshops, product demonstrations, and talks in downtown Boston for WWW4. Topics include Internet Security, Web Content Rating Systems, Virtual Reality, Spoken Language Interfaces, and the Future of Web-Based Education; a number of sessions throughout the conference cover W3C projects. Key sessions are also broadcast via Multicast Backbone (M-BONE) and live Web coverage is provided by Bellcore. Roy Fielding chairs the Birds of a Feather sessions, while Developers Day is chaired by W3C Visiting Scientist Jim Gettys and highlights emerging technologies. WWW4 co-sponsors are MIT's Laboratory for Computer Science and the Open Software Foundation. *http://www.w3.org/WWW4/*

Advisory Council Meeting

JANUARY 10-11, 1996, *Paris, France*
Advisory council meetings are held twice a year, to set the Consortium's future agenda. The first day is dedicated to a review of W3C activities specifically for new European members. On the second day, the members set W3C policy for the first half of 1996.

Fifth W3C Security Working Group Meeting

JANUARY 22, 1996, *San Jose, California*
W3C presents its current work on the Security Extension Architecture (SEA), built on top of the Protocol Extension Protocol (PEP). W3C proposes to build SEA as a set of large-scale modules, with the initial set being Signature, Key Exchange, and Encryption. Working drafts of these documents are available at *http://www.w3.org/pub/WWW/TR/WD-http-sea* and *http://www.w3.org/pub/WWW/TR/WD-http-pep*

The First JEPI General Meeting

JANUARY 23, 1996, *San Jose, California*

Nearly 100 representatives of several dozen W3C and Commerce.Net member companies come together at IBM's Almaden Research Center to agree on goals and structure for the project. Several subsequent design meetings are held around the country.

Workshop on Internet Survey Methodology and Web Demographics

JANUARY 29–30, 1996, *Cambridge, Massachusetts*

Co-sponsored by W3C and MIT's Political Science department, Artificial Intelligence Laboratory, and Laboratory for Computer Science, this workshop brings together a select group of survey and media researchers, methodologists, and Web technologists to assess the current state of the art in measurement of online demographics and suggest future directions. User privacy emerges as a universal concern. *Selected papers are discussed in this issue.*

Sixth Conference on Computers, Freedom, and Privacy

MARCH 27–30, 1996, *Cambridge, Massachusetts*

Co-sponsored by W3C and MIT, this conference features a number of lively and innovative panel discussions. Among them is "Before the Court: Unauthorized Encryption," which is set up as a moot Supreme Court examining the constitutionality of a hypothetical ban on the use of cryptography without key-escrow. The majority decision overturns the ban on First Amendment grounds. The concurrence overturns on Ninth Amendment grounds.

Web Style Sheets Announced

MARCH 5, 1996, *Paris, France*

As part of a W3C convergence initiative, Consortium members agree to develop a common way of integrating style sheets into the Web's hypertext documents. Participating members include: Adobe, America Online, CompuServe, Eastman Kodak, Grif S.A., Hewlett Packard, IBM, Matra Hachette, Microsoft, NCSA, Netscape, Oracle, O'Reilly & Associates, Reed-Elsevier, SoftQuad, and Spyglass. The style sheet efforts will be based on the Cascading Style Sheets (CSS) initiative.

AMAYA Team Joined W3C Staff

APRIL, 1996, *Grenoble, France*

As a result of a decision made by the Advisory Council in January, the Consortium's staff is augmented by a team from INRIA's Grenoble site. The group has many years of experience in the area of SGML editors and style sheets. Group Leader Vincent Quint also takes overall responsibility for W3C operations in Europe as Deputy Director for Europe.

Digital Signature Initiative Organizational Meeting

APRIL 15–16, 1996, *Mountain View, California*

Initiated by Microsoft and held at Netscape, this meeting features proposals from several companies. Discussion centers on digital signatures and signing of code distributed over open networks, the key issues being how to endorse both signatures and a pieces of code. In addition to the sponsors, representatives attend from Apple, GTE, IBM, Microsoft, Oracle, Sun, and Verisign.

Platform for Internet Content Selection (PICS) European Tour

MARCH 25–29, 1996, *Paris, Munich, Brussels, Hamburg, London*

PICS makes the front page of the London *Sunday Times* after Jim Miller gives demonstrations to European government officials, members of the press, and industry leaders. In mid-May, Jim makes a second trip to Paris and London with Paul Resnick of AT&T Research and Stephen Balkam of RSAC.

Al Vezza Testifies about PICS

APRIL 12, 1996, *Philadelphia, Pennsylvania*

Albert Vezza, Chairman of W3C, is called to testify in federal district court by the Citizens Internet Empowerment Coalition (CIEC) in its challenge to the Communications Decency Act. In his testimony to the court, Vezza explains the Platform for Internet Content Selection (PICS), and how it permits voluntary ratings for the Internet and commercial online services.

The full text of Al Vezza's testimony can be found at *http://www.aclu.org/court/4-12-96.txt* and the full text of the decision with an exhaustive explanation of the Internet itself is located at *http://www.cdt.org/ciec/decision_PA/decision_text.html*

Workshop on Web Efficiency and Robustness

APRIL 19, 1996, *Cambridge, Massachusetts*
Consortium member Digital Equipment Corporation's Cambridge Research Laboratory hosts a gathering that addresses the current state of the Internet and what, in terms of long term architecture, is necessary to ensure its robustness in the future. The workshop is organized and chaired by Jim Gettys. Notes and attendee list at *http://www.w3.org/pub/WWW/Propagation/ Meeting/960419_Notes.html*

W3C Workshop on High Quality Printing from the Web

APRIL 25, 1996, *Cambridge, Massachusetts*
This one day technical workshop focuses on improving the quality of printing from the Web. A font working group is formed, and a mailing list started for people to jointly discuss printing issues. Representatives from many major companies launch a font group. The workshop is chaired by W3C/HP Dave Raggett. A font working group led by W3C staffer Chris Lilley is launched. *http:// www.w3.org/pub/WWW/Printing/Workshop_960425*

5th International World Wide Web Conference

MAY 6-10, 1996, *Paris, France*
WWW5 was organized by INRIA in cooperation with the European Commission, ERCIM, and the WWW Consortium under the auspices of the International World Wide Web Conference Committee. The opening address is given by Conference Chairman Jean-François Abramatic of INRIA. More than 2,400 delegates attend the conference sessions and over 15,000 visit the exhibition. The W3C unveils Amaya, its Web browser/editor and Jigsaw, its extensible Java server. It is announced that WWW6 will take place April 7-12, 1997 in Santa Clara, California. *http:// www.w3.org/pub/Conferences/WWW5/*

6th Security Working Group Meeting

MAY 11, 1996, *Paris, France*
This meeting, which emphasizes European participation, marks the official launch of the Digital Signature Initiative. It is also the first security meeting held outside the U.S. *http://www.w3.org/ pub/WWW/Security/Activity*

Second JEPI General Meeting

MAY 13, 1996, *Paris, France*
The interim progress report on the Joint Electronic Payment Initiative protocols is presented. Discussion at the meeting emphasizes European and merchant participation. Additional design and implementation meetings are scheduled for key players.

Security Interest Group Meets

MAY 24, 1996, *Redwood Shores, CA and Cambridge, MA*
Started as an ad hoc group of invited software and hardware makers, the SIG meets to discuss industry priorities in developing security and encryption standards. Oracle sponsors the group's meeting on the West Coast, while MIT sponsors the East Coast gathering.

Workshop on Distributed Indexing and Searching

MAY 28-29, 1996, *Boston, Massachusetts*
The workshop brings together over 50 participants from a variety of backgrounds: Web search service providers, library science and digital library experts, search engine software vendors, and Web server vendors. Workshop chairs Michael Schwartz of @Home Network and Mic Bowman of Transarc Corp. agree to prepare a workshop report suggesting short-term, medium-term, and long-term opportunities to standardize mechanisms to improve the quality and efficiency of searching on the Web. *http://www.w3.org/pub/WWW/Search/9605-Indexing-Workshop/*

New Home Page Unveiled

JUNE 4, 1996, *Cambridge, Massachusetts*
The new W3C home page emphasizes the three new areas of Consortium work—User Interface, Technology and Society, and Architecture—as well the breadth of the W3C efforts. Webmaster Sally Khudairi's future plans for the site include incorporating richer, PNG-supported graphics and icons, the use of Cascading Style Sheets to enable more formalized type treatment and dynamic page layout, and various navigation tools. *Sally Khudairi is profiled in this issue.*

W3C Advisory Council Meeting

JUNE 10-11, 1996, *Peabody, Massachusetts*
W3C policy is discussed in detail over the two-day meeting. A decision is made to empanel a process subcommittee to examine how W3C creates activity areas, runs workshops, and approves W3C recommendations. A new three team structure is announced with leaders of each group presenting plans for 1996.

HTML in Editorial Review Board (ERB) Meeting

JUNE 17–18, 1996, *Toronto, Canada*

Representatives from Netscape, Microsoft, and other Consortium member companies meet to form a Math ERB. The project is code-named Wilbur and will be reflected in HTML 3.2.

Joint W3C/OMG Workshop on Distributed Objects and Mobile Code

JUNE 24–25, 1996, *Boston, Massachusetts*

A reception at the Boston Computer Museum celebrates the second workshop on Mobile Code. With the Object Management Group (OMG) and W3C as co-sponsors, the workshop's goal is to identify a range of software architectures for combining and scaling Web technology and object engineering, and collaboration. *http://www.w3.org/pub/WWW/OOP/9606_Workshop/*

7th Security Working Group Meeting

JULY 29, 1996, *Seattle, Washington*

Sponsored by Microsoft, the group works on the digital signature initiative; a technical subgroup meets to consider proposals on July 26.

As highlighted in Issue 2, well-written specifications are the alpha and omega of the Web's success. The W3C is working in several areas to advance interoperability. This section is the record of its efforts.

The <OBJECT> specification, edited by Dave Raggett, is a landmark of W3C's work on HTML. As the first product of the newly-launched HTML Editorial Review Board, it reflects consensus among most of the major commercial developers with a stake in HTML. OBJECT is the foundation for extending the Web using advanced component technologies like OLE and Java applets. Later this year, W3C will produce an HTML 3.2 specification (Wilbur), and an advanced version of HTML, which will include OBJECT (Cougar).

In addition to shepherding new developments in HTML, W3C is committed to encouraging adoption and enforcement of HTML standards already "on the books." To that end Dan Connolly, primary author of the HTML 2.0 proposed standard, put together a lexical analyzer for the language. It's an excellent operational complement to the abstract specifications of HTML and SGML.

After the W3C/MIT Demographics workshop this January, Phillip Hallam-Baker was inspired to issue three Working Drafts in the area. One in particular, describing a richer format for Web server logs, found support in the community and was implemented in the Apache server. Brian Behlendorf joined Phill as co-author of the March 23rd version of the proposal, which is presented here.

Inserting Objects into HTML

Dave Raggett, editor[*]

Abstract

[W3C Working Draft; WD-object-960422; April 22, 1996]

The HyperText Markup Language (HTML) is a simple markup language used to create hypertext documents that are portable from one platform to another. HTML documents are SGML documents with generic semantics that are appropriate for representing information from a wide range of applications. This specification extends HTML to support the insertion of multimedia objects including Java applets, Microsoft Component Object Model (COM) objects (e.g., ActiveX Controls and ActiveX Document embeddings), and a wide range of other media plug-ins. The approach allows objects to be specified in a general manner and provides the ability to override the default implementation of objects.

Status of This Document

This is a W3C Working Draft for review by W3C members and other interested parties. It is a draft document and may be updated, replaced, or obsoleted by other documents at any time. It is inappropriate to use W3C Working Drafts as reference material or to cite them as other than "work in progress." A list of current W3C Working Drafts can be found at *http://www.w3.org/pub/WWW/TR.*

Previous Work

This draft was previously known as the "INSERT" draft. However, on February 13, 1996, the authors decided, with input from various parties, to rename the elements defined by the specification. Thus the document was renamed from WD-insert to WD-object.

Introduction

HTML 2.0 defined only a single mechanism for inserting media into HTML documents: the IMG tag. While this tag has certainly proved worthwhile, the fact that it is restricted to image media severely limits its usefulness as richer and richer media finds its way onto the Web.

Developers have been experimenting with ideas for dealing with new media: Microsoft's DYNSRC attribute for video and audio, Netscape's EMBED tag for compound document embedding, and Sun's APP and APPLET tags for executable code.

Each of these proposed solutions attacks the problem from a slightly different perspective, and on the surface each are very different. In addition, each of these proposals falls short, in one way or another, of meeting the requirements of the Web community as a whole. However, we believe that this problem can be addressed with a single extension that addresses all of the current needs and is fully extensible for the future.

This specification defines a new tag, OBJECT, which subsumes the role of the IMG tag and provides a general solution for dealing with new media, while providing for effective backwards compatibility with existing browsers. OBJECT allows the HTML author to specify the data and/or properties/parameters for initializing objects to be inserted into HTML documents, as well as the code that can be used to display/manipulate that data. Here, the term *object* is used to describe the things that people want to place in HTML documents; other terms for these things include components, applets, plug-ins, and media handlers.

---

[*] A list of contributing authors can be found at the end of this paper.

The data can be specified in one of several ways: a file specified by a URL, inline data, or as a set of named properties. In addition, there are a number of attributes that allow authors to specify standard properties such as width and height. The code for the object is specified in several ways: by an explicit reference, or indirectly by the object's "class name" or media type.

This specification covers the syntax and semantics for inserting such objects into HTML documents but leaves out the architectural and application programming interface issues for how objects communicate with the document and other objects on the same page. It is anticipated that future specifications will cover these topics, including scripting languages and interfaces.

An Introduction to the OBJECT Tag

This section is intended to help readers get the feel of the insertion mechanism and is not a normative part of the specification. The OBJECT tag provides a richer alternative to the IMG tag. It may be used when the author wishes to provide an alternative for user agents that don't support a particular media. A simple example of using OBJECT is:

```
<OBJECT data=TheEarth.avi
    type="application/avi">
<img src=TheEarth.gif alt="The
    Earth">
</OBJECT>
```

Here the user agent would show an animation if it supports the AVI format; otherwise, it would show a GIF image. The IMG element is used for the latter as it provides for backwards compatibility with existing browsers. The TYPE attribute allows the user agent to quickly detect that it doesn't support a particular object and avoid wasting time downloading it. Another motivation for using the TYPE attribute is when the object is loaded off a local drive, as it allows the format to be specified directly rather than being inferred from the file extension.

A similar example for viewing a Macromedia Shockwave presentation, giving the intended width and height of the display area is shown here:

```
<OBJECT data=shocknew.dcr
    type="application/director"
    width=288 height=200>
<img src=shocknew.gif alt="Best
    with Shockwave">
</OBJECT>
```

The next example inserts an applet written in the Python language that displays a (rather large) analog clock. The CLASSID attribute gives a URL for the Python code implementing the applet. The PARAM element is used to pass named parameters to objects. Without `<PARAM NAME=size VALUE=40>`, the clock will measure only 200 pixels.

```
<OBJECT
    classid="http://
    monty.cnri.reston.va.us/grail/
    demo/clocks/analogclock.py"
>
<PARAM NAME=size VALUE=40>
fall back ...
</OBJECT>
```

The following example is a Java applet. The CLASSID uses the `java:` URL scheme [10] to name the Java class *program.start*. The value for the missing CODEBASE attribute, used to locate the implementation, defaults to same base URL as the document. The "main" method in the class *program.start* is invoked to start the Java applet. Unlike the APPLET element, no `.class` is permitted at the end of the CLASSID.

```
<OBJECT
    CLASSID="java:program.start"
    HEIGHT=100
    WIDTH=100
>
Your browser does not know how to
    execute Java applications.
</OBJECT>
```

In the next example, CODEBASE has been explicitly set, and an additional PARAM element has been provided. A browser can examine CODETYPE to determine whether or not to attempt to fetch the Java applet or go immediately to the apology section. It plays the same role for CLASSID as TYPE does for DATA.

```
<OBJECT
    CODETYPE="application/java-vm"
    CODEBASE="http://host/somepath/"
    CLASSID="java:program.start"
    HEIGHT=100
    WIDTH=100
>
<PARAM NAME="options" VALUE="xqz">
    Your browser does not know how
    to execute Java applications.
</OBJECT>
```

Here is another clock, but this time using an *ActiveX* control:

```
<OBJECT
    id=clock1
    classid="clsid:663C8FEF-1EF9-
    11CF-A3DB-080036F12502"
    data="http://www.acme.com/ole/
    clock.stm"
>
fall back ...
</OBJECT>
```

This uses the `clsid:` URL scheme [11] to specify the *ActiveX* class identifier. The ID attribute allows other controls on the same page to locate the clock. The DATA attribute points to data used to initialize the object's state. Note that *ActiveX* data streams include a class identifier that can be used by the *ActiveX* loader to find an implementation in the absence of the CLASSID attribute. The CODEBASE attribute can be used to give a URL as a hint to the *ActiveX* loader on where to find an implementation for this class.

For speedy loading of objects you can inline the object's state data using the URL `data:` scheme [9], for example:

```
<OBJECT
    id=clock1
    classid="clsid:663C8FEF-1EF9-
    11CF-A3DB-080036F12502"
    data="data:application/x-
    oleobject;base64, ...base64
    data..."
```

```
>
fall back...
</OBJECT>
```

Inline data is only recommended for small amounts of data.

A Walk Through the DTD

The Document Type Definition provides the formal definition of the allowed syntax for HTML inserts. The following sections provide an annotated listing of the DTD defining the semantics of the elements and their attributes. The complete listing appears at the end of this document.

Standard Units for Lengths

Length values can be specified as an integer representing the number of screen pixels, or as a percentage of the current displayable region, e.g., 50%. For widths, this is the space between the current left and right margins, while for heights, this is the height of the current window, table cell, etc.

You can also use fixed units by including a suffix after a floating point number, such as, "0.5in". The allowed suffixes are:

pt points

pi picas

in inches

cm centimeters

where 72pt = 6pi = 1in = 2.54cm.

Minimization of Attribute Values

HTML supports an SGML feature allowing minimization of attribute values.

1. If the attribute value is a token consisting of only name characters (for HTML these are a-z, A-Z, 0-9, - and .), then the quote marks may be omitted: `<foo bar="baz">` is equivalent to `<foo bar=baz>`.

2. If the values are declared as a group of one or more names, then the attribute name can

be omitted: `<foo bar="baz">` is equivalent to `<foo baz>`.

3. Attribute names are always case insensitive. If the values are declared as a group of one or more names, the attribute value is case insensitive: `<foo bar="baz">` is equivalent to `<foo BaR=BaZ>`.

The above means that attributes such as DECLARE and SHAPES can be abbreviated to just the attribute value, i.e., `declare="declare"` is equivalent to `declare` and to `DECLARE`. User agents must treat the permitted variant forms for attribute values as directly equivalent.

The OBJECT Tag

The OBJECT element is used to insert an object into an HTML document (see Example 1). It requires both start and end tags. The OBJECT element has the same content model as the HTML BODY element, except that one or more optional PARAM elements can be placed immediately after the OBJECT start tag and used to initialize the inserted object. The content of the OBJECT element is rendered if the object specified by the CLASSID, CODEBASE, and DATA

Example 1

```
<!-- Content model entities imported from parent DTD:
  %body.content allows objects to contain headers, paras,
  lists, form elements *and* arbitrarily nested objects.
-->
<!ENTITY % attrs -- ID plus additional attributes from parent DTD --
        "id  ID  #IMPLIED  -- element identifier --"
        >

<!ENTITY % URL "CDATA" -- uniform resource locator -->

<!ENTITY % Align "(texttop|middle|textmiddle|baseline|
                        textbottom|left|center|right)">

<!ENTITY % Length "CDATA" -- standard length value -->

<!-- OBJECT is a character-like element for inserting objects -->
<!ELEMENT object - - (param | %bodytext)*>
<!ATTLIST object
        %attrs        -- id, class, style, lang, dir --
        declare (declare) #IMPLIED  -- declare but don't instantiate flag --
        classid %URL      #IMPLIED  -- identifies an implementation --
        codebase %URL     #IMPLIED  -- some systems need an additional URL --
        data    %URL      #IMPLIED  -- reference to object's data --
        type    CDATA     #IMPLIED  -- Internet media type for data --
        codetype CDATA    #IMPLIED  -- Internet media type for code --
        standby CDATA     #IMPLIED  -- message to show while loading --
        align   %Align    #IMPLIED  -- positioning inside document --
        height  %Length   #IMPLIED  -- suggested height --
        width   %Length   #IMPLIED  -- suggested width --
        border  %Length   #IMPLIED  -- suggested link border width --
        hspace  %Length   #IMPLIED  -- suggested horizontal gutter --
        vspace  %Length   #IMPLIED  -- suggested vertical gutter --
        usemap  %URL      #IMPLIED  -- reference to image map --
        shapes  (shapes)  #IMPLIED  -- object has shaped hypertext links --
        name    %URL      #IMPLIED  -- submit as part of form --
        >
```

attributes can't be rendered (user agents may choose to display the content of the OBJECT element if displaying the actual element will take a long time to render). This provides for backwards compatibility with existing browsers and allows authors to specify alternative media via nested OBJECT elements.

Note that this doesn't provide the same level of flexibility as would be provided by a richer description of resource variants. For instance, several media types are available for resources, each in English, Spanish, French, and German.

In general, all attribute names and values in this specification are case insensitive, except where noted otherwise. OBJECT has the following attributes:

ID

> Used to define a document-wide identifier. This can be used for naming positions within documents for use as destinations of hypertext links. An ID attribute value is an SGML NAME token. NAME tokens are formed by an initial letter followed by letters in the range a-z and A-Z (no accented characters), digits, -, and . characters. It may also be used by the user agent or objects in the document to find and communicate with other objects embedded in the document.

DECLARE

> Used to indicate that the object is to be declared but not instantiated. A detailed description of the DECLARE attribute is given below.

CLASSID

> This is a URL that identifies an implementation for the object. In some object systems, this is a class identifier.

CODEBASE

> Some URL schemes used to identify implementations require an additional URL to find the implementation. CODEBASE allows you to specify that URL.

DATA

> This is a URL pointing to the object's data—for instance, a GIF file for an image. In the absence of the CLASSID attribute, the media type of the data is used to determine a default value for the CLASSID attribute. The implementation is then loaded as if the CLASSID attribute had been given explicitly.

TYPE

> This specifies the Internet Media Type [7] for the data referenced by the DATA attribute in advance of actually retrieving it. In the absence of the CLASSID attribute, this allows the user agent to retrieve the code implementing the object concurrently with the data and to skip over unsupported media types without needing to make a network access.

CODETYPE

> This specifies the Internet Media Type [7] of the code referenced by the CLASSID attribute in advance of actually retrieving it. User agents may use the value of the CODETYPE attribute to skip over unsupported media types without needing to make a network access.

STANDBY

> This allows you to specify a short text string the browser can show while loading the object's implementation and data. It can include character entities for accented characters, etc.

ALIGN

> This determines where to place the object. The ALIGN attribute allows objects to be placed as part of the current text line or as a distinct unit, aligned to the left, center, or right.

> The following values are chosen for their ease of implementation and their independence from other graphics occurring earlier on the same line:

For `ALIGN=TEXTTOP`, the top of the object is vertically aligned with the top of the current font.

For `ALIGN=MIDDLE`, the middle of the object is vertically aligned with the baseline.

For `ALIGN=TEXTMIDDLE`, the middle of the object is vertically aligned with the position midway between the baseline and the x-height for the current font. The x-height is defined as the top of a lowercase x in western writing systems. If the text font is an all caps style, then use the height of a capital X. For other writing systems, align the middle of the object with the middle of the text.

For `ALIGN=BASELINE`, the bottom of the object is vertically aligned with the baseline of the text line in which the object appears.

For `ALIGN=TEXTBOTTOM`, the bottom of the object is vertically aligned with the bottom of the current font.

NOTE

The proposed Netscape extensions for the align attribute of the IMG element are context sensitive, as are some of the implementations of ALIGN=TOP. See the test page at *http://www.w3.org/pub/ WWW/MarkUp/Test/Img/imgtest.html*.

The following alignment values allow the object to float rather than being treated as part of the current line:

For `ALIGN=LEFT`, the object is floated down and over to the current left margin. Subsequent text is flowed past the right hand side of the visible area of the object.

For `ALIGN=CENTER`, the object is floated to after the end of the current line and centered between the left and right margins. Subsequent text starts at the beginning of the next line.

For `ALIGN=RIGHT`, the object is floated down and over to the current right margin.

Subsequent text is flowed past the left hand side of the visible area of the object.

WIDTH

This gives the suggested width of a box enclosing the visible area of the object. The width is specified in standard units. User agents may use this value to scale an object to match the requested width if appropriate.

NOTE

Smooth scaling a small image to a larger size provides an effective solution to reducing the time needed to download an image, offering better subjective results when compared to color reduction.

HEIGHT

This gives the suggested height of a box enclosing the visible area of the object. The height is specified in standard units. User agents may use this value to scale an object to match the requested height if appropriate.

BORDER

This attribute applies to the border shown when the object forms part of a hypertext link, as specified by an enclosing anchor element. The attribute specifies the suggested width of this border around the visible area of the object. The width is specified in `"#units"`.

HSPACE

The suggested width of the space to the left and right of the box enclosing the visible area of the object. The width is specified in standard units. This attribute is used to alter the separation of preceding and following text from the object.

VSPACE

The suggested height of the space to the top and bottom of the box enclosing the visible area of the object. The height is specified in standard units.

USEMAP

This specifies a uniform resource locator for a client-side image map [4] in the format proposed by Spyglass, Inc. This is normally appropriate only for static images.

SHAPES

The presence of this attribute indicates that the contents of the OBJECT element contains anchors with hypertext links associated with shaped regions on the visible area of the object. See below for further information.

NAME

This provides a way for user agents that support FORMs to determine whether an object within a FORM block should participate in the "submit" process. If NAME is specified and the DECLARE attribute is absent, then the user agent should include the value of the NAME attribute and data obtained from the object along with the information derived from other form fields. The mechanism used to obtain the object's data is specific to each object system.

NOTE

As class identifiers in some object systems can be quite cumbersome, the CLASSID attribute may use a short URL to specify a class identifier indirectly. See the Internet Draft on Hypertext Link Relationships in HTML [3] for details on the "pointer" link relationship.

More About OBJECT DECLARE

OBJECT markup with the DECLARE attribute imply objects that are not created (instantiated) until needed by something that references them (i.e., late binding). Each such "binding" typically results in a separate copy of the object (this is class dependent). In other words, the OBJECT DECLARE is treated as a declaration for making an instance of an object.

If the declared object isn't supported, or fails to load, the user agent should try the content of the OBJECT DECLARE element, which is currently restricted to another OBJECT DECLARE element. The TYPE attribute can be used to specify the Internet Media Type for the object as a hint for this situation.

Examples of OBJECT DECLARE Usage

- To allow PARAM values to be "object valued"; that is, the value of the parameter is a pointer to an object. See Example 2 in the section entitled "PARAM Element" that follows.

- To allow hypertext links to point to objects that can't otherwise be addressed using a single URL.

For instance:

```
<OBJECT ID="obj1" DECLARE
    CLASSID=implementation >
<PARAM NAME=param1 VALUE=value1>
<PARAM NAME=param2 VALUE=value2>
</OBJECT>

<P>This points to an <A HREF=
    "#obj1">object</A>.
```

The meaning of the link in the anchor HREF="#obj1" depends on what it points to. In this case it points to an object declaration that is then used to replace the current page with a new instance of the specified object class and data. If the HREF points to an HTML element like <H1> or <P> or <A>, then the browser scrolls the document to that point.

NOTE

Anchors can exploit nested declared objects to provide alternative media for a given resource.

The PARAM Element

The PARAM element, shown in Example 2, allows a list of named property values (used, for example, to initialize an *ActiveX* control, plug-in

Example 2

```
<!ELEMENT param - O EMPTY -- named property value -->
<!ATTLIST param
        name      CDATA                 #REQUIRED   -- property name --
        value     CDATA                 #IMPLIED    -- property value --
        valuetype (DATA|REF|OBJECT) DATA            -- How to interpret value --
        type      CDATA                 #IMPLIED    -- Internet media type --
        >
```

module, or Java applet) to be represented as a sequence of PARAM elements. Note that PARAM is an empty element and should appear without an end tag.

The NAME attribute defines the property name. The case sensitivity of the name is dependent on the code implementing the object.

The VALUE attribute is used to specify the property value. It is an opaque character string whose meaning is determined by the object based on the property name. Note that CDATA attribute values need characters such as & to be escaped using the standard SGML character entities, e.g., & for &. It is also essential to escape the > character to defend against incorrect handling by many existing browsers (use >).

The VALUETYPE attribute can be one of REF, OBJECT, or DATA as described below:

REF

Indicates that the value is a URL. This allows support tools to identify URLs given as parameters. The value should be passed as is after dealing with any embedded character or numeric character entities; i.e., the URL should *not* be canonicalized before being passed to the OBJECT.

OBJECT

Indicates that the value is a URL of an OBJECT element in the same document. This is used primarily for object valued properties (where the value of a property is a pointer/reference to a running object).

DATA

Indicates that the value is to be passed directly to the object as a string, after dealing with any embedded character or numeric character entities. This is the default in the absence of an explicit value for VALUE-TYPE.

Note that the valuetype attribute value can be given without the corresponding attribute name, as seen in the examples below. This exploits a feature of SGML minimization.

The TYPE attribute is only valid for VALUE-TYPE=REF.

In Example 3, the string "Hello World!" is passed to the object as the value for the "Caption" property.

Example 4 is a hypothetical example of an applet for viewing poems. The poem is passed to the viewer applet via the DATA attribute. The applet recognizes a parameter named "font" that defines the font as an object. The VALUE attribute uses a URL fragment identifier *#tribune* to point to the font object, which is itself defined with an OBJECT DECLARE element.

Example 3

```
    <PARAM NAME="Caption" VALUE="Hello World!">
is equivalent to
    <PARAM NAME="Caption" DATA VALUE="Hello World!">
```

Example 4

```
<OBJECT DECLARE ID=tribune
        TYPE="application/x-webfont"
        DATA=tribune.gif>
</OBJECT>

<OBJECT CLASSID="http:// ..." DATA="KublaKhan.txt">
<PARAM NAME=font OBJECT VALUE="#tribune">
   <P>You're missing a really cool poem viewer ...
</OBJECT>
```

In the following example, the "Source" property of the object is passed the URL *images/foo.gif.*

```
<PARAM NAME="Source" REF VALUE=images/
    foo.gif>
```

Client-Side Image Maps

Image maps allow hypertext links to be associated with shaped regions on an image. The following mechanism extends the anchor element and provides backwards compatibility with all existing browsers. It removes the need to duplicate image maps with textual hypertext menus for non-graphical browsers.

Figure 1 is a navigation toolbar, which is represented as shown in Example 5.

On *all HTML 2.0 browsers* Example 5 would look like:

Access Guide | Go | Search | Top 10

The SHAPE and COORDS Attributes

If the OBJECT element includes a SHAPES attribute, then user agents need to parse the contents of the element to look for anchors. The anchor element (`<a href=...> ... </a>`) is

extended to permit a pair of new attributes SHAPE and COORDS. These attributes associate the hypertext link with a region on the image specified by the enclosing OBJECT element. The SHAPE and COORDS attributes take one of the general forms:

```
shape=default
shape=rect coords="left-x, top-
    y,right-x, bottom-y"
shape=circle coords="center-
    x,center-y, radius"
shape=poly coords="x1, y1, x2, y2,
    x3, y3,..."
```

Where x and y are measured in pixels from the left/top of the associated image. If x and y values are given with a percent sign (%) as a suffix, the values should be interpreted as percentages of the image's width and height, respectively. For example:

```
SHAPE=RECT COORDS="0, 0, 50%, 100%"
```

The ISMAP Attribute

When present with SHAPE and COORDS attributes, the ISMAP attribute causes the location clicked to be passed to the server. The user agent derives a new URL from the URL specified by the HREF attribute by appending ?, the x coordinate,

Figure 1   Navigational toolbar

Example 5

```
<object data="navbar.gif" shapes>
    <a href=guide.html shape=rect coords="0,0,118,28">Access Guide</a> |
    <a href=shortcut.html shape=rect coords="118,0,184,28">Go</a> |
    <a href=search.html shape=rect coords="184,0,276,28">Search</a> |
    <a href=top10.html shape=rect coords="276,0,373,28">Top Ten</a>
</object>
```

and the *y* coordinate of the location in pixels. The link is then followed using the new URL. For instance, if the user clicked at the location (10,27) for a link with:

```
HREF="http://www.acme.com/Guide/
    top10.html"
```

then the derived URL will be:

```
http://www.acm e.com/Guide/
    top10.html?10,27
```

The use of ISMAP for selected regions allows authors to exploit client-side and server-side imagemaps for the same image, e.g., regions that visually act as 3D beveled buttons can be handled locally, while for complex image maps, or where it is undesirable to pass the imagemap to the client, the location clicked can be dealt with by the server. An example can be seen in "Find the ball" competitions where sending the imagemap to the client would give the competition away.

The DTD Extensions for Anchors

The formal SGML definition of the ISMAP, SHAPE, and COORDS attributes is:

```
<!ATTLIST A
    ...
    shape
      (default|rect|circle|poly)
      #IMPLIED
    coords   CDATA   #IMPLIED
    ismap    (ismap)  #IMPLIE
>
```

The visually impaired community have argued strongly in favor of the shaped anchor mechanism, as it forces authors to provide a way for readers to follow the links regardless of which browser they are using.

Defining Overlapping Regions

In Figure 2, the rectangles are mapped to different URLs. Although the rectangles overlap, clicking on each rectangle loads the appropriate document.

If two or more regions overlap, the region defined first in the map definition takes precedence over other regions. For example, in the

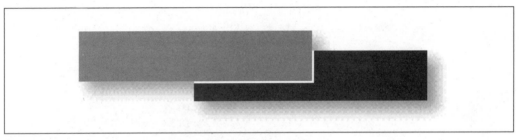

Figure 2   Two overlapped regions mapped to different URLs

Example 6

```
<object data="navbar1.gif" usemap="#map1">
</object>

<map name="map1">
   <area href=guide.html alt="Access Guide" shape=rect coords="0,0,118,28">
   <area href=search.html alt="Search" shape=rect coords="184,0,276,28">
   <area href=shortcut.html alt="Go" shape=rect coords="118,0,184,28">
   <area href=top10.html alt="Top Ten" shape=rect coords="276,0,373,28">
</map>
```

map definition for Figure 2, the leftmost rectangle is defined before the rightmost rectangle:

```
<object data="overlap.gif" shapes>
   <a href=green.html shape=rect
   coords="66,13,186,37">Green</a>
   |
   <a href=blue.html shape=rect
   coords="195,43,245,46">Blue</a>
</object>
```

In all cases shape=default has the lowest precedence. It extends to the whole of the visible region of the object.

Anchors can use the SHAPE attribute together with the TARGET attribute for designating the target user interface object (e.g., frame) for displaying the linked document or resource.

The MAP Element

The MAP element provides an alternative mechanism for client-side image maps. It was devel-

oped by Spyglass for use with the IMG element [4]. The SHAPE and COORDS attributes are the same as for the shaped anchor mechanism. The navigational toolbar becomes Example 6.

The OBJECT element references the MAP with a URL given with the USEMAP attribute. The SHAPE and COORDS attributes behave in the same way as for the shaped anchor proposal. The ALT attribute can be used to provide a few words describing each choice. This can't include markup but can include character entities. Note that MAP isn't backwards compatible with HTML 2.0 browsers.

HTML OBJECTs DTD

The DTD or Document Type Definition (Example 7) provides the formal definition of the allowed syntax for HTML objects. ∎

Example 7

```
<!-- Content model entities imported from parent DTD:
  %body.content allows objects to contain headers, paras,
  lists, form elements *and* arbitrarily nested objects.
-->
<!ENTITY % attrs -- ID plus additional attributes from parent DTD --
      "id  ID  #IMPLIED  -- element identifier --"
       >

<!ENTITY % URL "CDATA" -- uniform resource locator -->

<!ENTITY % Align "(texttop|middle|textmiddle|baseline|
                     textbottom|left|center|right)">

<!ENTITY % Length "CDATA" -- standard length value -->
```

Example 7 *(Continued)*

```
<!-- OBJECT is a character-like element for inserting objects -->
<!ELEMENT OBJECT - - (param | %bodytext)*>
<!ATTLIST OBJECT
        %attrs      -- id, class, style, lang, dir --
        declare (declare) #IMPLIED  -- declare but don't instantiate flag --
        classid %URL     #IMPLIED  -- identifies an implementation --
        codebase %URL    #IMPLIED  -- some systems need an additional URL --
        data    %URL     #IMPLIED  -- reference to object's data --
        type    CDATA    #IMPLIED  -- Internet media type for data --
        codetype CDATA   #IMPLIED  -- Internet media type for code --
        standby CDATA    #IMPLIED  -- message to show while loading --
        align   %Align   #IMPLIED  -- positioning inside document --
        height  %Length  #IMPLIED  -- suggested height --
        width   %Length  #IMPLIED  -- suggested width --
        border  %Length  #IMPLIED  -- suggested link border width --
        hspace  %Length  #IMPLIED  -- suggested horizontal gutter --
        vspace  %Length  #IMPLIED  -- suggested vertical gutter --
        usemap  %URL     #IMPLIED  -- reference to image map --
        shapes  (shapes) #IMPLIED  -- object has shaped hypertext links --
        name    %URL     #IMPLIED  -- submit as part of form --
        >

<!ELEMENT param - O EMPTY -- named property value -->
<!ATTLIST param
        name    CDATA            #REQUIRED  -- property name --
        value   CDATA            #IMPLIED   -- property value --
        valuetype (DATA|REF|OBJECT) DATA    -- How to interpret value --
        type    CDATA            #IMPLIED   -- Internet media type --
        >
```

References

1. Cascading Style Sheets. W3C's Working Draft specification on CSS1 can be found at *http://www.w3.org/pub/WWW/TR/WD-css1.html*

2. Attaching Rendering Information. W3C's Working Draft specification on how to attach rendering information to HTML documents can be found at *http://www.w3.org/pub/WWW/TR/WD-style.html*

3. Hypertext link Relationships in HTML. The proposed relationships for use with REL/REV attributes are described in the Internet Draft: *http://www.w3.org/pub/WWW/MarkUp/draft-ietf-html-relrev-00.txt*

4. Client-Side Image maps. Spyglass Client Side Image Maps: *http://www.spyglass.com/techspec/img_maps.html*

5. HTML3 Scripting. W3C's Working Draft specification on scripting in HTML documents can be found at *http://www.w3.org/pub/WWW/TR/WD-script.html*

6. HTML3 Forms. W3C's Working Draft specification on forms in HTML documents can be found at *http://www.w3.org/pub/WWW/TR/WD-forms.html*

7. Internet Media Types—RFC 1590. Postel, J., "Media Type Registration Procedure," RFC 1590, USC/ISI, March 1994. This can be found at *ftp://ds.internic.net/rfc/rfc1590.tx t*

8. MIME—RFC 1521. Borenstein N., and N. Freed, "MIME (Multipurpose Internet Mail Extensions) Part One: Mechanisms for Specifying and Describing the Format of Internet Message Bodies," RFC 1521, Bellcore, Innosoft, September 1993. This can be found at *ftp://ds.internic.net/rfc/rfc1521.txt.*

9. The data: URL scheme for inline data is defined by the Internet Draft *ftp://ds.internic.net/internet-drafts/draft-masinter-url-data-00.txt*

10. Java Applets. Complete specifications on Java can be found at *http://java.sun.com/*

11. The clsid: URL scheme is defined in *http://www.w3.org/pub/WWW/Addressing/clsid-scheme*

12. The Component Object Model Specification is available from *http://www.microsoft.com/intdev/inttech/comintro.htm*

13. The Microsoft Internet Technologies. Complete specifications can be found at *http://www.microsoft.com/intdev/default.htm*

14. OSF DCE. Further information about the OSF Distributed Computing Environment can be found at *http://www.osf.org/dce*

15. Grail and Python. Further information on using the python language for building applets can be found at *http://monty.cnri.reston.va.u s/grail/*

About the Author

Dave Raggett (W3C, Hewlett Packard)
MIT Laboratory for Computer Science
545 Technology Square
Cambridge, MA 02139
dsr@w3.org

Dave currently works at the World Wide Web Consortium (W3C) on secondment from Hewlett Packard's Corporate Research Laboratories in Bristol, England. His work is heavily involved with developing standards for the World Wide Web: as author of the HTML 3.0 draft specification and earlier the HTML+ Internet Draft, as the creator of the Arena browser, and as co-chair of the IETF working group for HTTP. He is also working on ideas for downloadable fonts, style sheets, and non-proprietary public domain protocols for micropayments (without export restrictions).

Contributing authors:
Charlie Kindel, Microsoft Corporation
Lou Montulli, Netscape Communications Corp.
Eric Sink, Spyglass Inc.
Wayne Gramlich, Sun Microsystems
Jonathan Hirschman, Pathfinder
Tim Berners-Lee, W3C
Dan Connolly, W3C

A Lexical Analyzer for HTML and Basic SGML

Dan Connolly

Abstract

[W3C Wroking Draft; WD-sgml-lex; June 15, 1996]

The Standard Generalized Markup Language (SGML) is a complex system for developing markup languages. It is used to define the Hypertext Markup Language (HTML) used in the World Wide Web, as well as several other hypermedia document representations.

Systems with interactive performance constraints use only the simplest features of SGML. Unfortunately, the specification of those features is subtly mixed into the specification of SGML in all its generality. As a result, a number of ad-hoc SGML lexical analyzers have been developed and deployed on the Internet, and reliability has suffered.

We present a self-contained specification of a lexical analyzer that uses automated parsing techniques to handle SGML document types limited to a tractable set of SGML features. An implementation is available as well.

Status of This Document

This is a W3C Working Draft for review by W3C members and other interested parties. It is a draft document and may be updated, replaced, or obsoleted by other documents at any time. It is inappropriate to use W3C Working Drafts as reference material or to cite them as other than "work in progress." A list of current W3C tech reports can be found at *http://www.w3.org/pub/WWW/TR/*.

Please direct comments and questions to *www-html@w3.org*, an open discussion forum. Include the keyword "sgml-lex" in the subject.

Introduction

"The hypertext markup language is an SGML format." —Tim Berners-Lee, in "About HTML"

The result of that design decision is something of a collision between the World Wide Web development community and the SGML community—between the quick-and-dirty software community and the formal ISO standards community. It also creates a collision between the interactive, online hypermedia technology and the bulk, batch print publications technology.

SGML, Standard General Markup Language, is a complex, mature, stable technology. The international standard, ISO 8879:1986 [1], is nearly ten years old, and GML-based systems predate the standard by years. On the other hand, HTML, Hypertext Markup Lanuage is a relatively simple, new, and rapidly evolving technology.

SGML has a number of degrees of freedom which are bound in HTML. SGML is a system for defining markup languages, and HTML is one such language; in standard terminology, HTML is an SGML application.

Lexical Analysis of Basic SGML Documents

The degree of freedom in SGML which the HTML 2.0 specification [4] binds can be separated into high-level, document structure considerations on the one hand, and low-level, lexical details on the other. The document structure issues are specific to the domain of application of HTML, and they are evolving rapidly to reflect new features in the Web.

The lexical properties of HTML 2.0 are very stable by comparison. With a few exceptions, HTML documents fit into a category termed *basic SGML documents* in the SGML standard. These properties are independent of the domain of HTML application. They are shared by a number of contemporary SGML applications, such as TEI [6], DocBook [9], HTF [10], and IBM-IDDOC [11].

The specification of this straightforward category of SGML documents is, unfortunately, subtly mixed into the specification of SGML in all its generality. The result is that a number of lexically incompatible HTML parser implementations have been developed and deployed [20].

The objectives of the document are to:

1. Refine the notion of "basic SGML document" to the precise set of features used in HTML 2.0.

2. Present a more traditional automated model of lexical analysis and parsing for these SGML documents [12].

3. Make a rigorous specification of this lexical analyzer, that can be understood without prior knowledge of SGML, freely available to the Web development community.

While this report focuses on the SGML features necessary for HTML 2.0 user agents, it should be applicable to future HTML versions and to extensions of the HTML standard [18], as well as other SGML applications used on the Internet [5]. See the "Future Work" section for discussion.

SGML and Document Types

SGML Documents

An SGML document is a sequence of characters organized as one or more entities for storage and transmission, with a logical hierarchy of elements imposed.

The organization of an SGML document into entities is analogous to the organization of a C program into source files [13]. This report does not formally address entity structure. We restrict our discussion to documents consisting of a single entity.

The element hierarchy of an SGML document is actually the last of three parts. The first two are the SGML declaration and the prologue.

The SGML declaration binds certain variables such as the character strings that serve delimiter roles, and the optional features used. The SGML declaration also specifies the document character set—the set of characters allowed in the document and their corresponding character numbers. For a discussion of the SGML declaration, see [8].

The prologue, or DTD, declares the element types allowed in the document, along with their attributes and content models. The content models express the order and occurrence of elements in the hierarchy.

Document Types and Element Structure

SGML facilitates the development of *document types*, or specialized markup languages. An *SGML application* is a set of rules for using one or more document types. Typically, a community such as an industry segment, after identifying a need to interchange data in a rigorous method, develops an SGML application suited to their practices.

The document type definition includes two parts: a formal part, expressed in SGML, called a document type declaration or DTD, and a set of application conventions. An overview of the syntax of a DTD follows. For a more complete discussion, see [7].

The DTD essentially gives a grammar for the element structure of the specialized markup language: the start symbol is the document element name; the productions are specified in element declarations, and the terminal symbols are start-tags, end-tags, and data characters. For example:

```
<!doctype Memo [
<!element Memo         - -
    (Salutation, P*, Closing?)>
<!element Salutation   O O (Date &
    To & Address?)>
<!element (P|Closing|To|Address) -
    O (#PCDATA)>
<!element Date - O EMPTY>
<!attlist Date
numeric CDATA #REQUIRED
]>
```

These four element declarations specify that a Memo consists of a Salutation, zero or more P elements, and an optional Closing. The Salutation is a Date, To, and optionally, an Address.

The notation - - specifies that both start and end tags are required; O O specifies both are optional, and - O specifies that the start tag is required, but the end tag is optional. The notation #PCDATA refers to parsed character data— data characters with auxiliary markup such as comments mixed in. An element declared EMPTY has no content and no end-tag.

The ATTLIST declaration specifies that the Date element has an attribute called numeric. The #REQUIRED notation says that each Date start-tag must specify a value for the Date attribute.

The following is a sample instance of the memo document type:

```
<!doctype memo system>
<Memo>
<Date numeric="1994-06-12">
<To>Third Floor
<p>Please limit coffee breaks to 10
    minutes.
<Closing>The Management
</Memo>
```

The following left-derivation shows the nearly self-evident structure of SGML documents when viewed at this level:

```
Memo -> <Memo>, Salutation, P,
    Closing, </Memo>
Salutation -> Date, To
Date -> <Date numeric="1994-06-12">
To -> <To>, "Third Floor"
P -> <P>, "Please limit coffee
    breaks to 10 minutes."
```

```
Closing -> <Closing>, "The
    Management"
```

The lexical analyzer in this report shows events at the level of start-tags, end-tags, and data.

Basic SGML Language Constructs

Basic SGML documents are like ordinary text files, but the text is enhanced with certain constructs called *markup*. The markup constructs add structure to documents.

The lexical analyzer separates the characters of a document into markup and data characters. Markup is separated from data charcters by delimiters. The SGML delimiter recognition rules include a certain amount of context information. For example, the delimiter string </ is only recognized as markup when it is followed by a letter.

For a formal specification of the language constructs, see the lex specification in the Appendix (which is part of the implementation source distribution [19]). The following sections contain an informal overview.

Markup Declarations

Each SGML document begins with a document type declaration. Comment declarations and marked section delcarations are other types of markup declarations.

The string <! followed by a name begins a markup declaration. The name is followed by parameters and a >. A [in the parameters opens a *declaration subset*, which is a construct prohibited by this report.

The string <!-- begins a comment declaration. The -- begins a comment, which continues until the next occurrence of --. A comment declaration can contain zero or more comments. The string <!> is an empty comment declaration.

The string <![begins a marked section declaration, which is prohibited by this report.

For example:

```
<!doctype foo>
<!DOCTYPE foo SYSTEM>
<!doctype bar system "abcdef">
<!doctype BaZ public "-//owner//DTD
    description//EN">
<!doctype BAZ Public "-//owner//DTD
    desc//EN" "sysid">
<!>
another way to escape < and &:
    <<!>xxx &<!>abc;
<!-- xyz -->
<!-- xyz -- --def-->
<!---- ---- ---->
<!------------>
<!doctype foo --my document type--
    system "abc">
```

The following examples contain no markup.
They illustrate that `<!` does not always signal
markup.

```
<! doctype> <!,doctype> <!23>
<!- xxx -> <!-> <!-!>
```

The following are errors:

```
<!doctype xxx,yyy>
<!usemap map1>
<!-- comment-- xxx>
<!-- comment -- ->
<!----->
```

The following are errors, but they are not
reported by this lexical analyzer.

```
<!doctype foo foo foo>
<!doctype foo 23 17>
<!junk decl>
```

The following are valid SGML constructs that are
prohibited by this report:

```
<!doctype doc [ <!element doc - -
    ANY> ]>
<![ IGNORE [ lkjsdflkj sdflkj
    sdflkj ]]>
<![ CDATA [ lskdjf lskdjf lksjdf ]]>
```

Tags

Tags are used to delimit elements. Most elements
have a start-tag, some content, and end-tag.
Empty elements have only a start-tag. For some
elements, the start-tag and/or end-tag are
optional. Empty elements and optional tags are

structural constructs specified in the DTD, not
lexical issues.

A start-tag begins with < followed by a name,
and ends with >. The name refers to an element
declaration in the DTD. An end-tag is similar, but
begins with </.

For example:

```
<x> yyy </X>
<abc.DEF   > ggg </abc.def >
<abc123.-23>
<A>abc def <b>xxx</b>def</a>
<A>abc def <b>xxxdef</b>
```

The following examples contain no markup.
They illustrate that the < and </ strings do not
always signal markup.

```
< x > <324 </234>
<==> < b>
<%%%> <---> <...> <--->
```

The following examples are errors:

```
<xyz!> <abc/>
</xxx/> <xyz&def> <abc_def>
```

These last few examples illustrate valid SGML
constructs that are prohibited in the languages
described by this report:

```
<> xyz </>
<xxx<yyy> </yyy</xxx>
<xxx/content/
```

Names

A name is a name-start characer—a letter followed by any number of name characters—letters, digits, periods, or hyphens. Entity names are
case sensitive, but all other names are not.

Attributes

Start tags may contain attribute specifications. An
attribute specification consists of a name, an
equals sign (=), and a value specification. The
name refers to an item in an ATTLIST declaration.

The value can be a name token or an attribute
value literal. A name token is one or more name
characters. An attribute value literal is a string de-

limited by double-quotes (") or a string delimited by single-quotes ('). Interpretation of attribute value literals is covered in the discussion of the lexical analyzer API.

If the `ATTLIST` declaration specifies an enumerated list of names, and the value specification is one of those names, the attribute name and "=" may be omitted.

For example:

```
<x attr="val">
<x ATTR ="val" val>
<y aTTr1= "val1">
<yy attr1='xyz' attr2="def"
    attr3='xy"z' attr4="abc'def">
<xx abc='abc&#34;def'>
<xx aBC="fred &amp; barney">
<z attr1 = val1 attr2 = 23 attr3 =
    'abc'>
<xx val1 val2 attr3=.76meters>
<a href=foo.html> ..</a> <a
    href=foo-bar.html>..</a>
```

The following examples illustrate errors:

```
<x attr = abc$#@>
<y attr1,attr2>
<tt =xyz>
<z attr += 2>
<xx attr=50%>
<a href=http://foo/bar/>
<a href="http://foo/bar/> ... </a>
    ... <a href="xyz">...</a>
<xx "abc">
<xxx abc=>
```

Character References and Entity References

Characters in the document character set can be referred to by numeric character references. Entities declared in the DTD can be referred to by entity references.

An entity reference begins with & followed by a name, followed by an optional semicolon (;).

A numeric character reference begins with &# followed by a number followed by an optional semicolon. (The string &# followed by a name is a construct prohibited by this report.) A number is a sequence of digits.

The following examples illustrate character references and entity references:

```
&#38; &#200;
&amp; &ouml;
&#38 &#200,xxx
&amp &abc() &xy12/..
To illustrate the X tag, write
    &lt;X&gt;
```

These examples contain no markup. They illustrate that & does not always signal markup.

```
a & b, a &# b
a &, b &. c
a &#-xx &100
```

These examples are errors:

```
&#2000000; &#20.7 &#20-35
&#23x;
```

The following are valid SGML, but prohibited by this report:

```
&#SPACE;
&#RE;
```

Processing Instructions

Processing instructions are a mechanism to capture platform-specific idioms. A processing instruction begins with <? and ends with >.

For example:

```
<?>
<?style tt = font courier>
<?page break>
<?experiment> ... <?/experiment>
```

The Application Programmer Interface (API) to the Lexical Analyzer

An implementation of this specification is available [19], in the form of an ANSI C library. This section documents the API to the library. Note that the library is undergoing testing and revision. *The API is expected to change.*

The client of the lexical analyzer creates a data structure to hold the state of the lexical analyzer with a call to `SGML_newLexer`, and uses calls to `SGML_lex` to scan the data. Constructs are reported to the caller via three callback functions.

`SGML_lexNorm` is used to set case folding of names and whitespace normalization, and `SGML_lexLine` can be used to get the number of lines the lexer has encountered.

The output of the lexical analyzer, for each construct, is an an array of strings, and an array of enumerated types in one-to-one correspondence with the strings.

Data Characters

Data characters are passed to the primary callback function as an array of one single string containing the data characters and `SGML_DATA` as the type.

Note that the output contains all newlines (record end characters) from the input verbatim. Implementing the rules for ignoring record end characters (as per section 7.6.1 of SGML) is left to the client.

Tags and Attributes

Start-tags and end-tags are also passed to the primary callback function.

For a start-tag, the first element of the output array is a string of the form `<name` with `SGML_START` as the corresponding type. If requested (via `SGML_lexNorm`), the name is folded to lowercase. As shown below, the remaining elements of the array give the attributes. For an end-tag, the first element of the array is a case-folded string of the form `</name` with `SGML_END` as the type.

The output for attributes is included with the tag in which they appear. Attributes are reported as name/value pairs. The attribute name is output as a string of the form `name` and `SGML_ATTRNAME` as the type. An omitted name is reported as NULL.

An attribute value literal is output as a string of the form "xxx" or 'xxx' including the quotes, with `SGML_LITERAL` as the type . Other attribute values are returned as a string with `SGML_NMTOKEN` as the type. For example:

```
<xX val1 val2 aTTr3=".76meters">
```

is passed as an array of six strings:

```
[Tag/Data]
Start Tag: '<xx'
  Attr Name: ''
  Name: 'val1'
  Attr Name: ''
  Name: 'val2'
  Attr Name: 'attr3'
  Name Token: '.76meters'
  Tag Close: '>'
```

Note that attribute value literals are output verbatim. Interpretation is left to the client. Section 7.9.3 of SGML says that an attribute value literal is interpreted as an attribute value by:

- Removing the quotes

- Replacing character and entity references

- Deleting character 10 (ASCII LF)

- Replacing character 9 and 13 (ASCII HT and CR) with character 32 (SPACE)

Character and Entity References

A character reference refers to the character in the document character set whose number it specifies. For example, if the document character set is ISO 646 IRV (aka ASCII), then `&#65;` is another way to write A.

A numeric character reference is passed to the primary callback as an event whose first token type is `SGML_NUMCHARREF` and whose string takes the form `&#999`. The second token, if present, has type `SGML_REFC`, and consists of a semi-colon (;) or a newline.

A general entity reference is passed as an event whose first token is of the form `&name` with `SGML_GEREF` as its type. The second token, if present, has type `SGML_REFC`, and consists of a semi-colon (;) or a newline.

The reference should be checked against those declared in the DTD by the client.

Other Markup

Other markup is passed to the second callback function.

A comment declaration is reported in the string `<!` with type `SGML_MARKUP_DECL`, followed by zero or more strings of the form

```
-- comment --
```

with `SGML_COMMENT` as the type, followed by `>` with type `MDC`.

Other markup declarations are output as a string of the form `<!doctype` followed by strings of type `SGML_NAME`, `SGML_NUMBER`, `SGML_LIT-ERAL`, and/or `SGML_COMMENT`, followed by `TAGC`.

For example:

```
<!Doctype Foo --my document type--
    System "abc">
```

is reported as:

```
[Aux Markup]
Markup Decl: '<!doctype'
  Name: 'foo'
  Comment: '--my document type--'
  Name: 'system'
  Literal: '"abc"'
  Tag Close: '>'
```

Processing instructions are passed as a string of the form `<?pi stuff>` with type `SGML_PI`.

Errors and Limitations

Errors are passed to the third callback function. Two strings and two types are passed. For errors, the first string is a descriptive message, and the type is `SGML_ERROR`. The second string is the offending data, and the type is `SGML_DATA`.

Limitations imposed in this report are output similarly, but with type `SGML_LIMITATION` instead of `SGML_ERROR`. The lexical analyzer skips to a likely end of the error construct before continuing.

For example:

```
<tag xxx=yyy ?>xxx <![IGNORE[
    a<b>c]]> zzz
```

causes six callbacks:

```
[Err/Lim]
!!Error!!: 'bad character in tag'
  Data: '?'
[Tag/Data]
Start Tag: '<tag'
  Attr Name: 'xxx'
  Name Token: 'yyy'
  Tag Close: '>'
[Tag/Data]
Data: 'xxx '
[Err/Lim]
!!Limitation!!: 'marked sections
    not supported'
  Data: '<!['
[Err/Lim]
!!Limitation!!: 'declaration
    subset: skipping'
  Data: 'IGNORE[ a<b>c'
[Tag/Data]
Data: ' zzz'
```

Differences from Basic SGML

In section 15.1.1 of the SGML standard, a Basic SGML document is defined as an SGML document that uses the reference concrete syntax and the `SHORTTAG` and `OMITTAG` features. A concrete syntax is a binding of the SGML abstract syntax to concrete values. The reference concrete syntax binds the delimiter role `UNKNOWN TAG:` `<VAR`.

Some of these exceptions are likely to be reflected in the ongoing revision of SGML [3].

Arbitrary Limitations Removed

The reference concrete syntax includes certain limitations (capacities and quantities, in the language of the standard). For most purposes, these limitations are unnecessary. We remove them:

Long Names

The reference concrete syntax binds the parameter `NAMELEN` to 8. This means that names are limited to 8 characters. We remove this limitation. Arbitrarily long names are allowed.

Long Attribute Value Literals

We similarly remove the limitation of setting `LITLEN` to 960 and `ATTSPLEN` to 240.

Simplifications

We require the SGML declaration to be implicit and the DTD to be included by reference only:

SGML declaration

The SGML declaration is generally transmitted out of band, and is assumed by the sender and the receiver. The lexical analyzer will accept an in-line SGML declaration, but it will not adhere to the declarations therein. The lexical analyzer client should signal an error.

Internal declaration subset

The DTD is often included by reference, but some documents contain additional entity, element and attribute declarations in the `<!DOCTYPE` declaration. We prohibit additional declarations in the `<!DOCTYPE` declaration (see "Internal Declaration Subsets" in the "Future Work" section).

Parameter entity reference

The `%name;` construct is a parameter entity reference—similar to a reference to a C macro. There is little use for these entity references given the above limitations. An occurrence of a parameter entity in a markup declaration is prohibited.

Named character references

The construct `&#SPACE;` refers to a space character. This construct is not widely supported, and is reported as a limitation.

Marked sections

The construct `<![ IGNORE [ ... ]]>` is similar to the `#ifdef` construct in the C preprocessor. It is a novel construct that can be used to represent effectivity (applicability of parts of a document to various environments, depending on locale, client capabilities, user preferences, etc.). We expect that it will be deployed eventually (see "Marked Sections"), but to avoid interoperability issues, we prohibit its use.

Shorthand Markup Prohibited

Some constructs save typing, but add no expressive capability to the languages. And while they technically introduce no ambiguity, they reduce the robustness of documents, especially when the language is enhanced to include new elements. The SHORTTAG constructs related to attributes are widely used and implemented, but those related to tags are not.

These are relatively straightforward to support, but they are not widely deployed. While documents that use them are conforming SGML documents, they will not work with the deployed HTML tools. This lexical analyzer signals a limitation when encountering these constructs.

```
NET tags
     <name/.../

Unclosed Start Tag
     <name1<name2>

Empty Start Tag
     <>

Empty End Tag
     </>
```

In addition, the lexical analyzer assumes no short references are used.

Future Work

This report presents technology that is usable, but not complete. Work is ongoing in the following areas. Contributions are welcome. Send a note to *www-html@w3.org* with "sgml-lex" in the subject.

Marked Sections

Support for marked sections is an integral part of a strategy for interoperability among HTML user agents supporting different HTML dialects [18]. It has other valueable applicatoins, and it is a straightforward addition to the lexical analyzer in this report.

Internationalization

Support for character encodings and coded character sets other than ASCII is a requirement for production use. Support for the X Windows compound text encoding (related to ISO-2022) and the UTF-8 or perhaps UCS-2 encoding of Unicode (ISO-10646), with extensibility for other character encodings seems most desirable.

Internal Declaration Subset Support

Internal declaration subsets are not expected to become a part of HTML. But the technology in this report is applicable to other SGML applications, and internal declaration subsets are a straightfoward addition to this lexical analyzer. Relevent mechanisms include:

- General entity declarations with URIs as system identifiers

- General entity declarations as "macros"

- Parameter entity declarations for "switches" and "hooks"

Short References and Empty End-tags

While they may increase the complexity of the lexical analyzer, short references may be necessary to support math markup in HTML. Empty end-tags are not likely to be used in HTML, as they interact badly with conventions for handling undeclared element tags. But in other SGML applications, they are a useful feature.

Appendix: Flex Specification and Source Distribution

A formal specification of the lexical analyzer discussed in this report is given in the form of a flex input file in Example 1.

The flex input file is part of the sgml-lex source distribution, which contains an implementation of the API discussed above, and some test materials.

The source distribution is provided under the W3C copyright, which allows unlimited redistribution for any purpose. ∎

Example 1

```
/* $Id: sgml.l,v 1.9 1996/02/07 15:32:28 connolly Exp $ */
/* sgml.l -- a lexical analyzer for Basic+/- SGML Documents
 * See: "A Lexical Analyzer for HTML and Basic SGML"
 */


/*
 * NOTE: We assume the locale used by lex and the C compiler
 * agrees with ISO-646-IRV; for example: '1' == 0x31.
 */


/* Example 1 -- Character Classes: Abstract Syntax */

Digit   [0-9]
LCLetter[a-z]
Special ['()_,\-\./:=?]
UCLetter[A-Z]

/* Example 2 -- Character Classes: Concrete Syntax */
```

Example 1 *(Continued)*

```
LCNMCHAR[\.-]
/* LCNMSTRT[] */
UCNMCHAR[\.-]
/* UCNMSTRT[] */
 /* @# hmmm. sgml spec says \015 */
RE       \n
 /* @# hmmm. sgml spec says \012 */
RS       \r
SEPCHAR \011
SPACE   \040

/* Example 3 -- Reference Delimiter Set: General */

COM "--"
CRO "&#"
DSC "]"
DSO "["
ERO "&"
ETAGO"</"
LIT \"
LITA"'"
MDC ">"
MDO "<!"
MSC "]]"
NET     "/"
PERO    "%"
PIC ">"
PIO "<?"
REFC";"
STAGO"<"
TAGC">"

/* 9.2.1 SGML Character */

/*name_start_character{LCLetter}|{UCLetter}|{LCNMSTRT}|{UCNMSTRT}*/
name_start_character{LCLetter}|{UCLetter}
name_character{name_start_character}|{Digit}|{LCNMCHAR}|{UCNMCHAR}

/* 9.3 Name */

name    {name_start_character}{name_character}*
number  {Digit}+
number_token{Digit}{name_character}*
name_token{name_character}+

/* 6.2.1 Space */
s       {SPACE}|{RE}|{RS}|{SEPCHAR}
ps      ({SPACE}|{RE}|{RS}|{SEPCHAR})+

/* trailing white space */
ws      ({SPACE}|{RE}|{RS}|{SEPCHAR})*

/* 9.4.5 Reference End */
```

Example 1 *(Continued)*

```
reference_end({REFC}|{RE})

/*
 * 10.1.2 Parameter Literal
 * 7.9.3  Attribute Value Literal
 * (we leave recognition of character references and entity references,
 *  and whitespace compression to further processing)
 *
 * @# should split this into minimum literal, parameter literal,
 * @# and attribute value literal.
 */
literal ({LIT}[^\"]*{LIT})|({LITA}[^\']*{LITA})




/* 9.6.1 Recognition modes */

/*
 * Recognition modes are represented here by start conditions.
 * The default start condition, INITIAL, represents the
 * CON recognition mode. This condition is used to detect markup
 * while parsing normal data charcters (mixed content).
 *
 * The CDATA start condition represents the CON recognition
 * mode with the restriction that only end-tags are recognized,
 * as in elements with CDATA declared content.
 * (@# no way to activate it yet: need hook to parser.)
 *
 * The TAG recognition mode is split into two start conditions:
 * ATTR, for recognizing attribute value list sub-tokens in
 * start-tags, and TAG for recognizing the TAGC (">") delimiter
 * in end-tags.
 *
 * The MD start condition is used in markup declarations. The COM
 * start condition is used for comment declarations.
 *
 * The DS condition is an approximation of the declaration subset
 * recognition mode in SGML. As we only use this condition after signalling
 * an error, it is merely a recovery device.
 *
 * The CXT, LIT, PI, and REF recognition modes are not separated out
 * as start conditions, but handled within the rules of other start
 * conditions. The GRP mode is not represented here.
 */

 /* EXCERPT ACTIONS: START */

/* %x CON == INITIAL */
%x CDATA

%x TAG
%x ATTR
%x ATTRVAL
```

Example 1 *(Continued)*

```
%x NETDATA
%x ENDTAG
/* this is only to be permissive with bad end-tags: */
%x JUNKTAG

%x MD
%x COM
%x DS

 /* EXCERPT ACTIONS: STOP */

%%

  int *types = NULL;
  char **strings = NULL;
  size_t *lengths = NULL;
  int qty = 0;

     /*
      * See sgml_lex.c for description of
      *   ADD, CALLBACK, ERROR, TOK macros.
      */


 /*
  * 9.6 Delimiter Recognition and
  * Figure 3 -- Reference Delimiter Set: General
  *
  * This is organized by recognition mode: first CON, then TAG,
  * MD, and DS. Within a mode, the rules are ordered alphabetically
  * by delimiter name.
  */


  /* &#60; -- numeric character reference */
<INITIAL,NETDATA>{CRO}{number}{reference_end}? {
                reference(yytext, yyleng, SGML_NUMCHARREF, 0,
                        1, tokF, tokObj);
            }

  /* &#60xyz. -- syntax error */
<INITIAL,NETDATA>{CRO}{number_token}{reference_end}?{
                            ERROR(SGML_ERROR,
                    "bad character in character reference",
                    yytext, yyleng);
                }


  /* &#SPACE; -- named character reference. */
<INITIAL,NETDATA>{CRO}{name}{reference_end}?{
                if (l->restrict) {
                    if (l->compat)
            /* old-style user agents use it as data. */
```

Example 1 *(Continued)*

```
                        TOK(tokF, tokObj, SGML_DATA, yytext, yyleng);
            else{
                    ERROR(SGML_LIMITATION,
                "named character references are not supported",
                yytext, yyleng);
            }
                }else{
                    reference(yytext, yyleng, SGML_NAMECHARREF, l->normalize,
                            l, tokF, tokObj);
                }
            }

    /* &amp; -- general entity reference */
<INITIAL,NETDATA>{ERO}{name}{reference_end}?{
                        reference(yytext, yyleng, SGML_GEREF, 0,
                                l, tokF, tokObj);
                    }

    /* </name <  -- unclosed end tag */
<INITIAL,CDATA>{ETAGO}{name}?{ws}/{STAGO} {
            if (l->restrict){
                ERROR(SGML_LIMITATION,
                    "unclosed end tag not supported",
                                yytext, yyleng);
            }else{
                        ADDCASE(SGML_END, yytext, yyleng);
                        CALLBACK(tokF,tokObj);
                    }
                }

    /* </title> -- end tag */
<INITIAL,CDATA>{ETAGO}{name}{ws} {
                                ADDCASE(SGML_END, yytext, yyleng);
                    if (l->restrict && l->compat) {
                        BEGIN(JUNKTAG);
                    }else {
                        BEGIN(ENDTAG);
                    }
                }

    /* @# HACK for XMP, LISTING? */
    Date: Fri, 19 Jan 1996 23:13:43 -0800
    Message-Id: <v01530502ad25cc1a251b@[206.86.76.80]>
    To: www-html@w3.org
    Subject: Re: Daniel Connolly's SGML Lex Specification
    */

    /* @@ all these are recognized in NETDATA too. Need a stack? */

    /* </> -- empty end tag */
{ETAGO}{TAGC}{
            if (l->restrict) {
                if (l->compat)
```

Example 1 *(Continued)*

```
                                    TOK(tokF, tokObj, SGML_DATA, yytext, yyleng);
            else
            ERROR(SGML_LIMITATION,
                    "empty end tag not supported",
                    yytext, yyleng);
                    }else{
                        TOK2(tokF, tokObj,
                            SGML_START, yytext, yyleng-1,
                            SGML_TAGC, yytext + yyleng - 1, 1);
                }
            }

  /* <!DOCTYPE -- markup declaration */
{MDO}{name}{ws}{
                                    ADDCASE(SGML_MARKUP_DECL, yytext, yyleng);
                BEGIN(MD);
                }

  /* <!> -- empty comment */
{MDO}{MDC}  {
                                TOK(auxF, auxObj, SGML_MARKUP_DECL,
                    yytext, yyleng);
                }

  /* <!-- -- comment declaration */
{MDO}/{COM} {
                                ADD(SGML_MARKUP_DECL, yytext, yyleng);
                BEGIN(COM);
                }

  /* <![ -- marked section */
{MDO}{DSO}{ws}{
                        ERROR(SGML_LIMITATION,
                    "marked sections not supported",
                    yytext, yyleng);
            BEGIN(DS); /* @# skip past some stuff */
                }

  /* ]]> -- marked section end */
{MSC}{MDC}  {
                        ERROR(SGML_ERROR,
                    "unmatched marked sections end",
                    yytext, yyleng);
                }

  /* <? ...> -- processing instruction */
{PIO}[^>]*{PIC}{
                                    if (l->restrict && l->compat){
                                    /*@# issue warning? */
                                    TOK(tokF, tokObj, SGML_DATA,
                    yytext, yyleng);
                }else{
                                        TOK(auxF, auxObj, SGML_PI,
```

Example 1 *(Continued)*

```
                              yytext, yyleng);
                                            }
                }
  /* <name -- start tag */
{STAGO}{name}{ws}{
                                    ADDCASE(SGML_START, yytext, yyleng);
                BEGIN(ATTR);
                }


  /* <> -- empty start tag */
{STAGO}{TAGC}{
            if (l->restrict) {
                if (l->compat)
                    TOK(tokF, tokObj, SGML_DATA, yytext, yyleng);
                else
                ERROR(SGML_LIMITATION,
                        "empty tag not supported",
                        yytext, yyleng);
            }else {
                ADDCASE(SGML_START, yytext, yyleng - 1);
                CALLBACK(tokF, tokObj);
            }
}

  /* abcd -- data characters */
([^<&]|(<[^<&a-zA-Z!->?])|(&[^<&#a-zA-Z]))+|.{
                                    TOK(tokF, tokObj, SGML_DATA, yytext, yyleng);
                }

  /* abcd -- data characters */
<CDATA>[^<]+|.{
                                    TOK(tokF, tokObj, SGML_DATA, yytext, yyleng);
                }

<NETDATA>{NET}{
                        TOK(tokF, tokObj, SGML_NET, yytext, yyleng);
            BEGIN(INITIAL);
                }

  /* <em/ ^abcd  / -- data characters within null end tag */
<NETDATA>([^/&<])+|. {
                                    TOK(tokF, tokObj, SGML_DATA, yytext, yyleng);
                }

/* 7.4 Start Tag */
/* Actually, the generic identifier specification is consumed
 * along with the STAGO delimiter ("<"). So we're only looking
 * for tokens that appear in an attribute specification list,
 * plus TAGC (">"). NET ("/") and STAGO ("<") signal limitations.
 */

/* 7.5 End Tag */
```

Example 1 *(Continued)*

```
/* Just looking for TAGC. NET, STAGO as above */

  /* <a ^href = "xxx"> -- attribute name */
<ATTR>{name}{s}*={ws}{

                                if(l->normalize){

                                   /* strip trailing space and = */
                                   while(yytext[yyleng-1] == '='
                          || isspace(yytext[yyleng-1])){
                          --yyleng;
                        }
                                }

                                ADDCASE(SGML_ATTRNAME, yytext, yyleng);
                   BEGIN(ATTRVAL);
                 }

  /* <img src="xxx" ^ismap> -- name */
<ATTR>{name}{ws}{
                                ADD(SGML_ATTRNAME, NULL, 0);
                                ADDCASE(SGML_NAME, yytext, yyleng);

                 }

  /* <a name = ^xyz> -- name token */
<ATTRVAL>{name_token}{ws}{
                                ADD(SGML_NMTOKEN, yytext, yyleng);
                   BEGIN(ATTR);
                 }

  /* <a href = ^"a b c"> -- literal */
<ATTRVAL>{literal}{ws}{
                                if(yyleng > 2 && yytext[yyleng-2] == '='
                     && memchr(yytext, '>', yyleng)){
                    ERROR(SGML_WARNING,
                      "missing attribute end-quote?",
                      yytext, yyleng);
                  }
                                ADD(SGML_LITERAL, yytext, yyleng);
                   BEGIN(ATTR);
                 }

  /* <a name= ^> -- illegal tag close */
<ATTRVAL>{TAGC}{
                                ERROR(SGML_ERROR,
              "Tag close found where attribute value expected",
                  yytext, yyleng);
                                /* @@ need test for this */
                ADD(SGML_TAGC, yytext, yyleng);

                                CALLBACK(tokF,tokObj);
                   BEGIN(INITIAL);
                 }
```

Example 1 *(Continued)*

```
  /* <a name=foo ^>,</foo^> -- tag close */
<ATTR,TAG>{TAGC}{
                              ADD(SGML_TAGC, yytext, yyleng);
                              CALLBACK(tokF,tokObj);
             BEGIN(INITIAL);
           }

  /* <em^/ -- NET tag */
<ATTRVAL>{NET}{
                         ERROR(SGML_ERROR,
                   "attribute value missing",
                 yytext, yyleng);

            ADD(SGML_NET, yytext, yyleng);
            CALLBACK(tokF, tokObj);
            BEGIN(INITIAL);
              }

  /* <em^/ -- NET tag */
<ATTR>{NET}{
            if (l->restrict) {
               CALLBACK(tokF, tokObj);
               ERROR(SGML_LIMITATION, "NET tags not supported",
                 yytext, yyleng);
               BEGIN(INITIAL);
            }else{
              ADD(SGML_NET, yytext, yyleng);
              CALLBACK(tokF, tokObj);
              BEGIN(NETDATA);
            }
}

  /* <foo^<bar> -- unclosed start tag */
<ATTR,ATTRVAL,TAG>{STAGO}{
                         /* report pending tag */
            CALLBACK(tokF, tokObj);
            BEGIN(INITIAL);

                      if(l->restrict){
                          ERROR(SGML_LIMITATION,
                   "Unclosed tags not supported",
                 yytext, yyleng);
                      }else{
                          /* save STAGO for next time */
#ifdef FIX_YYLESS /*@@*/
                          yyless(leng-1); /*@# length of STAGO assumed 1 */
#endif
                          BEGIN(INITIAL);
                      }
              }

  /* <a href = ^http://foo/> -- unquoted literal HACK */
```

Example 1 *(Continued)*

```
<ATTRVAL>[^ "\t\n\r>]+{ws}{
                            ERROR(SGML_ERROR,
                "attribute value needs quotes",
                yytext, yyleng);
                            ADD(SGML_LITERAL, yytext, yyleng);
                BEGIN(ATTR);
              }

<ATTR,ATTRVAL,TAG>.{
                        ERROR(SGML_ERROR,
                "bad character in tag",
                yytext, yyleng);
              }

  /* end tag -- non-permissive */
<ENDTAG>{TAGC} {
                        ADD(SGML_TAGC, yytext, yyleng);
                        CALLBACK(tokF,tokObj);
          BEGIN(INITIAL);
          }

<ENDTAG>. {
        ERROR(SGML_ERROR, "extraneous character in end tag",
            yytext, yyleng);
        }

  /* permissive search for tag close */
<JUNKTAG>[^>]+ {
          /* skip */
          }

<JUNKTAG>{TAGC} {
        BEGIN(INITIAL);
            }


 /* 10 Markup Declarations: General */

 /* <!^--...-->   -- comment */
<MD,COM>{COM}([^-]|-[^-])*{COM}{ws}{
                            ADD(SGML_COMMENT, yytext, yyleng);
          }

 /* <!doctype ^%foo;> -- parameter entity reference */
<MD>{PERO}{name}{reference_end}?{ws}{
          if (l->restrict) {
                    ERROR(SGML_LIMITATION,
                "parameter entity reference not supported",
                yytext, yyleng);
                }
          ADD(SGML_PERO, yytext, yyleng);
            }
```

Example 1 *(Continued)*

```
/* <!entity ^% foo system "..." ...> -- parameter entity definition */
<MD>{PERO}{ps}{
                if (l->restrict) {
                    ERROR(SGML_LIMITATION,
               "parameter entity definition not supported",
                      yytext, yyleng);
                }
                ADD(SGML_PERO, yytext, yyleng);
            }

/* The limited set of markup delcarations we're interested in
 * use only numbers, names, and literals.
 */
<MD>{number}{ws}{
                            ADD(SGML_NUMBER, yytext, yyleng);
            }

<MD>{name}{ws}{
                            ADDCASE(SGML_NAME, yytext, yyleng);
            }

<MD>{number_token}{ws}{
                            ADD(SGML_NUMTOKEN, yytext, yyleng);
            }

<MD>{name_token}{ws}{
                            ADDCASE(SGML_NMTOKEN, yytext, yyleng);
            }

<MD>{literal}{ws}        {
                            ADD(SGML_LITERAL, yytext, yyleng);
            }

<MD,COM>{MDC}{
                            ADD(SGML_TAGC, yytext, yyleng);
                            CALLBACK(auxF, auxObj);
                BEGIN(INITIAL);
                }

/* other constructs are errors. */
   /* <!doctype foo ^[  -- declaration subset */
<MD>{DSO}   {
                        if(l->restrict){
                            ERROR(SGML_LIMITATION,
                  "declaration subset not supported",
                  yytext, yyleng);
                        }
            ADD(SGML_DSO, yytext, yyleng);
            CALLBACK(auxF, auxObj);
            BEGIN(DS);
                }

<MD,COM>.        {
```

Example 1 *(Continued)*

```
                        ERROR(SGML_ERROR,
                "illegal character in markup declaration",
                yytext, yyleng);
        }


/* 10.4 Marked Section Declaration */
/* 11.1 Document Type Declaration Subset */

/* Our parsing of declaration subsets is just an error recovery technique:
 * we attempt to skip them, but we may be fooled by "]"s
 * inside comments, etc.
 */

/* ]]> -- marked section end */
<DS>{MSC}{MDC}{
                BEGIN(INITIAL);
                }
/* ] -- declaration subset close */
<DS>{DSC}   { BEGIN(COM); }

<DS>[^\]]+ {
                        ERROR(SGML_LIMITATION,
                "declaration subset: skipping",
                yytext, yyleng);
        }

/* EXCERPT ACTIONS: STOP */

%%
```

References

1. Goldfarb, C.F., *The SGML Handbook*, Y. Rubinsky, ed., Oxford University Press, 1990.

2. ISO 8879, Information Processing—Text and Office Systems—Standard Generalized Markup Language (SGML), 1986.

3. Goldfarb, C.F., ed., ISO/IEC JTC1/SC18/WG8 N1351, Request for contributions for review of ISO 8879, , 11, October 1991.

4. Berners-Lee, T., and D. Connolly, "Hypertext Markup Language—2.0" RFC 1866, MIT/W3C, November 1995.

5. *rfc1874.txt*—SGML Media Types, E. Levinson, December 1995.

6. Sperberg-McQueen, C. M., and Lou Burnard, eds., "Guidelines for Electronic Text Encoding and Interchange," 16, May 1994.

7. The SGML PRIMER SoftQuad's Quick Reference Guide to the Essentials of the Standard: The SGML Needed for Reading a DTD and Marked-Up Documents and Discussing Them Reasonably.

8. Wohler, Wayne L. "The DTD May Not Be Enough: SGML Declarations," 5/10 (October 1992) 6-9, 6/1 (January 1993) 1-7; 6/2 (February 1993) 1-6.

9. Eve Maler, "DocBook V2.3 Maintainer's Guide," ArborText, Inc., Revision 1.1, 25 September 1995.

10. Online documentation of HTF (Hyper-G Text Format), 94/09/21.

11. Wholer, Wayne, Don R. Day, W. Eliot Kimber, Simch Gralla, and Mike Temple "IBM ID Doc Language Reference, Draft 1.4," February 13, 1994.

12. Aho, Alfred V., Ravi Sethi, and Jeffrey D. Ullman, *Compilers, Principles, Techniques, and Tools*, Addison-Wesley, 1988.

13. Kernighan, Brian W. and Dennis M. Ritchie, *The C Programming Language*, Prentice Hall, 1988.

14. Kaelbling, Mike, "On Improving SGML, Electronic Publishing—Origination, Dissemination and Design," 3(2)93—98, May, 1990; also available as Ohio State Tech Report 88-22.

15. Vern Paxson Systems Engineering Bldg. 46A, Room 1123 Lawrence Berkeley Laboratory University of California Berkeley, CA 94720, *vern@ee.lbl.gov*

16. Connolly, Dan, "SGML and the Web"—Work in Progress. W3C, January 1996.

17. Connolly, Dan, "HTML Dialects: Internet Media and SGML Document Types," W3C, Work in progress, January 1996.

About the Author

Dan Connolly
World Wide Web Consortium
MIT Laboratory for Computer Science
545 Technology Square
Cambridge, MA 02139
connolly@w3.org

Dan discovered the Web project in 1991 soon after graduating from U.T. Austin while he was at Convex. His industry experience in online documentation tools, distributed computing, and information delivery kept him in touch with the project while he was at Dazel and HaLSoft.

In March 1995, Dan joined the W3C, utilizing his background in formal systems to work on the specification of HTML and other parts of the Web. He was the editor of Issue 2 of the *World Wide Web Journal* (W3J), and is currently editor of *Web Programmer* magazine.

EXTENDED LOG FILE FORMAT

Phillip M. Hallam-Baker, Brian Behlendorf

Abstract

[W3C Working Draft; WD-logfile-960323; March 23, 1996]

An improved format for Web server log files is presented. The format is extensible, permitting a wider range of data to be captured. This proposal is motivated by the need to capture a wider range of data for demographic analysis and also the needs of proxy caches.

Status of This Document

This is a W3C Working Draft for review by W3C members and other interested parties. It is a draft document and may be updated, replaced or obsoleted by other documents at any time. It is inappropriate to use W3C Working Drafts as reference material or to cite them as other than "work in progress." A list of current W3C working drafts can be found at *http://www.w3.org/pub/WWW/TR.*

Introduction

Most Web servers offer the option to store log files in either the *common log format* or a proprietary format. The common log file format is supported by the majority of analysis tools but the information about each server transaction is fixed. In many cases it is desirable to record more information. Sites sensitive to personal data issues may wish to omit the recording of certain data. In addition ambiguities arise in analyzing the common log file format since field separator characters may in some cases occur within fields. The extended log file format is designed to meet the following needs:

- Permit control over the data recorded

- Support needs of proxies, clients, and servers in a common format

- Provide robust handling of character escaping issues

- Allow exchange of demographic data

- Allow summary data to be expressed

In particular the common log file format does not record the HTTP `referer` field that informs a server of the resource in which the client discovered the URI being requested. The extended log file format permits any header field value to be recorded, including that of the `referer` header.

The log file format described permits customized log files to be recorded in a format readable by generic analysis tools. A header specifying the data types recorded is written out at the start of each log.

This work is in part motivated by the need to support collection of demographic data. This work is discussed at greater length in companion drafts describing session identifier URIs [6] and more consistent proxy behavior [7].

Notational Conventions and Generic Grammar

Augmented BNF

All of the mechanisms specified in this document are described in both prose and an augmented Backus-Naur Form (BNF) similar to that used by RFC 822 [4], a strict subset of that used in RFC 1945 [3], which describes HTTP/1.0. Implementors will need to be familiar with the notation in order to understand this specification. The augmented BNF includes the following constructs:

name = definition

The name of a rule is simply the name itself without any enclosing brackets (< and >) and is separated from its definition by the equal character (=). Whitespace is only significant in that indentation of continuation lines is used to indicate a rule definition that spans more than one line. Certain basic rules are in uppercase, such as SP, LWS, HT, CRLF, DIGIT, ALPHA, etc. Angle brackets are used within definitions whenever their presence will facilitate discerning the use of rule names.

"literal"

Quotation marks surround literal text. Unless stated otherwise, the text is case-insensitive.

rule1 | rule2

Elements separated by a bar (|) are alternatives, e.g., yes | no will accept yes or no.

(rule1 rule2)

Elements enclosed in parentheses are treated as a single element. Thus, (elem (foo | bar) elem) allows the token sequences elem foo elem and elem bar elem.

*rule

The asterisk character (*) preceding an element indicates repetition. The full form is <n>*<m>element indicating at least <n> and at most <m> occurrences of element. Default values are 0 and infinity so that *(element) allows any number, including zero; 1*element requires at least one, and 1*2element allows one or two.

[rule]

Square brackets enclose optional elements; [foo bar] is equivalent to *1(foo bar).

N rule

Specific repetition: <n>(element) is equivalent to <n>*<n>(element); that is, exactly <n> occurrences of (element). Thus 2DIGIT is a 2-digit number, and 3ALPHA is a string of three alphabetic characters.

#rule

A construct # is defined, similar to *, for defining lists of elements. The full form is <n>#<m>element indicating at least <n> and at most <m> elements, each separated by one or more commas (,) and optional linear whitespace (LWS). This makes the usual form of lists very easy; a rule such as "(*LWS element *(*LWS element))" can be shown as 1#element. Wherever this construct is used, null elements are allowed but do not contribute to the count of elements present. That is, (element), , (element) is permitted but counts as only two elements. Therefore, where at least one element is required, at least one non-null element *must* be present. Default values are 0 and infinity so that #(element) allows any number, including zero; 1#element requires at least one, and 1#2element allows one or two.

; comment

A semicolon (;), set off some distance to the right of rule text, starts a comment that continues to the end of line. This is a simple way of including useful notes in parallel with the specifications.

implied *LWS

The grammar described by this specification is word-based. Except where noted otherwise, linear whitespace (LWS) can be included between any two adjacent words (token or quoted-string) and between adjacent tokens and delimiters (tspecials), without changing the interpretation of a field. At least one delimiter (tspecials) *must* exist between any two tokens, since they would otherwise be interpreted as a single token. However, applications *should* attempt to follow "common form" when generating HTTP constructs, since some implementations fail to accept anything beyond the common forms.

Example 1

```
OCTET           = <any 8-bit sequence of data>
       CHAR        = <any US-ASCII character (octets 0 - 127)>
       UPALPHA     = <any US-ASCII uppercase letter "A".."Z">
       LOALPHA     = <any US-ASCII lowercase letter "a".."z">
       ALPHA       = UPALPHA | LOALPHA
       DIGIT       = <any US-ASCII digit "0".."9">
       CTL         = <any US-ASCII control character
                     (octets 0 - 31) and DEL (127)>
       CR          = <US-ASCII CR, carriage return (13)>
       LF          = <US-ASCII LF, linefeed (10)>
       SP          = <US-ASCII SP, space (32)>
       HT          = <US-ASCII HT, horizontal-tab (9)>
       <">         = <US-ASCII double-quote mark (34)>

       CRLF        = CR LF

       word        = token | quoted-string

       token       = 1*<any CHAR except CTLs or tspecials>

       tspecials   = "(" | ")" | "<" | ">" | "@"
                   | "," | ";" | ":" | "\" | <">
                   | "/" | "[" | "]" | "?" | "="
                   | "{" | "}" | SP | HT
```

Basic Rules

Example 1 above shows the rules used throughout this specification to describe basic parsing constructs. The US-ASCII coded character set is defined by [1].

Format

An extended log file contains a sequence of *lines* containing ASCII characters terminated by either the sequence LF or CRLF. Log file generators *should* follow the line termination convention for the platform on which they are executed. Analyzers MUST accept either form. Each line may contain either a *directive* or an *entry*.

Entries consist of a sequence of *fields* relating to a single HTTP transaction. Fields are separated by whitespace; the use of tab characters for this purpose is encouraged. If a field is unused in a particular entry, a dash (–) marks the omitted field. Directives record information about the logging process itself.

A variation of BNF is used to describe the syntax of the log file format.

Directives

Lines beginning with the # character contain directives. The following directives are defined:

Version: *<integer>.<integer>*
> The version of the extended log file format used. This draft defines version 1.0.

Fields: [*<specifier>*...]
> Specifies the fields recorded in the log.

Software: *string*
> Identifies the software that generated the log.

Start-Date: *<date> <time>*
> The date and time at which the log was started.

End-Date:*<date> <time>*
> The date and time at which the log was finished.

Date:*<date> <time>*

> The date and time at which the entry was added.

GMT-Offset:*<time-offset>*

> Offset of times recorded from GMT. If local time is used for logging the offset from GMT *must* be specified using this field.
>
> **NB**: The time offset is *only* applied to fields of type *<time>* . If the value of a header field is recorded as a string the offset *must not* be applied.

Remark: *<text>*

> Comment information. Data recorded in this field MUST be ignored by analysis tools.

The directives `Version` and `Fields` are required and one directive of each type *must* precede all entries in the log. The `Fields` directive specifies the data recorded in the fields of each entry.

The scope of a directive begins on the line that is defined and continues until the next directive of the same name. Thus a file may have multiple `Date` or `fields` directives. The `start-date` and `End-Date` directives are an exception to this rule. These directives may occur at any position in a file, and their scope is global to the whole file. Thus a log file generator *may* write an `End-Date` directive to the start of a file as a convenience to users scanning through large numbers of logs.

Example

The following is an example file in the extended log format:

```
#Version: 1.0
#Date: 1996-01-12 00:00:00
#Fields: time cs-method cs-uri
00:34:23 GET /foo/bar.html
12:21:16 GET /foo/bar.html
12:45:52 GET /foo/bar.html
12:57:34 GET /foo/bar.html
```

Fields

The `#Fields` directive lists a sequence of *field identifiers* specifying the information recorded in each entry. Field identifiers may have one of the following forms:

identifier

> Identifier relates to the transaction as a whole.

prefix-identifier

> Identifier relates to information transfer between parties defined by the value *prefix*.

prefix(header)

> Identifies the value of the HTTP header field `header` for transfer between parties defined by the value *prefix*. Fields specified in this manner always have the value *<string>*.

The following prefixes are defined:

c	Client
s	Server
r	Remote
cs	Client to server
sc	Server to client
sr	Server to remote server—this prefix is used by proxies.
rs	Remote server to server—this prefix is used by proxies.
x	Application-specific identifier

The identifier `cs-method` thus refers to the method in the request sent by the client to the server while `sc(Referer)` refers to the `referer:` field of the reply. The identifier `c-ip` refers to the client's IP address.

Identifiers

The following identifiers do not take a prefix:

date

> Date at which transaction completed, field has type *<date>*.

time

Time at which transaction completed, field has type *<time>*.

time-taken

Time taken for transaction to complete in seconds, field has type *<fixed>*.

bytes

Bytes transferred, field has type *<integer>*.

cached

Records whether a cache hit occurred, field has type *<integer>* 0 indicates a cache miss.

The following identifiers require a prefix:

ip [c-ip, s-ip, r-ip]

IP address and port, field has type *<address>*

dns [c-dns, s-dns, r-dns]

DNS name, field has type *<name>*.

status [sc-status, rs-status]

Status code, field has type *<integer>*.

comment [sc-comment, rs-comment]

Comment returned with status code, field has type *<string>*.

method [cs-method, sr-method]

Method, field has type *<id>*.

uri [cs-uri, sr-uri]

URI, field has type <uri>.

uri-stem [cs-uri, sr-uri]

Stem portion alone of URI (omitting query), field has type *<uri>*.

uri-query [cs-query, sr-query]

Query portion alone of URI, field has type *<uri>*.

auth-id [c-auth-id, s-auth-id, r-auth-id]

Records the authorization identifier of the specified party; field has type *<string>*. This field permits a single field to be used to record all authorization information, regardless of the mechanism used to obtain it.

Special Fields for Log Summaries

Analysis tools may generate log summaries. A log summary entry begins with a count specifying the number of times a particular event occurred. For example, a site may be interested in a count of the number of requests for a particular URI with a given `referer:` field but not be interested in recording information about individual requests such as the IP address.

The following field is mandatory and *must* precede all others and does not take a prefix:

count

The number of entries for which the listed data, field has type *<integer>*.

The following fields may be used in place of *time* to allow aggregation of log file entries over intervals of time; none take prefixes:

time-from

Time at which sampling began, field has type *<time>*.

time-to

Time at which sampling ended, field has type *<time>*.

interval

Time over which sampling occurred in seconds, field has type *<integer>*.

Entries

This section describes the data formats for log file field entries. These formats are chosen so as to avoid ambiguity, minimize the difficulty of generation and parsing, and provide for human readability.

Each log file entry consists of a sequence of fields separated by whitespace and terminated by a CR or CRLF sequence. The meanings of the fields are defined by a preceding #Fields directive. If a field is omitted for a particular entry, a single dash (–) is substituted.

Log file parsers *should* be tolerant of errors. If an entry contains corrupt data or is terminated unexpectedly the parser *should* resynchronize using the end of line marker and continue to parse the following entries. Entries *must not* contain any ASCII control characters.

```
<entry> = *<field> <end-of-line>

<field> = <integer> | <fixed> |
    <uri> | <date> | <time> |
    <string> | <text> | <name> |
    <address>

<digit> = "0" | "1" | "2" | "3" |
    "4" | "5" | "6" | "7" | "8" |
    "9"
```

ID

```
<id>  =  1*<alpha>
```

Alpha identifier.

Integer

```
<integer>      = 1*<digit>
```

Integers are represented as a sequence of digits.

Fixed Format Float

```
<fixed> = 1*<digit> [. *<digit>]
```

URI

A URI or fragment thereof as specified by RFC 1738; relative URIs are specified by RFC 1808. URIs cannot by definition include whitespace or ASCII control characters. Consequently, no ambiguity arises from their use.

Date

```
<date>  = 4<digit> "-" 2<digit> "-"
    2<digit>
```

Dates are recorded in the format YYYY-MM-DD where YYYY, MM, and DD stand for the numeric year, month, and day, respectively. All dates are specified in GMT. This format is chosen to assist collation using *sort*.

Time

```
<time>  = 2<digit> ":" 2<digit>
    [":" 2<digit> ["." *<digit>]
```

Times are recorded in the form HH:MM, HH:MM:SS, or HH:MM:SS.S where HH is the hour in 24-hour format, MM is minutes, and SS is seconds. All times are specified in GMT unless the GMT-Offset directive is used.

Time-Offset

```
<time-offset>  = (+ | -) 4<digit>
```

Used in the GMT-Time directive to specify an offset to be added to all *<time>* fields.

String

```
<string>        = '"' *<schar> '"'

<schar> = xchar | '"' '"'
```

Strings are output in quoted form. If a string contains a quotation character, the character is repeated. This format is unambiguous since fields are by definition separated by whitespace. The dash character *must not* be used as an abbreviation for an empty string.

No mechanism for incorporating control characters is defined.

Text

```
<text>  =  <char>*
```

The text field is used only by directives.

Name

```
<name>  =  <alpha> [ "." *<alpha> ]
```

DNS name.

Address

```
<name>  =  <integer> [ "."
    *<integer> ] [ ":" <integer> ]
```

Numeric IP address and optional port specifier.

Further Work

Geographical Location

The present specification does not have a provision for stating the geographical location of a user. Unfortunately, although it is highly desirable to obtain and record this information, it is very difficult to determine from network information alone more than the continent from which a connection was made.

It is unlikely that this situation will improve. Many Internet Service Providers (ISPs) consider the internal topology of their networks to be commercially sensitive information and are reluctant to provide such information. A number of ISPs serve an entire continent from one or two centralized control centers using dedicated long distance phone connections to allow connection via a "local" call. Such systems are likely to require substantial and expensive modification to permit capture of the original number dialed. ∎

References

1. ANSI, US-ASCII, *Coded Character Set— 7-Bit American Standard Code for Information Interchange.* Standard ANSI X3.4-1986, 1986.

2. Berners-Lee, T., and L. Masinter, "Uniform Resource Locators (URL)," RFC 1738, December 1994, *ftp://ds.internic.net/rfc/rfc1738.txt*

3. Berners-Lee, T., R. Fielding, and H. Frystyk, Hypertext Transfer Protocol—HTTP/1.0," RFC 1945, May 1996.

4. Crocker, D.H., "Standard for the Format of ARPA Internet Text Messages," STD 11, RFC 822, UDEL, August 1982.

5. Fielding, R., "Relative Uniform Resource Locators," RFC 1808, June 1995, *ftp://ds.internic.net/rfc/rfc1808.txt*

6. Hallam-Baker, P.M., "Session Identification URI," World Wide Web Consortium Working Draft, WD-session-id.

7. Hallam-Baker, P.M., "Notification for Proxy Caches," World Wide Web Consortium Working Draft, WD-proxy.

8. Luotonen, A., "The Common Logfile Format," 1995, *http://www.w3.org/pub/WWW/Daemon/User/Config/Logging.html*

Acknowledgments

Robert Thau provided useful advice and some code. John Mallery and Roger Hurwitz helped develop many of the ideas. Daniel DuBois provided many useful comments while finalizing the draft. In addition the following members of the *www-logging* working group helped comment during the development of this specification:

James E. Calloway, *jcallowa@nando.net*
Gerald L. Despain, *g.despain@az05.bull.com*
Rohit Khare, *khare@w3.org*
John Line, *jml4@cus.cam.ac.uk*
Magnus Mengelbier, *magnusm@maths.lth.se*
Josh M. Osborne, *stripes@va.pubnix.com*
David L. Smith, *smith@mail.wco.com*
Niel G. Smith, *ngs@sesame.hensa.ac.uk*

About the Authors

Phillip M. Hallam-Baker
MIT Artificial Intelligence Laboratory
545 Technology Square
Cambridge, MA 02139
hallam@w3.org

Phil Hallam-Baker is a computer scientist who has been active in W3 issues since 1992. He has contributed to the HTML 3.0 Maths markup and is currently active in Web security issues. Before working on the Web, he worked on parallel processing, code synthesis, and formal methods. He joins the W3C/MIT team from the CERN Programming Techniques Group (which is also active in W3 development).

Brian Behlendorf
Organic Online
510 3rd Street, Suite 540,
San Francisco, CA 94107
brian@organic.com

Brian Behlendorf is a Founder and the Chief Technology Officer at Organic Online. Prior to that he was Lead Engineer at HotWired and

Wired Magazine, where he set up Wired's first Web server in 1993. Prior to that he was a student of computer science at the University of California at Berkeley. Brian is a founding member of the Apache Web Server Project, the most widely implemented Web server on the Internet, and also co-founded the VRML development effort in 1993.

In the past year, Web-based advertising has achieved critical mass, focusing the nascent industry's attention on standards and practices for measuring Web site usage. The media world discovered that the Web offered a unique new medium: mass customization, individual measurement, and consumer interactivity.

At the same time, technologists realized that these practices can exacerbate existing weaknesses in Web infrastructure (by making caching more difficult, for example). Both communities also realized the ethical challenges associated with this brave new world.

Over the last several months, researchers, startup companies, public policy organizations, regulators, and consortia have all joined the fray to lead and control the development of demographic analysis on the Internet. The W3C, together with several MIT academic departments, assembled a workshop in January, 1996 to take a first look at these issues. This area has also become a significant part of mainstream Web research, as represented by our selections from WWW5.

From these two events, our Special Section Editor, Roger Hurwitz (MIT AI Lab), helped select and edit a handful of relevant papers. Taken together, they provide a survey of the challenges ahead as the Web grows into a mass, commercial medium.

Note: Some papers in this section have been selected from the proceedings of the Fifth International World Wide Web Conference, held in Paris in May, 1996 . The complete proceedings of record were published by Elsevier as a special issue of "Computing Networks and ISDN Systems," Volume 28, Numbers 7–11, May 1996, pages 893–1579.

AN INTRODUCTION TO THE
TECHNICAL PAPERS

Roger Hurwitz, Special Section Editor

. . . the Internet may fairly be regarded as a never-ending worldwide conversation. The government may not. . . interrupt the conversation. As the most participatory form of mass speech yet developed, the Internet deserves the highest protection from governmental intrusion. (ACLU vs. Reno)

—Judge Dalzell, declaring that the Communications Decency Act violated the Constitution of the United States

This praiseworthy opinion, which Judge Dalzell's colleagues shared, reflects a serious effort to characterize the Net and the Web. The need for that effort should not surprise us, since the growth of the Web has outstripped the ability of our familiar models to understand it. Indeed, those who remember the Internet before the Web know that cozy world is forever gone. But who knows how many people now or in the future will participate in this much larger form of mass speech? And who knows how the Net and Web will survive, without governmental intrusion or the funding that helped start them?

Together we will find the answers, since they will help ground in reality the engineering, administrative, and business plans for tomorrow's Web. Because the Web is growing explosively, we cannot simply make assumptions about its demographics. We can neither estimate numbers of users accurately, nor can we assume that projections of revenues will inevitably be realized through growth alone. A Web built on such assumptions may prove inconsistent with its future applications and financial models.

The papers in this section are a major step toward satisfying the need for answers. They review efforts to identify and/or measure current and future Web services and use, as well as efforts to adapt or design Web infrastructure to support them. Their diversity reflects the fact that the Web's growth and transformation into a broadcast medium surprised nearly everyone—a necessity that birthed inventions of tools for measuring, managing, and even defining the demand for this new medium. The papers here are based on presentations and submissions to the *Workshop on Internet Survey Methodology and Web Demographics* in Cambridge, Massachusetts, and the *Fifth International World Wide Web Conference* in Paris, France.

The workshop brought together Web developers, survey researchers, social scientists, and media consultants to discuss means of measuring Web use and their results, implications, and problems (see the summary at *http://www.ai.mit.edu/projects/iiip/conferences/survey96/cfp.html*). The means include on- and off-line surveys to measure diffusion and demographics of users (see Harkness et al.; Kehoe and Pitkow; Bonchek, Hurwitz, and Mallery), and logging the use of individual sites and clients (see the panel interview with loggers; Abrams and Williams). The workshop presentations revealed disagreement about the size of Net and Web use, but basic agreement about its demographic profile. While a Find/SVP survey estimated that 9.2 million Americans use the Internet, the preliminary result of the Nielsen/CommerceNet survey reported 24 million Internet users, including 18 million Web users, in the United States and Canada. (The latter figures were reduced about 10% through restratification of the survey sample; see Harkness et al.) Despite their differences, the numbers indicate that diffusion has moved beyond the pioneers to early adopters. Moreover, the various surveys and studies converge on their findings that Net and Web users tend to be high income, high education, white, male, English speaking, technologically oriented, and career minded—a very attractive population segment for advertisers, but perhaps too narrow for political pollsters and organizers.

As noted in the workshop, the discovery of the Web as an advertising medium and the possibility of using it for passive collection of consumer data has both increased the importance of logging and highlighted its problems. The latter includes undercounting file access due to caching proxy servers, difficulties in tracking within and across sites due to the statelessness of HTTP, inadequacy of current logging protocols, and legal and ethical limits on data collection. Though alternative approaches, such as registering users and adaptive or branching online surveys, can exploit the Web's interactivity, they also have problems such as self-selection, response bias to the medium, and analytic bias. While oversampling, weightiness (see Danes), and approval voting schemes (see Urken) provide a few possible solutions, before the Web can become a good survey research tool, we must study and calibrate responses to similar questions online and through traditional media.

The papers from the Paris conference propose representations or paradigms for the anticipated large scale of activity on the Web. Two projects attempt to visualize Web topology and traffic in a virtual reality space. Bray represents the size and distribution of sites according to their relative number of accessible pages and their links to and from other sites. This method provides a highly intelligible, data-driven means of capturing the changing shape of cyberspace. The second system, *Avatar* (described by Lamm, Reed, and Scul-

lin), adapts a geographical information system perspective to usage measurement.

Smith describes one spontaneous creature of the Web that is rapidly becoming another paradigmatic institution, namely, the large caching proxy server; Neal provides a similar perspective from the antipodes in New Zealand. Both argue that caches are the primary defense against network saturation and server overload. In addition, Bolot and Hoschka examine performance analysis and modeling of such services.

Kohda and Endo customize the proxy server to become an advertisement server. This technique merges an ad which is specific to the registered user's interest with a page she is downloading from another server. Under this proposal, less visible, peripheral sites could benefit from an advertising revenue stream without having to compete with larger sites, which could help stabilize the shape of cyberspace.

The editors wish to thank the MIT Artificial Intelligence Laboratory, the Laboratory for Computer Science, the MIT Political Science Department, and the World Wide Web Consortium for organizing the workshop, as well as additional sponsorship by ANYwhere Online, Ceridian/Arbitron, and the Gallup Organization. We also thank all the presenters, panelists, discussants, and attendees, who made it a success, and are particularly grateful to the presenters and panelists who responded to the call for participation in this volume. Finally, we warmly acknowledge the work of INRIA and the W3C in organizing the Fifth World Wide Web Conference. ∎

Roger Hurwitz
June 1996, Cambridge, Massachusetts

Surveying the Territory

GVU's Five WWW User Surveys

Colleen M. Kehoe, James E. Pitkow

Abstract

The Graphics, Visualization and Usability (GVU) WWW User Surveys have been conducted every six months since January 1994 and have received over 55,000 responses. In the course of conducting the surveys, we have attempted to advance on-line surveying technology and methodology and to document the changing profile of Web users. This paper first describes the history of our technology including our recently tested Java survey applet. Next, we detail our methodology and address some issues raised by non-random sampling. Finally, we summarize some of the trends we have observed in the basic demographics of the Web population.

Five years is not very long on most historical scales, but for the World Wide Web (WWW) it constitutes a lifetime. A question almost as old as the Web itself is, "Who is using it, and for what?" One way to answer this question is to use the same methods used to measure the audiences of other one-way media such as television and radio. However, something interesting happened in early 1994: the implementation of HTML Forms turned the Web into a two-way medium, which made it possible to contact the audience directly. To test the viability of the Web as a survey medium and collect preliminary data on the Web population, the first GVU WWW User Survey was conducted in January 1994. Subsequent surveys have been conducted approximately every six months. Having collected results from over 55,000 Web users over five surveys has given us a unique perspective on the advances in surveying technology and methodology and changes in the Web population itself. In the following sections, we discuss what we have learned in each of these areas.

Evolving Technology

With each survey, we have attempted to advance the state of surveying technology and take advantage of new Web capabilities. Our first survey was the first publicly accessible Web-based survey, and it pushed browsers that supported HTML Forms to their limits. Error reports from respondents and garbled results in our database quickly revealed differences between the various browsers in their handling of Forms. Although most major differences have been resolved, some minor ones persist, and as a result, the data usually contains some errors that must be corrected by hand.

Many important features of the architecture were introduced in the second survey: adaptive questioning, enforcing questionnaire completion, and allowing user-selected IDs. Adaptive questioning means that the questions a user is asked depend on his or her answers to previous questions. In the questions adapted in a "batch mode" using CGI scripts, respondents answered a set of questions, submitted their answers, and got back a new set of questions that were follow-ups to the ones they had submitted. Also, questions from the original set that the respondent did not answer were returned along with the follow-up questions. Questionnaires were not accepted until all of the questions asked had been answered, preventing users from accidentally skipping questions. (For sensitive questions, we provided a "Rather Not Say" option.) The final feature introduced in the second survey was user-selected IDs that were used to relate a particular user's answers across different sections of the survey. After entering an ID, users were given a URL that contained their ID to add to their hot-list and that they could use to participate in future GVU surveys. This simple mechanism would allow us to do a longitudinal analysis of users who participated in several surveys.

Longitudinal tracking was tested during the third survey and fully deployed during the fourth. When users identified themselves as having previously participated in a GVU survey, either by using the URL they had stored or by remembering their ID, we used a weak challenge-response mechanism to verify their identity. Users were asked their location and age during the last survey, and if their responses matched those in our database, we considered them verified. Note that this was not an attempt at true, reliable authentication; it was simply designed to minimize errors in identification and to discourage blatant mis-identification attempts. Users who did not want to participate in the longitudinal study were asked to simply choose a new ID for each survey. To make it more convenient for users who participate in multiple surveys, we filled in as much of the general demographics questionnaire as possible with their previous answers. Users could then simply review their answers and change them when necessary.

The recent introduction of Java to the Web has opened a variety of possibilities for improving the survey technology. Originally, because of the Web's limited interactivity, the vision of truly adaptive questioning could not be fully realized. While "batch mode" adaptability was a reasonable solution, it did not have the natural, conversational progression of questions we were aiming for. We felt a natural progression of questions would help respondents to give better answers because the preceding questions would provide a context for the current question. Java made it possible to have the desired degree of adaptability—each mouse click had the potential to trigger new questions that could be asked immediately. To test this idea, we implemented a prototype survey applet that was offered as an option in the fifth survey. Since the survey applet has not been discussed in any of our previous publications, we describe it in more detail in the next section.

Prototype Survey Applet

There are three distinct portions of the survey applet: the adaption engine, the user interface, and the server interface. At the heart of the adaption engine is a simple production rule system. The survey designer specifies the way the survey adapts by creating a set of rules of the form: "if the answer to question X is A, then ask question Y." Rules may have multiple conditions, "(X is A) and (Y is B) and (Z is C)," but they can only test for equality and not arbitrary expressions. Every time a user answers a question, a "fact" is asserted, such as "the answer to question Z is D." The list of rules is then evaluated to see if this new fact satisfies any of the conditions. When all of the conditions for a rule are satisfied, the rule "fires," and the new question is added to the list of questions currently asked. If the question is already currently asked, it is not asked again. This situation can occur if the same question appears on the right-hand side of more than one rule. Questions that have no conditions for being asked (i.e., the initial questions) are given a condition of "NIL," which is always considered to be satisfied. Facts may also be retracted if a user changes an answer to a question. Any questions that were asked as a result of the fact having been asserted are then "unasked."

When the applet is loaded, the questions and adaption rules are read in, and the initial questions are displayed. The applet supports the standard types of survey questions: checkbox, radio button, scrolling list, selection pop-up, and text entry. All of these can have follow-up questions that, when triggered, are placed on the screen slightly indented and immediately following the question that triggered them. Another strategy would be to append the new question to the end of the survey. We chose the first placement strategy because it places the new question (or questions) in the user's current area of attention, making the connection between the user's action (clicking) and the system's action (adding the question) explicit. Connecting a particular answer to a particular follow-up question also helps the user understand why that question is being asked and provides a context for interpreting it. As with the Forms version of the survey, the applet enforces question completion. If a user tries to submit an incomplete questionnaire, the unanswered questions are highlighted in red and can be easily spotted when scrolling back through the survey.

The applet integrates seamlessly with the CGI scripts used to collect the results. To submit the results, the applet creates a URL that mimics the format of Forms output. The name-value pairs are created from the answers to the currently asked questions and appended to the URL for the CGI script to create a GET-style URL. The applet then calls the `showDocument()` method on this new URL, submitting the results and returning the user to the same point they would have reached if they had used the Forms version of the same questionnaire.

Evaluation of Prototype

Making the survey applet available to a large number of users revealed some interesting technical issues. First, we expected that use of the applet would decrease the load on our Web server since adapting questions and verifying completeness could be done locally, without a call to the server. This was not the case, however, because each class needed by the survey applet was retrieved by a separate call to the server. Approximately 25 classes are used in the applet, which currently must be retrieved with 25 separate calls. Not only did this make loading the applet very slow, but it required many more calls to the server than the Forms version does. (Granted, the classes only have to be retrieved once even if the applet is run several times for different questionnaires. Even taking this into account, the Forms version requires fewer calls to the server to complete the main part of the survey.) A solution to this problem would be to allow an entire set of classes, perhaps in a compressed format, to be retrieved with only one call to the server. Another interesting revelation, which is probably well-known to most Java programmers by this point, is that different browsers (and different versions of the same browser) do not handle Java applets the same way, thereby defeating their cross-platform benefits. This situation is very similar to the differences in the handling of Forms a few years ago and will probably be resolved as these browsers become more mature.

Evolving Methodology

How can we ensure that the results of the survey are meaningful and valid? The field of distributed, electronic surveying is still very new, and consequently any results obtained must be interpreted conservatively. Our survey suffers two problems that limit our ability to generalize from the results: self-selection and sampling. When a person decides to participate in a survey, they select themselves. Researchers can do very little to persuade someone to participate if they simply prefer not to. The potential problem is that this decision not to participate may reflect some systematic judgment by a segment of the population being studied, causing them to be excluded from the results. However, all surveys have this problem to some extent; when a potential respondent hangs up on a telephone survey or does not return a direct-mail survey, self-selection has occurred.

The more fundamental problem is sampling. There are basically two types of sampling: random and non-random. Random sampling uses various techniques to ensure that the people who answer the survey are representative of the larger population being studied. The data obtained from the survey can then be corrected if necessary and used to make statistically valid estimates about the larger population. Surveys that can make statements about the number of people in the U.S. who use the Internet or the WWW, for example, are using random sampling. Our survey uses non-random sampling, which means we rely on users to see announcements of the survey in order to participate. Obviously, only those users who see the announcements ever have the chance to participate. As a result, all segments of the Web population may not be represented in our sample. This reduces the ability of the gathered data to generalize to the entire Web population. At the heart of the problem is the fact that the Web does not yet have a broadcast mechanism nor a way of registering individual users (with digital signatures, for example) that makes it impossible to draw a random sample from a complete, or nearly complete, list of Web users. Over the course of the surveys we have used several methods to maximize the chances that our respondents do represent the larger Web population and to measure how well they do.

The first method we began using was promoting the survey through diverse media to attract respondents, including:

- Links to the survey from high-exposure, general-interest Web sites, such as NCSA's "What's New," Yahoo, Lycos, CNN, etc.

- Announcements on WWW and Internet-related Usenet newsgroups

- Coverage in national and local newspapers and trade magazines

- An announcement on the *www-surveying* mailing list that we maintain for users who would like to be notified about GVU survey activities

We felt that by providing many channels to bring respondents to the survey, we would attract a larger and more diverse set of users.

To determine if the different channels were indeed attracting different sets of users, starting in the third survey, we have included a question asking how the respondent found out about the survey. This allows us to group respondents accordingly and to look for differences between the different populations, specifically gender differences. For the third survey, we reported that

the same percentage of men and women found out about the survey through the following sources:

- Remembering to participate because of the last survey

- Following links from other Web pages

- Reading about it in a newspaper

- Hearing about it from some other sources

- Receiving a listserve announcement about it

The percentages were different for:

- Hearing about the survey from friends

- Reading about it in a magazine

- Seeing a posting in a WWW-related newsgroup

- Receiving an announcement from the www-surveying mailing

Differences were even more pronounced in the fourth survey, and we expect to find the same in the fifth.

Given the low effectiveness of all but other Web pages and Usenet news announcements, which account for well over 50% of the respondents, most of these differences lead to nominal effects. To be conclusive, we would need to examine other basic demographics (e.g., age, location, income) across the different populations, as well. The differences in gender across the populations, however, are a positive indication that the different channels are reaching different sets of Web users.

Another method we rely on is oversampling: collecting data from many more users than are required for a valid random sample. For the third and fourth surveys, we were able to collect data from approximately 1 out of every 1000 Web users (based on current estimates of the number of people with Web access). For random sample surveys, having a large sample size does not increase the degree of accuracy of the results. Instead, the accuracy depends on how well the sample was chosen and other factors [4]. Since we use non-random sampling and do not explicitly choose a sample, having a large sample size makes it less likely that we are systematically excluding large segments of the population. Oversampling is a fairly inexpensive way to add more credibility to a non-random Web-based survey. The cost to actually collect data from extra users is minimal compared to other surveying methods; most of the expense is in the fixed costs of survey development and equipment and does not depend on the number of users surveyed.

When conducting a survey, it is also valuable to know something about those who had the opportunity to respond, but did not. Ideally, we would like to know why they did not respond, but in most cases this is impossible. Instead, most surveys simply measure the *rate* of non-response—the number of users who chose not to respond. For the third survey, we developed a similar measure of attrition rates. Attrition can best be thought of in terms of the paths taken by users through an information space. These paths are determined by the underlying structure of hyperlinks, that is, which pages are connected to which other pages. We know that some users will visit a page and not continue traversing the hyperlinks contained in that page. Others, however, will proceed to traverse the presented links, thus continuing down a path. Attrition for a particular survey can be understood as a measure of the percentage of users who began that survey, but who did not complete it. Attrition is calculated across a group of users. Attrition curves are defined as the plot of attrition ratios for all pages along a certain path. A complete discussion of the attrition analysis can be found in [9]. Excluding one questionnaire that had technical problems with submission, attrition rates for the third survey ranged from 4.54% to 12.58%. These rates are extremely low and support the notion that the effects of self-selection on the data are minimal.

Around the time that the fourth survey was completed, several other North American random-sample surveys released the results of their studies of Web and Internet users [5, 3, 6]. An obvious method of investigating the biases introduced by non-random sampling is to compare our results to theirs. The fourth survey's ratios for gender and other core demographic characteristics like income, marital status, etc., are almost exactly those reported by these other surveys. While our surveys do attract heavier Web users than do random phone-based surveys, it does not appear that frequency of Web use is a differentiating characteristic within the population. This result is both surprising and encouraging for Web-based surveying.

These methods when coupled with conservative interpretation of the data, lend a great deal of credibility to the results from the survey. One possible improvement that we are considering for future surveys is to select a random sample from the collected results. Data from other questions in the survey, such as the number of hours spent on the Web, could be used to take into account the probability of selecting each person in the sample. Results obtained with this method could then be used to make statistically valid statements about the Web population as a whole. Still, we remain unconvinced that the survey's sampling methodology is optimal and welcome suggestions and further comments on this subject.

Evolving Population

One of the most interesting aspects of studying the Web population is documenting the swift changes that it has gone through. While certain characteristics of the Web users sampled in the surveys have remained the same or changed slightly, other characteristics have changed dramatically. More than ever, the users in the most recent surveys represent less and less the "technology developers/pioneers" (primarily young, computer-savvy users) of the earlier surveys and more of what we refer to as the "early adopters/

seekers of technology." The adopters do not typically have access to the Web through work or school but actively seek out local or major Internet access providers. As the Web continues to expand its horizon of users, we expect, and indeed, find that more and more users from diverse segments of the population participate in the surveys. Please refer to the results from the individual surveys for more complete results.

Age

The average age of respondents in the fifth survey is 32.95 years, which is very close to the average from the fourth (32.7 years) and down two years from the third (35.0). Although the average age is relatively stable, we do notice dramatic changes in the age distribution. With each survey, the curve becomes flatter as more people in both ends of the age spectrum start using the Web.

Gender

The gender ratio continues to become more balanced with females representing 31.45% of the respondents and males representing 68.55% in the fifth survey. The percentage of females using the Web has more than doubled since the second survey (15.5% female, 80.3% male, 2.6% chose not to answer). Also, the U.S. is integrating female users into the Web user population faster than Europe (U.S.: 34.35% female, Europe: 15.2% female). The increase in female users is occurring largely in college students and K-12 educators.

Location

When classifying users by major geographic location, we find that the Web is slowly becoming less U.S. dominated (U.S. respondents: 80.6% third survey, 76.2% fourth, 73.5% fifth). Although Canada and Mexico showed a surge in the fourth survey (5.8% third, 10.2% fourth, 8.44% fifth), Europe has the second highest response rate in the fifth (9.8% third, 8.4% fourth, 10.82% fifth). All other areas of the world continue to show

increases in the fifth survey including Oceania with 3.63% of respondents and Asia with 1.81%.

Education

Overall, the distribution of educational level has shifted slightly towards lower levels as indicated by less advanced degrees and more high school and some college level education. This trend toward more and more Web users without advanced degrees has continued since the second survey, where for example, over 13% of the users had doctoral degrees, compared to 7% for the third survey and 4% for the fourth and fifth. The education level of users is still high, in general, with over 80% of respondents in the fifth survey having at least some college education.

Primary Computing Platform

Unix was the primary platform of most users in the second survey (44% second, 10.4% third, 8.76% fourth, 6.67% fifth), but some flavor of Windows has held this position since the third (29% second, 51.98% third, 61.5% fourth, 63.63% fifth). The Macintosh platform has accounted for between 20% and 30% of the users in each survey.

Years on the Internet

There seems to be a fairly steady stream of new users to the Internet as indicated by the percentage of users who have been on less than twelve months: 50.2% for the third survey, 60.3% for the fourth, and 43.14% for the fifth. The rise in the number of new users in the fourth survey can probably be attributed to users who have gained access through local online providers.

Nature of Internet Provider

The nature of respondents' Internet providers has shown substantial change throughout the surveys. (There was a link from Prodigy to the Third GVU survey, so results from that survey are probably biased for this question and are excluded from this analysis.) The percentage of users gaining access through educational institutions has dropped from 51.0% in the second survey to 31.59% in the fourth, to 26.8% in the fifth. The most popular method of gaining access in the fourth and fifth surveys is through local Internet providers (41.64% and 48.53%, respectively) while access from major providers accounts for only 8.1% in the fourth and 9.24% in the fifth.

Willingness of Users to Pay for Access

One of the most stable characteristics of the earlier surveys has been that one of five users stated outright that they would not pay for access to WWW sites. This number has increased from 22.6% in the third survey to 31.8% in the fourth. For the fifth survey, we changed the question somewhat to test the interest of respondents in some of the business models currently being proposed. As a consequence, it is not fair to directly compare the results from the fifth survey to the others. However, an amazing 64.95% replied that they would not pay for access to WWW pages. This may reflect the perceived value of the material and resources currently available on the Web and could change as users become more aware of high-quality sites. It may also be related to the fact that 57.64% of the users in the fifth survey are already paying for their own Internet access and are not willing to pay an additional fee for content. For those who were willing to pay, the largest percentage (12.06%) favored a subscription model.

Conclusion

Measuring and describing the Web population has turned out to be an interesting and challenging task. A primary goal of ours has always been to provide quality data, with the limitations clearly defined, and to make it available to support a variety of research agendas within the Web community. We feel that through our technology and methodology, we have been able to reach this goal. We hope that as more researchers enter this field, new ideas and collaborations

will continue to raise the quality of the data being collected. ∎

References

1. Alao, F., "Pilot Study of Network Surveying Techniques," unpublished manuscript, 1994.

2. Catledge, L., and J. Pitkow, "Characterizing Browsing Strategies in the World-Wide Web," *Journal of Computer Networks and ISDN Systems*, 27, 6, 1995.

3. FIND/SVP, "The American Internet Users Survey," 1995, *http://etrg.findsvp.com/index.html*

4. Fowler, F. *Survey Research Methods*, 2d edition, Newbury Park, SAGE Publications, 1993.

5. Nielsen Media Research/CommerceNet, "The CommerceNet Nielsen Internet Demographics Survey," 1995, *http://www.nielsenmedia.com/*

6. O'Reilly Research, "Defining the Internet Opportunity," 1995, *http://www.ora.com/survey/*

7. Pitkow, J., and M. Recker, "Results from the First World-Wide Web Survey," *Journal of Computer Networks and ISDN systems*, 27, 2, 1994.

8. Pitkow, J., and M. Recker, "Using the Web as a Survey Tool: Results from the Second World-Wide Web User Survey," *Journal of Computer Networks and ISDN systems*, 27, 6, 1995.

9. Pitkow, J., and C. Kehoe, "Results from the Third WWW User Survey," *World Wide Web Journal*, 1, 1, 1995.

Acknowledgments

Georgia Tech's Graphics, Visualization, and Usability (GVU) Center operates the surveys as a public service and as part of its commitment toward the Web and Internet communities.

This material is based upon work supported under a National Science Foundation Graduate Research Fellowship. Thanks to all members of the GVU, its director Dr. Jim Foley, and staff for their support and help. Special thanks are extended to Kipp Jones, Dan Forsyth, Dave Leonard, Randy Carpenter, and the entire Computer Network Services staff for their technical support, and to Sun Microsystems for their generous donation of equipment.

About the Authors

Colleen Kehoe
Georgia Institute of Technology
Atlanta, GA 03002-0280
colleen@cc.gatech.edu

Colleen Kehoe received her B.S. in Computer Science from Stevens Institute of Technology in Hoboken, N.J. in 1994. She is currently a Ph.D. student in the Graphics, Visualization, and Usability Center of the College of Computing at the Georgia Institute of Technology. Her current interests include educational technology, visualization, cognitive science, and Web-related technologies.

James Pitkow
Georgia Institute of Technology
Atlanta, GA 03002-0280
pitkow@cc.gatech.edu

James Pitkow received his B.A. in Computer Science Applications in Psychology from the University of Colorado Boulder in 1993. He is a Graphics, Visualization, & Usability (GVU) Center graduate student in the College of Computing at Georgia Institute of Technology. His research interests include event analysis, user modeling, adaptive interfaces, and usability.

NIELSEN/COMMERCENET INTERNET DEMOGRAPHIC STUDY
ANALYSIS OF POSTSTRATIFICATION WEIGHTING PROCEDURES

David H. Harkness, Paul B. Lindstrom, Timothy E. Dolson,
Edward A. Schillmoeller, Barry P. Cook

The Nielsen/CommerceNet Internet (NCID) study is a survey based on a probability sample of persons 16 years or older among telephone households in the U.S. and Canada. Internet users and nonusers were included in the sample. A key objective of the study was to provide estimates of the number and characteristics of Internet users. Other objects include the following:

- Much of the research, prior to the NCID survey, related to estimating the characteristics of Internet users has been based on surveys using convenience type samples on the Internet. Typically, a questionnaire has been placed on a Web site, and individuals visiting the site could complete the questionnaire. The NCID survey questionnaire was also placed on the CommerceNet and Nielsen Web sites with links from various other Web sites. This online survey was available to visitors for approximately the same period as the probability sample based survey. The objective was to compare the results of the two survey approaches to estimate the bias that results when using a nonprobability based online survey.

- Another objective was to provide an open environment for researchers to analyze the results of the survey and share this information with interested parties. Respondent level data was provided to various individuals and groups in the academic and research community.

- Providing respondent level results of the survey allowed us to achieve our final objective of enabling the research community to eval-

uate the survey procedures, including sampling, data collection, and computational methods for estimating the number and characteristics of Internet users. Recommendations related to adjusting the respondent weights to reduce the variance of the weights and poststratification adjustments to reduce the bias of the survey estimates have been received.

This paper addresses poststratification adjustments to reduce bias in the survey estimates.

The NCID survey was based on a sample selected from an unrestricted random digit sampling frame of phone numbers from exchanges operating in the U.S. and Canada. Prior to selection of the sample of phone numbers the frame was stratified by geography. Over 280,000 phone numbers were selected with equal probability. All 280,000 phone numbers were dialed to identify non-residential and non-working phone numbers. Approximately 167,000 phone numbers were excluded using this process. The remaining 113,000 phone numbers were randomly assigned to 215 equal size sub-samples or replicates. This was done to provide control of the sample size while still achieving a probability sample. The objective was to achieve a desired sample size in each of the cells in Table 1.

Approximately 19,000 households were interviewed and assigned to one of the three cells. Interviews were completed with over 4,200 persons 16 years or older.

The data collection period was August 3–September 3, 1995. Up to eight attempts were made to reach a household. When a household was

Table 1

	Cell Description
1	Persons 16+ with direct access and have used the Internet in the last 3 months
2	Persons 16+ with access to an online service only
3	Persons 16+ with no direct access or have not used the Internet in the last 3 months and do not have access to an online service

reached, a respondent was randomly selected with equal probability among all household members 16 years or older. The interview was conducted with the randomly selected respondent. Due to the need for projectable survey estimates, it was essential to conduct the interview with the selected respondent. Therefore, additional attempts were made if the selected respondent was not available during the initial contact. Household members included students temporarily living away from home in a dormitory or sorority or fraternity house. If a student was selected, the number where he or she could be reached was obtained, and additional attempts were made to the new number. A computer assisted telephone interviewing system was used to control the attempts to reach a household and administer the interview when a household was contacted.

Computing the estimates included assigning a weight to each respondent. The respondent weight was computed as follows.

$$W_i = W_{1i} \times W_{2i} \times W_{3j}$$

Where:

W_i = Initial weight for respondent i

W_{1i} = The number of household members 16+ from household i

W_{2i} = 1 if household i has one residential phone number, 0.5 if household i has more than one residential phone number

W_{3j} = Total sample phone numbers
Number of phone numbers in the replicates used for cell j

NOTE

Cells (j = 1, 2, or 3) are defined in Table 1 above.

The initial respondent weights were adjusted such that the sum of respondent weights was equal to the population estimates for males 16+ and females 16+ in the U.S. and Canada.

The above weighting procedures include an initial weight which adjusts for the different probability of selecting respondents. A poststratification adjustment was applied to compensate for differences between the sample and population characteristics due to frame undercoverage, nonresponse and sampling variability. The poststratification adjustment described in the previous paragraph adjusted the initial weight to compensate for differences in the gender distribution between the sample and population estimates. This paper discusses analyses to evaluate the advantages and disadvantages of other possible poststratification weighting variables.

The following criteria were used to evaluate the possible weighting variables:

- The correlation of the weighting variable and Internet usage. There would be little effect on estimates if the percent of Internet users is uniform or nearly so across the individual categories of the variable.

- The differences between the sample and population distributions.

- Accuracy of responses for the characteristics used for weighting. Response error may lead to misclassifying respondents and distort the weights.

- Accurate and current population estimates used for weighting controls are available.

Total survey error includes two components—bias and variance. Bias is the difference between

Table 2   Percent of Persons 16+ Using the Internet in the Last 3 Months by Gender

Gender	%
Male	14.4
Female	7.5

the population value and the survey estimate that is constant for repeated surveys. Variance is the difference between the population value and the survey estimate that changes direction and size over repeated surveys. Applying poststratification adjustments may decrease the bias component of total survey error but at the same time may increase the variance due to an increase in the variance of the respondent weights. The objective for poststratification adjustments should be a reduction of total survey error.

The variables considered in these analyses included gender (male, female), age (16–24, 25–34, 35–44, 45–49, 50–54, 55–64, 65+), education (high school or less, some college, college degree and post graduate), income (11 household income categories), region (northeast, midwest, west, south and Canada), occupation (12 occupation categories) and presence of nonadult.

A CHI-squared Automatic Interaction Detector (CHAID) analysis [1] was used to identify variables correlated with the percent of users of the Internet in the last three months. The following variables were identified:

- Age
- Education
- Gender
- Income
- Occupation
- Region

Tables 2–7 compare the percent of persons in the U.S. portion of the sample that used the Internet in the last three months for each category within each variable. The percent of U.S. persons 16+ that used the Internet in the last three months is 10.8%.

Table 2 compares the percent of persons 16 years or older that used the Internet in the last three months among males and females. The table shows that the ratio of male to female users of the Internet is almost 2 to 1.

Table 3 compares the percent of persons that used the Internet in the last three months by age. The table shows that the percent of Internet users tends to decrease as age increases and is substantially lower among persons 55 and older compared to persons 16–54.

Table 4 compares the percent of Internet users by education. This table shows that the percent of Internet users varies by educational attainment. Persons with at least some college educa-

Table 3   Percent of Persons 16+ Using the Internet in the Last 3 Months by Age

Age	%
16–24	14.1
25–34	14.2
35–44	12.4
45–49	11.7
50–54	9.9
55–64	4.7
65+	1.5

Table 4   Percent of Persons 16+ Using the Internet in the Last 3 Months by Education

Education	%
High School/Technical	3.9
Some College	11.0
College Graduate	19.3
Post Graduate	29.4

tion have used the Internet in the last three months at a substantially higher rate than persons with no college education, and Internet usage increases as educational attainment increases.

Table 5 compares the percent of persons that used the Internet by household income. Again this table shows that the percent of Internet users is not uniform across income levels. The percent of persons using the Internet in the last three months increases as the household income level increases.

Table 6 provides the percent of persons 16+ using the Internet in the last three months by region. There is some variation of Internet use between regions with the west region showing the highest percent of Internet usage.

Table 7 shows the percent of persons using the Internet in the last three months by occupation. Persons with professional, technical, managerial or military occupations have above average Internet use while the persons in the remaining occupations show below average use.

Tables 8–12 provide a comparison of the sample distribution to the March 1995 Current Population Survey (CPS) distribution to identify variables with sample and population distribution differences. The NCID sample includes only U.S. households for comparison to the CPS.

Table 8 compares the gender distribution of the NCID survey sample to March 1995 CPS. A post-stratification adjustment has been made to the respondent weights using population estimates by gender for U.S. and Canada.

Table 9 shows that NCID survey sample has a higher percent of persons 16–24 and a lower percent of persons 55+ than the March 1995 CPS results.

Table 10 shows that persons with a high school/technical school education or less are underrepresented in the NCID survey sample when compared to the CPS. This table shows that persons with a post graduate degree are slightly overrepresented. These differences are possibly due to frame undercoverage and nonresponse. However, analyses done by Nielsen suggest that these differences are, to a large extent, due to response error.

Table 5   Percent of Persons 16+ Using the Internet in the Last 3 Months by Household Income

Household Income	%
Less Than $20,000	3.6
$20,000–39,999	7.4
$40,000–59,999	11.8
$60,000+	20.7

Table 6   Percent of Persons 16+ Using the Internet in the Last 3 Months by Region

Region	%
Northeast	11.3
Midwest	10.7
South	9.5
West	14.0
Canada	9.1

Table 7   Percent of Persons 16+ Using the Internet in the Last 3 Months by Occupation

Occupation	%
Professional	20.6
Technical	17.4
Managerial	16.0
Clerical	7.4
Sales	7.7
Service	7.7
Laborer	4.4
Craftsman	3.6
Military	21.0
Student	23.1
Not Working	2.4

Table 8   Percent Distribution NCID Sample and March 1995 CPS by Gender

Gender	NCID Survey	March '95 CPS
Male	46.9	48.1
Female	53.1	51.9

Table 9   Percent Distribution NCID Sample and March 1995 CPS by Age

Age	NCID Survey	March '95 CPS
16–24	18.3	16.3
25–34	20.9	20.8
35–44	22.8	21.3
45–49	9.3	8.7
50–54	7.2	6.7
55–64	8.6	10.4
65+	13.0	15.7

Table 10   Percent Distribution NCID Sample and March 1995 CPS by Education

Education	NCID Survey	March '95 CPS
High School/Technical	45.7	54.2
Some College	25.5	25.6
College Graduate	20.5	13.7
Post Graduate Degree	8.3	6.5

Table 11

Income	NCID Survey	March '95 CPS
Less Than $20,000	19.3	23.8
$20,000–39,999	31.9	27.9
$40,000–59,999	23.9	20.4
$60,000+	24.9	27.9

Table 11 also shows that persons in low and high income households are underrepresented and persons in middle income households are over-represented in the NCID survey sample when compared the CPS results. Again, these differences may be due to frame undercoverage and nonresponse. Although, as discussed in the previous paragraph, these differences are probably, in large part, due to response error.

Table 12 provides a comparison of persons 16+ by region between the NCID survey sample and March 1995 CPS. It shows persons in the northeast and west are underrepresented and persons in the midwest are overrepresented in the NCID survey sample as compared to the March 1995 CPS. Since the persons were assigned to region based on the area code of their telephone number, this variable is not subject to response error. Therefore, these differences are due to frame undercoverage or nonresponse or sampling variability.

The distribution of the NCID sample was not compared to the CPS results for occupation because the categories identified in the NCID questionnaire were not comparable to the CPS. As a result, occupation was not considered for use as a poststratification adjustment variable.

As stated earlier, poststratification adjustments are used to attempt to compensate for differences between the sample and population due to frame coverage, nonresponse bias and sampling variability. However, some differences may be due to misclassification because of response error. Poststratification adjustments using variables subject to response error may result in incorrect adjustments. Nielsen research described in the Appendix has shown that collecting education and household income from respondents is subject to response error. Some respondents with low educational attainment and low income tend to overstate their education and income levels. Further, some respondents such as the children of the head may not know the household

Table 12   Percent Distribution NCID Sample and March 1995 CPS by Region

Region	NCID Survey	March '95 CPS
Northeast	16.9	20.0
Midwest	27.6	23.3
South	35.6	35.1
West	19.9	21.6

Table 13　Effect of Weighting Variables on Estimate of Internet Usage. Percent of Persons 16+ Using the Internet in the Last 3 Months

Variables Added	%	Standard Error
Gender	11.1	0.7
Gender + Age	10.7	0.7
Gender + Age + Region	10.8	0.7
Gender + Age + Region + Education (4 category)	9.1	0.7

income. The income question also showed a high level of item nonresponse. Approximately 600 respondents did not provide income. The income question was also substantially different than the question used in the CPS which may have also contributed to the difference between the sample and the population.

URL here?

Appendix 1 provides a description of Nielsen's research related to education and income response error. While Nielsen's research was based on an independent sample using a different sample frame, design, and data collection mode, the conclusions are applicable to the NCID survey results.

Nielsen recommends that the following variables be used when computing the poststratification adjustments.

- Gender

- Age

- Region

The income and occupation variables should not be used for the reasons discussed in this paper.

Table 13 shows the effect of adding each variable to the poststratification adjustment procedures. Again, these estimates are based on U.S. sample households only.

Again, Nielsen recommends the respondent weighting should be based on the three variables, gender, age, and region for the reasons previously specified. Using education for weighting may not be as effective as the other variables in reducing bias because of errors in the weights

due to response error. Controlling on education may understate the number of Internet users because some respondents that should be in the lowest education category are erroneously assigned to a higher education category resulting in over weighting the lowest education category. However, the amount of understatement is unknown because the extent that frame undercoverage and nonresponse versus response error contributes to the difference between the education distribution of the sample respondents and the CPS is unknown. However, the correlation between education and Internet usage cannot be ignored. Nielsen will provide, as its best estimate, an estimated range of the number of persons that used the Internet. The maximum estimate will only use gender, age, and region as poststratification weighting variables. The minimum estimate will include education as the fourth weighting variable.

In summary, frame coverage errors and nonresponse errors affect the quality of Internet usage estimates. Weighting adjustments are used in attempt to compensate for the exclusion of persons in nontelephone households and the inability to measure all the persons selected for the sample. These adjustments assume the groups used for adjustment are homogenous regarding Internet usage and there are no errors in assigning persons to the correct weighting group. Departures from these assumptions will reduce the effectiveness of weighting adjustments to reduce bias of the estimates. Further research will address these weighting issues, as well as issues related to improving the level of survey cooperation and improving the questionnaire design to make the weighting controls more comparable to independent population estimates. ■

References

1. Barksdale, Hiram C., Jr., and William D., Perreault, Jr., "A Model-Free Approach for Analysis of Complex Contingency Data in Survey Research," *Journal of Marketing Research* 27, November 1980, pp. 503–515.

2. Magidson, Jay, "Some Common Pitfalls in Causal Analysis of Categorical Data," *Journal of Marketing Research* 19, November 1982, pp. 461–471.

3. Kish, L., *Survey Sampling*, New York, Wiley & Sons, Inc., 1965.

About the Authors

David H. Harkness, Senior Vice President, Nielsen Media Research, is responsible for the development and marketing of measurement services for online computer services and the Internet.

Paul B. Lindstrom, Vice President, Nielsen Homevideo Index, Nielsen Media Research, is responsible for the design of the recent CommerceNet-Nielsen Internet Demographic Study.

Timothy E. Dolson, Statistical Research Operations Manager for Nielsen Media Research, has been involved in the analysis and evaluation of the Commercenet/Nielsen Internet Demographic Survey results.

Edward A. Schillmoeller, Senior Vice President of Nielsen Media Research, is in charge of statistical operations and research.

Dr. Barry P. Cook, Senior Vice President, Chief Research Officer, Nielsen Media Research, is responsible for design, testing, and implementation of all research methods.

WILL THE WEB DEMOCRATIZE OR POLARIZE THE POLITICAL PROCESS?

A WHITE HOUSE ELECTRONIC PUBLICATIONS SURVEY

Mark S. Bonchek, Roger Hurwitz, John Mallery

Noting widespread mistrust of government and declining civic and political involvement [5], some observers have seen the Internet as a means of reinvigorating the political process [3]. According to this view, the Internet can become an electronic agora or new public space, directly connecting citizens with government officials, making political information more accessible, and facilitating debate over public issues [1] [4]. However, in an alternative view, the Internet will have a polarizing effect on the democratic process. Economic, educational, and cultural barriers to the Internet, together with its growing importance for politics, will widen the gap between the information "haves" and "have nots" in political work as well as elsewhere

To test these views, we have been conducting an email and Web based survey of the people who use a new source of political information enabled by the Internet. We want to understand the demographics of the users, their uses of the information, and the effects of this access on their political activity. We selected for the survey a source that is relatively well-used and mainstream, and with which we are quite familiar, namely the White House electronic publications service (hereafter the service). This service was established in affiliation with the Artificial Laboratory at MIT. Since January 20, 1993, it has distributed daily transcripts of speeches and remarks by the President, briefings by his staff, press releases, executive orders and other presidential documents. By July 1996, over 6400 documents had been distributed and electronically archived for retrieval. To support retrievals and users' subscriptions according to their interests, the service categorizes each document for type and contents and adds a descriptive subject line.

The documents are distributed to over 4000 direct email subscribers, including private individuals, journalists, organizations, and redistributors such as on-line services, government agencies, libraries and newsgroups. Together with redistribution, the email stream was estimated in early 1994 to bring about 150,000 people into contact with one or more electronic documents on a near daily basis [2]. In addition, the service's Web and email retrieval interfaces handle several thousand requests per day. The web interface is directly linked into the highly visible White House website (*www.whitehouse.gov*), which is pointed to by more than 30,000 web pages and is an early stop for web newcomers. The interface thus serves both regular retrievers and casual, onetime visitors.

The service is supported by the COMLINK system developed primarily by Mallery and utilizes a categorization scheme by Hurwitz. (The automatic surveying system we are using is, in fact, an extension of COMLINK and is described by Mallery, elsewhere in this volume.) As developers, we were consequently also interested in how well the service met users' information needs and what improvements users' wanted.

The Survey

In January 1996, we initiated a hierarchical, multipart branching survey by mailing initial survey instruments to 18,000 current subscribers, past subscribers and other mail contacts. Survey recipients who redistribute documents via their mailing lists, Web pages, or bulletin boards were asked to post or inform their audiences about the survey. We had planned to conduct soon thereafter a complimentary web based survey of White

House website visitors, to capture users of the retrieval interface, as well as casual visitors. Unfortunately that survey had to be postponed. The present research note reports our findings on a population which accesses the service and responded to the survey predominantly through email. We do report here data on web use by this population and what we expect to learn from the complementary survey.

Results

1472 people returned the top level survey. Each received one of 38 possible follow-up surveys. The selection was automatic and rule based, according to answers to particular questions, which indicated the respondent's usage profile. 1071 people returned the follow up survey. Survey recipients could either respond to the email instruments or connect to our Web server and reply through an HTML interface. 79% of the respondents chose email, while 21% replied via the Web (at both levels). (The proportion probably reflects the higher transaction costs of using the Web in this case.)

The survey administration enforced completion on both surveys. Questions with no or out-of-range answers at the top level were retried before the follow up survey was sent, and unanswered questions at the second level were retried, although no enforcement was possible. To deter "ballot-stuffing," only one survey was accepted from each email address. Survey recipients who chose to answer on the Web were sent a password by email to authenticate their email address.

Respondents were categorized according to whether they used the documents on behalf of organizations or just for their personal ends (individuals), and whether they redistributed the documents or were the principal end user. The majority of active respondents get the documents for personal use. They do not redistribute the documents on any large scale (over 25 people), although many pass them or information in them along in some form to several others. In contrast, those getting documents for their organizations generally redistribute the documents. See Table 1.

Respondents were also classified according to the method by which they obtain their documents. Receivers obtain their documents automatically by subscription to an email mailing list, while retrievers actively seek out documents on Web sites, usenet groups, gopher sites, or other Internet resources. Despite the bias of the present sample to email subscribers, past and current, 41% of users reported obtaining their documents by active retrieval, and another 16% obtain documents both by subscription and by retrieval. 90% of retrieval is over WWW, (75% at the White House site, 15% at other sites), with Gopher, Usenet, ftp, bulletin boards, and WAIS accounting for the remaining 10%. The tendency to retrieve was stronger among newer users. In brief, then, about 60% of these users got documents over the Web, and the trend is toward more Web retrieval, and apparent displacement of email.

Like studies of general Internet and Web users, our surveys show that document users are wealthier, more educated, younger, and more likely to be white and male than the general U.S. population. However when we compared these findings with those for the 1994 survey, we found, as the GVU surveys (Kehoe & Pitkow, this volume) have, that these differences, with the exception of gender, have diminished. See Table 2.

Transaction costs associated with network access and usage explain some of the differences between document users and the on-line population. Students and information workers, who are disproportionately represented among document users, have lower Internet access costs. Put another way, if their costs were higher their use would be lower, or conversely, if the access costs were lower for others with comparable incomes, those others would seek more political information. We assume here high income groups are

Table 1   Individual and Organizational Distribution

	Percent of Responding Users by Affiliation	Percent of Affiliation Type Distributing
Individual	72%	6%
Organizational		
Governmental	12%	78%
Corporate	7%	69%
Political	5%	81%
Educational	4%	72%
Informational	1%	78%
Sub-total	28%	75%
Total	100%	25%

more politically involved because their members can afford the costs of the activities.

The under-representation of women relative to even the Internet population in self-selection surveys is puzzling, but may be due to their lower interest in public affairs relative to men (see the URL *http://www.umich.edu/~nes/resourcs/nesguide/2ndtables/t6d_5_1.htm*).

Political Participation

Party affiliation and political ideology of the document users reveals a mainstream, but Democratic and liberal, audience among U.S.-based document users (90% of the sample). See Tables 3 and 4.

Political ideology shows a similar distribution around the center. Thirty-three percent of document users are moderate, compared to 27% in the general population. Fourteen percent of the document users can be considered out of the mainstream as either very liberal or very conservative.

White House document users are more politically active than the general population. Whereas voter turnout was 45% in the 1992 Presidential election, voter turnout was 78% among document users. Much of this effect can be attributed to the income and educational disparities already mentioned. The greatest disparity in voter turnout rates is among younger document users. Average

turnout for 18–29 year olds is 15%, but among White House document users turnout is 69%.

Document users are also significant consumers of news and information. Fifty-one percent spend more than an hour a day with political news and information, and another 26% spend between a half-hour and an hour. The World Wide Web is an important and frequently utilized source of political information for document users. Thirty-two percent consider the on-line sources to be one of their most important sources of political information. 33% report visiting at least weekly an on-line newspaper, 27% visit the CNN site, 15% the White House home page, 12% Time/Pathfinder, 10% Thomas, and 10% a campaign home page. These figures are relatively high compared to that of 54% for a visit to a Web search engine at least once a week.

One question of interest is whether Web users differ from email users either because of differences between Web vs. Email users or because of differences between information receivers vs. retrievers. Web retrievers retrieve fewer documents and spend less total time reading documents than email receivers. Demographically, Web and email users are quite similar. Web and email users have similar income, partisanship, gender, student status, and are equally likely to report an improvement in political awareness as a result of using the Internet. However, Web users are more educated and politically active

Table 2   Demographics of Active Document Users

	U.S.	'96 Survey	'94 Survey
Income: Over $50,000	27%	47%	NA
Education:			
College graduate	28%	69%	75%
Post-graduate	8%	36%	50%
Age:			
Under 35	39%	46%	53%
Over 55	21%	8%	3%
Race/Ethnicity: White	75%	82%	NA
Gender: Male	49%	80%	80%

Table 3   Partisanship

	U.S.	96 Survey
Democrat	47%	51%
Independent	10%	8%
Republican	42%	33%
Other	8%	

online and offline, spend more time reading and listening to news each day, and are more likely to have sent email to the President.

Use of Documents

Among individuals, the documents are primarily used as a first-hand, direct news sources (48%), as additional information on issues that interest them (43%), and for more information about the political process (35%). Other reasons include inputs to political discussions and material for work or research. The median individual retriever obtains four documents every 10 days. The median individual receiver receives four documents per day and spends fifteen minutes reading them.

Reasons for using the electronic document service over other sources include it being quicker (32%), more complete (23%), easier to use (21%), cheaper (20%), more accurate (19%), and not

Table 4   Active Users' Online and Offline Political Activity

On-line:	Active	Active	Inactive	Inactive
Off-line:	Active	Inactive	Active	Inactive
Contacting	39%	13%	14%	34%
Information	19%	12%	11%	57%
Petition	15%	6%	32%	47%
Campaigning	15%	2%	30%	53%
Join Group	3%	2%	14%	81%
Meeting	2%	1%	30%	67%
Contribute	1%	0%	17%	81%

available elsewhere (15%). The majority of users rate search and retrieval by subject line and category tags as important features, indicating that users have specific information needs and are not just browsing. This finding strongly suggests that more refined search and retrieval methods would be a major improvement of the service for them.

Reasons why organizations use the service vary according to the organizational type and whether the organization actively redistributes the documents. Overall, the primary reason for using the documents is as a way of staying informed themselves (for end-users) and keeping other individuals and organizations informed (for distributors). The value of the documents as a first-hand news source and as a valuable information source was cited by all types of organizations. Government organizations primarily redistribute documents to other government officials or employees; educational organizations primarily use the documents for research or classroom purposes; and advocacy organizations generally redistribute documents to members of the press, their own organization, and other organizations as an effort to promote awareness for their cause. Some advocacy organizations post documents on their own Web sites or post hyperlinks to the White House site from their site.

Overall, the White House document service demonstrates that the Web and the Internet provide a valuable and useful mechanism for connecting citizens directly with their government. Electronic media's timeliness, completeness, immediacy, ease of use, and ability to pass the information along to others provides a decided advantage over other media.

Effects on Political Activity

There is evidence from the survey that the World Wide Web, the White House document service, and the Internet are changing the way that people feel about and participate in politics. As a result of using the Web and the Net, 37% of individual respondents report that they have become more connected with people like themselves,

62% find government to be more personal and accessible, 61% have become more aware of issues that affect them, and 43% have become more involved in issues that affect them. Half of the individuals have sent email to the White House, and 68% redistribute documents on-line. Interestingly, respondents were more likely to pass along the documents on-line than to either pass them along off-line or discuss them in person.

Contacting government officials, obtaining or distributing political information, and petitioning are the most common forms of on-line political activity engaged in by document users. Interestingly, a significant proportion of those who engage in these activities on-line do not participate in the same activities off-line, suggesting that on-line activity is a distinctive form of participation among some users. See Table 4.

Overall, the survey responses suggest that the Web and the Internet are altering the flow of political information and creating new and distinct forms of political participation. Contacting government officials, organizing on-line petitions, retrieving political information, and coordinating political activities are made significantly easier by the Web and other electronic media. The Net is bypassing traditional intermediaries such as the press, contributing to an improvement in feelings of political efficacy. Finally, the Net provides an important mediating function, allowing citizens and organizations with similar interests to find each other.

Discussion

Especially with this low rate of response, self-selection is a salient problem of our survey methodology. There are two aspects of this problem: a) whether findings for the respondents generalize to the entire group of service users (generalization); b) whether differences we find in attributes or behaviors for users and non-users of the service are real or artifacts of self-selection. Regarding the first aspect, we note

- The demographic profile of responding users, in most respects, resembles that for general Internet users, found by stratified telephone surveys (Nielsen, Find/SVP).

- The changes in the profile from that found in the 1994 survey of users correspond in most respects to the trends found in the larger GVU surveys of general Web users (Kehoe & Pitkow, this volume)

- The finding that just over half the respondents have been using the Internet for less than a year is consistent with recent growth patterns for Internet use.

- The distribution over frequency of retrieval of documents (for those retrieving) and over time spent reading documents does not indicate a bias in the sample toward heavy users.

Hence we believe that the demographic profile for individual users approximates the profile of that produced by a random sampling of users, if that were possible. However, the survey findings may over-represent redistributors. Since users on behalf of those entities are professionally involved with the Internet communications, they probably have a higher propensity than others to respond to a survey about such communications.

In regard to the difference aspect, note that although there was no formal control group of non-users, some individuals who do not use the service did respond to the survey. Their group can be used for comparison, because, although slightly younger, it matches the users in income, education, race, gender, and occupation (viz., the variables we would match for a control group). We can therefore take as real the finding that users are more likely than non-users to be Democrats and liberal (which agrees with our expectations of who would seek releases from the Clinton administration). However, we are less certain of the validities that users are more likely to engage in on-line and off-line political activity, and more likely to feel more aware of and more interested in political issues as a result of being on the Net. But these differences are artifacts of the survey being less likely to reach politically active Republicans and/or such type having a lower propensity than other non-users to respond to a survey about a service of a Democratic administration.

Summary

The 1996 survey of White House electronic publication users indicates that hopes and fears about electronic democracy are coming true. The World Wide Web and the Internet can improve the democratic process by making it easier for citizens to be informed about politics and to communicate with each other, government agencies, and representatives in government. At the same time, the citizens who are utilizing these new media are predominantly those who are already privileged and politically active. This is puzzling and troubling. Does it mean that the cost barrier has not fallen low enough? The overrepresentation of students among users might suggest that. The low rate of computer diffusion and connectivity among minority, low income and inner-city groups also supports that idea. Yet, the fact that people who can already access the Web are not flocking to political sites reminds us that there are barriers besides cost to political participation. Can Web technology help people overcome the various cultural, educational, technological and social barriers, as well as economic ones? Or are these barriers preventing use of Web technology in the first place? For the moment, one thing is clear, unless the population using the Web becomes more democratic, any democratizing effect of the use will be limited to an elite subset of the population. ∎

References

1. Habermas, Jurgen., *The Structural Transformation of the Public Sphere*, translated by Thomas Burger and Frederick Lawrence (Cambridge, Mass.: M.I.T. Press, 1989); original paper published 1962.

2. Hurwitz, Roger, and John Mallery, "Of Public Cyberspace: A Survey of Users and Distributors of Elec-

tronic White House Documents." April 1994. *http://www.ai.mit.edu/projects/iiip/doc/surveys/report.html/*

3. Toffler, Alvin, and Heidi Toffler, *Creating a New Civilization: The Politics of the Third Wave* (Washington D.C./Atlanta: Progress and Freedom Foundation, 1994).

4. Oldenburg, Ray, *The Great Good Place: Cafes, Coffee Shops, Community Centers, Beauty Parlors, General Stores, Bars, Hangouts, and How They Get You Through the Day* (New York: Paragon, 1989).

5. Putnam, Robert D., "Tuning In, Tuning Out: The Strange Disappearance of Social Capital in America" *PS: Political Science and Politics*, December 1995, pp. 664–682.

About the Authors

Mark S. Bonchek
MIT Artifical Intelligence Lab
545 Technology Square
Cambridge, MA 02139
bonchek@ai.mit.edu

Mark S. Bonchek is a Ph.D. Candidate in Political Economy and Government at Harvard University and a Research Associate at the Artificial Intelligence Laboratory at MIT.

Roger Hurwitz
MIT Artifical Intelligence Laboratory
545 Technology Square
Cambridge, MA 02139
rhhu@ai.mit.edu

Roger Hurwitz is a research scientist at the M.I.T. Artificial Intelligence Laboratory, an architect of the Open Meeting System, and a contributor to COMLINK Development. His work focuses on the modeling, measurement, and management of collective actions, public communications flows, and organizational intelligence. Hurwitz holds a Ph.D. from M.I.T., has taught at M.I.T. and the Hebrew University (Jerusalem), and has consulted for major communication companies and U.N. agencies.

John Mallery
MIT Artifical Intelligence Lab
545 Technology Square
Cambridge, MA 02139
jcma@ai.mit.edu

John Mallery is technical director of the Intelligent Information Infrastructure Project at the Artificial Intelligence Laboratory of the Massachusetts Institute of Technoloy. An electronic publications system that he developed for use during the 1992 presidential campaign currently serves as the primary distribution hub for press releases by the U.S. White House. His current research explores intelligent information access, wide-area collaboration, knowledge-based organizations, and global knowledge Webs.

COMPLEMENTING SURVEYING AND DEMOGRAPHICS WITH AUTOMATED NETWORK MONITORING

Marc Abrams, Stephen Williams

Abstract

Two complementary ways of learning about who uses the Web and how they use it are surveying and logging. Logging provides exhaustive information on what a population of users is doing, while surveying provides demographics of who those users are. The pros and cons of four logging methods are described: server-based, proxy-based, client-based, and network based. Network-based logging has not been used before in the World Wide Web and is discussed in detail. Two tools for network-based logging are described: httpfilt, based on tcpdump, and httpdump. Examples of what we can learn from network-based logs are given and contrasted with information available in the ubiquitous Web server log.

Introduction

With the explosive growth in the number of World Wide Web (WWW or Web) users has come a desire to characterize who uses the Web and what those users access in the Web. For example, advertisers and marketers want rating numbers of Web pages reflecting how often they are accessed and how long they are viewed [17]. Content providers could use Web user demographics to tailor information to their audiences. To assist in planning for the growth of computer networks, network managers want information on present and projected Web-generated traffic. To answer questions like these, two complementary techniques are available:

Logging

A sequence of machine-observable events is automatically recorded in a file. Typically the events are requests (e.g., for document retrieval, script execution, applet downloading) or responses (e.g., containing documents, output from scripts, applet code). Web server logs are an example of logging. Technically, logging can be done without the knowledge of users (a common occurrence for Web servers today), although legal

or ethical concerns eventually may prohibit this.

Surveying

People are asked to voluntarily answer a series of survey questions, often by a Web form, through electronic mail, or by telephone.

Logging

Logging and surveying each collect data that is inaccessible to the other. Logging can represent a nearly perfect record of what requests reached a Web server or proxy, were sent across a network, or were typed into a Web browser. We say "nearly perfect" because the device collecting the log may crash, the collection device (e.g., software) may have bugs, or the collected logs may be maliciously modified or fabricated (e.g., by someone who gains permission to modify files on the machine storing the log).

However, very little information can be derived about *who* generated requests from logs. For example, Web server logs contain an Internet Domain Name System (DNS) host name or IP address of the client computer. Many computers in the Internet are single-user systems, so the DNS name or IP address is likely to correspond to one person, but there is no readily available method to learn who the individual is. Even the geographic location of the client is questionable: an Internet Service Provider (ISP) may connect users in other cities to the Internet. Or the client logged by a Web server log may have been modified by a proxy server [14] in one country sending requests on behalf of clients on another continent.

Web server logs contain a user name if the client computer or ISP runs the `ident` protocol [18]. Even if a user name is given, and even if the name is not falsified, there is no guarantee that the individual named was the actual user (e.g., a child may use a parent's user id at home). But even if the user can be identified, to learn anything about the user requires another method, such as surveying.

Surveying

Surveying, unlike logging, can provide demographic information on who uses the Web, such as gender, education level, and income. Thus logging and surveying provide almost mutually exclusive information: logging provides exhaustive data on what the population is doing with the Web, and surveying provides a sample of who's doing it.

In contrast to the automated and transparent collection of (albeit limited) data done with logging, survey methods must gather information from individuals through questions. Potential problems in surveys are listed below.

- Surveys are subject to self-selection of respondents. For example, the method of advertising a forms-based Web survey might bias what types of Web users complete the survey.

- Respondents might give inaccurate or even false answers.

- Survey outcomes are affected by the questions used, the order of the questions, and how the questions are phrased.

Logging can complement surveying by helping to validate data collected from surveys. For example, if respondents are asked what fraction of the time they use commercial (.*com*) Web sites, or even how many hours a week they use the Web, the responses from surveys can be compared to estimates of those numbers derived independently from logs of Web requests made by those clients.

Taxonomy of Logging

The focus of this paper is "Automated Network Monitoring" as a complement to survey methods. Henceforth we discuss only logging. Logging methods may be categorized based on *where* in the Web a log is collected. Therefore we review the basic Web architecture before presenting our taxonomy.

Web users run browser programs on client machines. Each time a client sends a request, a Hypertext Transfer Protocol (HTTP) [3] packet is sent on the Internet from the client to the server named in the Universal Resource Locator (URL) field of the request (see Figure 1). The server then returns one or more packets containing either the response or one packet containing an error code.

The picture is complicated when organizations use *proxy servers* [14], either to act as firewalls, caches, or both (Figure 2). A firewall may prohibit Internet users from directly reaching a machine in the organization or may limit access of the organization's clients to the Internet. A cache keeps copies of some responses requested in the past, which reduces both the time that users wait and the Internet bandwidth consumed if the responses are requested again.

There are four possible places to collect logs, corresponding to four categories of logging: at the server, at a proxy, at a client, and on the network. These methods and the information each produces are explained below.

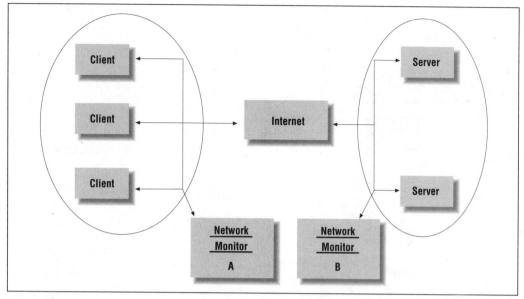

Figure 1 Alternate locations of a network monitor to generate network logs when no proxy server is used

Server Logs

Logging by a server is the most widely used form. It yields information about requests to a single Web site from clients anywhere in the world. Web servers can collect a log of document requests by logging each HTTP GET, POST, or HEAD that they receive.

For example, NCSA *httpd* collects four logs: an access log, an agent log, an error log, and a referer log.

- The access log, in the NCSA and CERN "common log format" [20], is used most often by tools to analyze servers (e.g., wwwstat [8]), and contains the remote client's host name, specified as either a DNS name or an IP address; the user "name" as specified by RFC 931 [18] if the client runs the ident protocol; the date and time when the request was received; the URL requested; the status code of the server's response (see [16] for a list); and the number of bytes transferred, if available.

- The error log lists error messages that the server and executable scripts generate, and identifies each time the server is started and terminated.

- The agent log identifies the Web browser used in each HTTP request received by the server; sometimes Web browsers also identify in this string the type of computer used (e.g., "Mozilla/2.0b6a (WinNT; I)").

- The referer log contains information on links between Web pages and local documents.

There are limits on the information that Web server logs provide. First, many of the requests may have come from proxy servers. Therefore the client's host name may be made anonymous because the server log contains the proxy's host name. Second, the user name field, even if present in the log, may contain incorrect information, because the `ident` daemon running on a client host that identifies user names may report incorrect information. Third, a Web administrator may turn off collection of the client host name and user name for one of several reasons: collecting

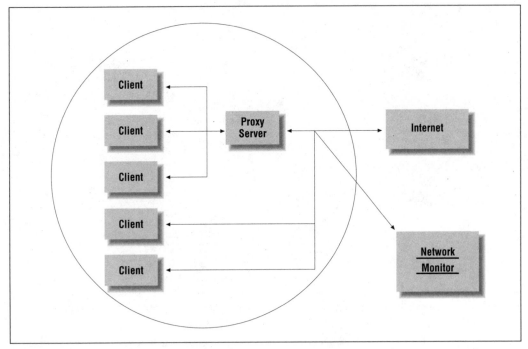

Figure 2   Possible location of a network monitor when a proxy server is used

the user name by the `ident` protocol slows server performance, and the collection of client host names and user names may be unethical or, in the case of the European Union's Directive on the Protection of Individuals [2], perhaps illegal. (See the section entitled "Privacy Issues" in this paper.) Fourth, the server log only contains those requests that actually reach the server, and exclude cases when users examine a document from the server that is cached by a proxy server or by the client Web browser. As the use of caches, particularly proxy caches, becomes more widespread in the Web, the accuracy of server logs as a measure of Web page usage declines.

Proxy Logs

Logging yields information on the requests that reach a proxy server, and thus characterizes the set of requests made by a particular population of clients to servers anywhere in the world, namely browsers configured to use the proxy.

For example, the CERN proxy generates all the information in the common log format used by servers, because it is simply a normal CERN server with its configuration file appropriately set.

Proxy logs also have limitations. First, many Web browsers automatically create caches in the memory and even on the disk of the machine running the browser. Thus user requests for URLs that are satisfied by a memory or disk cache on the client are not sent to a proxy, and thus are missing from a proxy log. Second, unlike Web browser caches that are created automatically, Web browsers today only use a proxy when a user has explicitly configured the browser to use a proxy (e.g., by entering the browser name in a field of a preferences form). Therefore a proxy log may represent a biased sample of clients in that only users sophisticated enough to know what a proxy is and to know how to reconfigure their browser will be logged. (However the sample would not be biased in this manner in organizations that prohibit direct access from a client hosts to the Internet, and in an ISP that distributes Web browsing software with the configuration preset to use a proxy.) Third, users may turn access to the proxy off in their Web browsers whenever they wish. This is a particular problem because Web browsers today require a user to determine when a proxy has crashed, and to turn off use of the proxy, and to turn it back on later when the proxy is up again.

Client Logs

A log is collected on a client machine, either by the Web browser itself or by a separate monitoring process running on the client machine. Client logging is rare, but has been done in research projects (e.g., [6]). The logs can be an accurate characterization of every document that a user examines on servers anywhere in the world. Examples of client logs are available from [7].

Web clients today normally have no facility for generating logs. Thus there is no "standard" format or sets of information listed for client logs. However, it is technically feasible to do so. For example, NCSA Mosaic Web browsers have been modified at universities to collect client logs, such as at Boston University [6] [7], where the following items are logged: machine name; time; URL; size; retrieval time; client window name; and whether the reference URL was retrieved directly, as an inlined image, or from an anchor in another URL. Another example of the potential for client logging is HindSite [11], a plug-in for Netscape Navigator that stores in a database the URL, title, date, and time of access, date and time of last modification to document, and document size of each URL requested by a user.

The advantage of client-based logging is that it overcomes a problem mentioned earlier for server logging, namely that a server log contains only those requests that were satisfied by a browser or proxy cache. This is because a client-based log could record all accesses as a user enters them, before they are dispatched to a cache or Web server.

The obvious limitation of client logging is that information can be collected only from those clients that are willing to run a Web browser that logs. Another limitation of client logs is that we can never be sure who is actually using a Web browser. For example, a Web browser in a home might be used by several family members, and so it may be difficult to correlate information collected from client logs with the demographics of users.

Network Logs

In this paper, we propose collecting logs of URL requests from within the network itself. A network monitor machine (also called a *network sniffer*) is attached to a network. The monitor listens passively to all traffic that travels over the network, identifies packets containing parts of HTTP messages, and constructs a log of URL requests in those packets. The population that network-based logging can be characterized depends on where the network monitor is attached. A network monitor attached to a network of client hosts running Web browsers (Network Monitor A in Figure 1) logs information about that set of Web clients. Alternately, a Network Monitor attached to a network connecting one or more Web servers (Network Monitor B in Figure 1) logs information about requests destined to any of those servers. Network monitoring may also augment proxy logging; for example in Figure 2 the network monitor logs requests made by clients which are configured not to use the proxy and clients that are not connected to networks with proxies.

The network monitoring device can be either a monitoring instrument (e.g., a LANalyzer for Ethernet) or a general purpose computer. An example of using a general purpose computer for monitoring is the *tcpdump* [12] tool. To use *tcpdump*, a user must configure the operating system of a Unix workstation to put its network adaptor into "promiscuous" mode, so that it accepts all packets appearing on the network, rather than just the ones destined to the workstation's network address. *tcpdump* decodes the packets to produce a list of the fields in the protocol headers (e.g., TCP and IP).

Monitoring networks is not new, and has been widely used to analyze problems in communication networks. Network monitoring has several advantages.

1. It is transparent: no change is required to any client, proxy, or server to do the monitoring, and network monitoring has no impact on the performance of clients, proxies, servers, or networks.

2. It is secure: no one has access to the monitored data except the owner of the network monitoring device. For example, a firm that audits usage of server logs could bring in their own network monitor to a server's site, attach it to a server network, and then collect a network log to compare to the server log to independently verify the information in the server log.

3. A network monitor could be programmed to log protocols other than HTTP that are becoming popular in the Web, such as those for Real Audio and other forms of multimedia.

4. There is no sampling or self-selection problem: the monitor collects all document requests, or, if the monitor is too slow to log bursts of packets on the network, a random sample.

5. A rating number for a monitored set of clients can be computed, because a network log reveals the number of distinct client machines that were active and the number of requests from each client that went to each URL. Finally, a network monitor can dump all HTTP message header fields, and even perform computation based on multiple packets, to produce more information about Web usage than a proxy or server log in the common log format. (The section

"Network Monitors for the Web" explains more on this.)

The main drawback of network monitoring is it either requires a broadcast network, such as an Ethernet, token ring, or FDDI ring, or else it requires the network monitor to be configured as a gateway on a point-to-point network link.

One concern in network monitoring is the rate at which the monitor can log network Web packets. There is a limit to the number of clients and servers that one network monitor can monitor. However, multiple network monitors may be used together on the same network by configuring each to log a different set of client or server host addresses. To get an idea of how much server traffic a network monitor can handle, consider use of a general purpose computer as a network monitor. The network monitor will be able to handle at least the traffic that the fastest Web server running on the same hardware could handle. That is because the network monitor reads but never writes network packets, while a Web server must read packets, find a document on disk, and write packets.

Privacy Issues

Any form of logging—be it server, client, proxy, or network—raises an issue of privacy. For example, in the Web today, servers and proxies routinely collect access logs that identify users indirectly by recording client host names and even, when available, user names. Web users, especially novice users, may be unaware that such logs are being collected. The logs are retained for an indeterminate period of time. Information about users in logs may be combined with other databases (e.g., online address listings) to infer further information. There are no legal rules or ethical guidelines in most countries addressing what use may be made of the logs, such as selling them to other organizations. These issues are discussed in [5].

Several issues of individual privacy arise in logging data:

- Are users individually notified when information about their Web requests is being collected? Must the users give written consent?

- Do access logs identify the requests on a per-client machine or even per-user basis, or only the aggregate behavior of the population of requests?

- For what period of time are logs that identify client machines or users retained?

- What uses are made of the information in logs that identify client machines or users retained? What information is published in any form about users based on logs?

- Do we overlog information—for example, would it be sufficient to record which requests in a log correspond to the same client host and (if available) user name without recording the names themselves?

Although these issues arise for any form of Web logging, they are particularly germane for network monitoring because network monitoring is done transparently, without modification to clients or servers.

Network monitoring and proxy logging both record Web usage by some population of clients (although a user can elect not to use a proxy, unless the proxy acts as a firewall and outside HTTP connections from client machines are prohibited). This would allow, for example, an unscrupulous employer to use network monitoring to observe what employees are doing.

Balanced against these issues is a valid need to identify the sequence of URL requests that individual users make for various reasons, such as rating Web content for advertisers, performance monitoring of the Web, product development, and sociological and psychological research into the behavior of Web users. These needs are often satisfied by knowing *which URL requests are made by the same client machine or user,* without knowing the identity of that client machine or user. Therefore we could satisfy both commercial and privacy concerns by recording random (but unique) numeric "session" identifiers to all URLs that correspond to the same client host or user and that cannot be mapped to an individual.

Network Monitors for the Web

We have developed two tools that allow a UNIX workstation to collect network logs of Web traffic: *httpfilt* and *httpdump*. Each tool will log all HTTP requests that appear on the network to which the analyzer is attached. *httpfilt* can log HTTP requests at a faster rate, but *httpdump* provides more extensive information about each request and can be extended to log traffic from protocols other than HTTP used for delivery of multimedia services from a Web page.

Log Tool Design Issues

Several issues arise in the design of logging tools, which we address for our two tools in subsequent sections:

- Is the log format generated by the tool compatible with existing Web log analysis software?

- Can logs be displayed in real time as they are collected, or must they be collected first and analyzed off-line?

- For network monitors, what fraction of traffic on the network is captured in logs?

Extended Common Log File Format

Web server access logs only record a portion of information that appear in HTTP messages. Our logging tools record all information that appears in HTTP messages and additionally estimates the amount of time required to transfer a response to a user. We log information that is absent from the common log format:

- A Web content provider might want to know how a user reached a Web page; the answer is called the "referer" URL, defined as the URL that contained the link to the requested document. One field of an HTTP message is the referer URL, and this is logged by our tools. (In contrast, NCSA *httpd* 1.4 generates a referer log with the content of this field when present. However, there is no easy way to collate the referer log with the access log.)

- The common log format records time of document request in units of seconds. Because this sometimes is insufficient for performance studies of the Web, we log the time in milliseconds.

- It is not always possible to infer the type of a document (e.g., audio, mpeg, text) appearing in a common log format, because this must be done based on the URL alone. Hence we log the MIME type of the URL.

- It is not always possible to tell if a Web page was dynamically generated by a script. Hence we log the date and time that the URL was last modified. This information is also useful in studies of caching in the Web to identify if cached documents are outdated.

- In performance studies of the Web, one important measure is latency, or the time from when a user requested a document until the user's browser began displaying the document. We log two measures of latency: the network latency (the time between when the network monitor saw the first packet of a client HTTP GET, POST, or HEAD message and the server's first reply packet) and the file transfer time (the time between when the network monitor saw the server's first reply packet and the server's disconnection request). These are illustrated as T1 and T2 in Figure 3, respectively.

- We also log the type of browser a client used, the type of server that responded, and information on the proxy gateway used (if available in the HTTP message header).

- The common log format often records a zero for document size, because it merely reports the `Content-Length` field of an HTTP header. Servers often set the `Content-Length` field to zero, for example for dynamically generated Web pages. In contrast, in one of our network monitors (*http-dump*), we examine each packet on the network and add the length of all packets comprising a document to obtain the correct document length, ignoring the `Content-Length` field.

Our extended common log format is described in the Appendix to this paper. It consists of one line per URL request, just like the common log format. However we append the information above as space-separated fields on each line. Therefore the many tools available to analyze common log format files (e.g., [4], [8], [13]) can still be used with our extended common log format files by stripping off our extra fields.

httpfilt

httpfilt, the first of our two network monitoring tools, filters the output from the popular *tcpdump* utility [12] to produce one of two output files. *tcpdump* is executed with settings that only pass packets with a host on port 80 (the standard `http` daemon port). Then, the output is piped to a series of three Perl scripts as shown in Figure 4 that run as separate, concurrent processes. Each filter (left-to-right) performs the following operations:

- Filter 1 invokes *tcpdump* to capture all network packets destined to port 80 on any IP address. (Upon invocation of *httpfilt*, one can specify additional port numbers to monitor.) The initial 128 bytes of the TCP data field of each captured packet are passed to Filter 2.

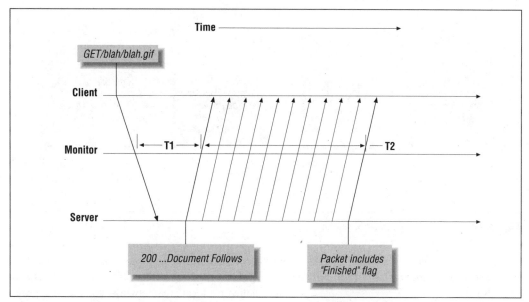

Figure 3   Network latency (T1) and file transfer time (T2) logged by network monitoring tools. Thick arrow from client to server denotes first packet of an HTTP GET, POST, or HEAD. Leftmost thick arrow from server to client denotes first packet of an HTTP response message, containing a return code (e.g., 200). Thin arrows denote additional packets required to send remaining bytes of response. Rightmost thick arrow is TCP packet containing connection disconnect.

- Filter 2 converts the packet contents from hex to ASCII and passes them to Filter 3.

- Filters 1 and 2 pass on *all* packets destined to port 80 (and other ports specified during invocation of *httpfilt*). However, only *some* of those packets contain the header of an HTTP message. (For example, a requested document often does not fit in one network packet. *httpfilt* ignores all packets but those containing HTTP headers. Also some packets may not even contain HTTP traffic.) Thus Filter 3 scans the initial characters of the data field of each packet, looking for one of the strings GET, HEAD, HTTP, and POST to identify packets containing a HTTP header. Packets containing these strings are passed to Filter 4.

- Filter 4 categorizes each packet as a request (i.e., starts with GET, HEAD, or POST) or a

response (i.e., starts with HTTP). For each packet, Filter 4 generates a six-tuple (client IP address, client port, server IP address, server port, direction, HTTP header) from the TCP header of each packet passed by Filter 3, where direction is either "request" or "response" and "HTTP header" is an ascii string representing the packet's HTTP header. In order to compute the network latency field of the output log (field 17 in the Appendix), Filter 4 must match two packets appearing on the network at different times, namely the URL request and the first packet of the server response. Thus Filter 4 maintains a table of unmatched request/response pairs. The six-tuple is added to the table if it matches no (client IP, client port, server IP, server port) tuple in the table. Otherwise, the matching six-tuple is removed from the table, and the two six-tuples are combined

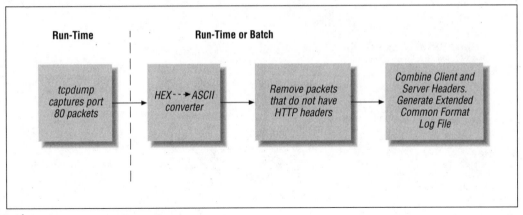

Run-Time | **Run-Time or Batch**

tcpdump captures port 80 packets → HEX→ASCII converter → Remove packets that do not have HTTP headers → Combine Client and Server Headers. Generate Extended Common Format Log File

Figure 4   Block diagram of httpfilt

to yield all fields of one line in the output log (except, currently, field 18 in the Appendix).

Note that *httpfilt* takes advantage of the fact that each URL request by a Web browser uses a different, dynamically selected TCP port number than the last request. Therefore it is possible to match HTTP requests and responses for the same URL, even though they are in different packets that appear on the network. Otherwise, it would be impossible to generate a complete log file entry.

Upon termination, *httpfilt* can also generate a log of all requests for which a response was never seen, by simply dumping out the remaining client request entries in the table in Filter 4. This log indicates what user requests were aborted by the user or timed out by the user browser due to a server that did not respond.

httpdump

A limitation of *httpfilt* is that it only monitors traffic to and from specified server ports. Therefore one must know *a priori* which port numbers on any network are running Web servers. Also, the more port numbers that are monitored, the greater the total volume of network traffic that *httpfilt* must filter. Meanwhile, traffic to Web serv-

ers on ports not specified on invocation of *httpfilt* will not be logged. Therefore *httpdump* is best suited for local area networks containing a group of servers, where the server port numbers are known. A second limitation of *httpfilt* is that it cannot be extended to monitor protocols that use HTTP as a "communications-agent" (e.g., Real-Audio and VDO).

The second tool is *httpdump*, which overcomes these limitations. In particular, *httpdump* is based on a highly optimized *packet-filter* [15] rather than on *tcpdump*, and hence monitors all port numbers to filter for packets containing HTTP headers. Also *httpdump* can be extended to monitor communications-agent protocols. Another advantage of *httpdump* is that it can compute the size of documents sent in HTTP responses itself by adding the length of each packet sent by a server, rather than depending on the HTTP Content-Length, which we said earlier was often equal to zero. However, our present implementation of *httpdump* has lower performance than *httpfilt*, and its present implementation is specific to a DECstation running the Ultrix operating system.

httpdump currently consists of two C programs run concurrently to produce a network log of Web requests. As shown in Figure 4, program *tcppf* (TCP packet filter) creates a packet filter that monitors network packets to identify TCP packets and sends to the second program, *httpc*, the timestamp, source, and destination IP address and port, size, and flags (e.g, the TCP FIN flag) of each TCP packet. In addition, if the first two bytes of the data field of the TCP packet are the characters "GE", "HE", "HT", or "PO" (for GET, HEAD, HTTP, and POST, respectively), then the packet is suspected to contain an HTTP header, and the entire data portion of the TCP packet is sent to *httpc* for further analysis.

Program *httpc* tries to identify *sessions*; each session corresponds to one output line in the extended common log file that is eventually written. A session represents the process of a client sending a request and a server sending a response. In particular, a session begins with the first packet of an HTTP GET, POST or HEAD message and ends with the server sending a TCP disconnection request (i.e., a TCP packet with FIN set).

Each time *httpc* receives a packet from the *tcppf* whose first two characters are "GE", "HE", or "PO", it parses the packet to ensure that it is an HTTP client request, and then creates a new thread to keep track of the following information for the session: the client and server IP addresses and port numbers, the total size of data transferred from server-to-client so far, the time at which the server sent the first packet response (to compute network latency), and the time when a packet containing FIN appeared (to compute file transfer time).

For all other packets received from *tcppf*, *httpc* sees if their source and destination IP and port numbers match that of any active session. If not, the packet is discarded. If there is a match and if the packet contains "HTTP" in its first four bytes, it is a server response and that packet's time is recorded to compute network latency. Otherwise, if the packet is from the server to the client, the length field is added to the total size of data transferred so far. If the packet contains a FIN, the time is recorded to compute file transfer time, one line is written in extended common log file

format, and the thread frees itself to await a new session to monitor.

Performance Considerations

A network monitor such as *httpfilt* or *httpdump* is run on a computer attached to a network. The current design of our tools requires that the network be a broadcast medium, such as an IEEE 802.3 (e.g., Ethernet), 802.5 (token ring), or FDDI network. Can a network monitor capture all packets containing pieces of HTTP messages, or will it miss some? If the monitor misses some, the log will contain a sample of the network traffic, rather than an exhaustive listing. (In comparison, a Web server log is an exhaustive listing.)

In the worst case, *every* packet appearing on the network would contain part of an HTTP message. In this case the computer must have a network adaptor that is capable of receiving packets at the network's maximum rate of packet transfer. In addition the computer running the network monitor must have a sufficiently fast processor, memory, and disk so that execution of the network monitor software (e.g., *httpfilt* and *httpdump*) will not be a bottleneck. The network monitor computer must also have sufficient main memory to hold the monitoring software and any necessary data structures and code (e.g., the table used in Filter 4 of *httpfilt* and the threads used in *httpdump*).

Another consideration is whether the network monitor will write the log to a disk file, or will instead send the log data as it is generated to a log analyzer for real-time display. In the former case, there must also be sufficient disk space to hold the log. In the later case, the analyzer program will degrade the network monitor's performance, unless the log is transferred in real time to another machine, in which case it will degrade network performance (unless a separate network is used to communicate with the host running the log analysis software).

To measure what fraction of HTTP messages are captured by *httpfilt* and *httpdump*, an experiment was conducted in an local area network in a lab with a average of 715 accesses per day. We could compute the fraction of captured packets because the lab uses a proxy as a firewall for HTTP traffic. The firewall collects a count of HTTP messages (i.e., requests and responses); the ratio of the number of HTTP messages in an *httpfilt* or *httpdump* log to the firewall count yields the fraction of monitored HTTP messages. The network monitor was a relatively slow machine for the network (10Base2 IEEE 802.3), a DECstation 5000/125 with a 25MHz R3000 processor and only 20MB of main memory. Consider a scenario in which logs are written to disk for later analysis. Then *httpfilt* can be configured to run just Filter 1 (see Figure 4) during monitoring, and write Filter 1's output to disk. After collection, Filters 2 through 4 can be run. In this setting *httpfilt* collects almost all HTTP traffic. On the other hand, if the scenario is real-time analysis of the data, then all four filters must be run concurrently, and *httpfilt* drops in performance to log about 78% of the HTTP traffic.

Another setting in which the performance of *httpfilt* has been evaluated is an eight-month traffic collection project of HTTP messages in the *.cs.vt.edu* domain used in the proxy cache simulation studies in [19]. An average of 5950 accesses per day were collected on the monitored network with a maximum of 7920 per day. In these cases, we run Filters 1 to 3 of *httpfilt* concurrently during the collection, and run filter 4 as a batch process later (on a different machine). This reduces the amount of disk space required by a factor of 30 from that required by Filter 1 alone. The fourth filter, which creates the log file, is run after the collection process is complete. In order to reduce the size of the intermediate file in this study, we only save TCP/IP packets containing HTTP headers, and thus do not compute file transfer time (i.e., field 18 in the Appendix).

Addressing Privacy with httpfilt and httpdump

We developed *httpfilt* and *httpdump* to log Web requests in various networks at Virginia Tech and for performance studies of caching in the Web and for traffic characterization (e.g., [1], [19]). We collect our logs in anonymous name mode. We also treat the URLs as sensitive information for the institution as a whole, and do not disclose our raw logs to anyone outside our research group. However we plan to distribute a "sanitized" version of our log files to other researchers in which each unique field in any URL in the log is mapped to a unique random number, and to withhold the mapping algorithm that was used to prevent reverse mapping.

In designing *httpfilt* and *httpdump* we followed three principles to address the concerns raised previously in the section entitled "Privacy Issues":

1. Only information from packet headers (e.g., HTTP and TCP headers) should be analyzed for logging. The body of an HTTP message should never be examined by a network monitor algorithm.

2. Logging information with client host or user names should only be done with written consent of individual users.

3. We regard it as necessary and acceptable for a tool to examine client host and user names in memory (without user permission), as long as they are never written to a disk file—even a temporary file—without user permission. We take this view because communication protocol software in any computer today already examines at least client host names in memory. But whoever has access to a network monitor machine would be able to easily copy disk files, so it is unreasonable to write client host and user names to a file without user permission.

4. We try to make it difficult for people to maliciously log client and user names without their permission. Of course we cannot make it impossible, because a determined individual could simply buy a hardware network monitor or use *tcpdump* directly to log anything they want about Web traffic.

Adhering to the first principle is important because the body can contain information sensitive to a user. However, this poses a technical problem because HTTP headers have variable length, and the length of the header can only be determined by reading the TCP data field (containing HTTP header and body) character by character, parsing the header along the way, until the entire header has been read.

Given these principles, our tools are designed to log in one of three modes:

Anonymous mode

Do not log client and user information. (This mode should be used when user permission is not obtained, and only information about the aggregate population is required.)

Client name mode

Log client host names and, when available, user names. (This mode should be used only if permission was obtained from users to log this information.)

Anonymous client mode

Map each value of client host and (if present) user name to a unique and random integer *requester number*. The resultant log therefore shows which log entries correspond to the same client host and (if available) user names, but without disclosing the actual names. The mapping is uninvertible. (This mode is used when permission is not obtained from users to log host and user names, but subsequent log analysis requires identification of which URL requests came from the same client and user.)

Obviously someone could misuse *httpfilt* and *httpdump* by turning on client and user name logging without obtaining permission of users. Therefore we only put a version of *httpdump* without client name mode on our Web page (described in the section "Conclusion and Future Work") for anonymous downloading. We will distribute the full version of *httpdump* as well as *httpfilt* upon written request by individuals. If the written request specifies that the requester has obtained written consent from users, we provide the client name mode; otherwise, we provide an implementation without that mode. The rationale behind this distribution method is that we do not want to make it easy for an unscrupulous individual to download and misuse our network monitors.

We do not make *httpfilt* available for anonymous downloading from the Web because it is trivial to change its code to log client host and user names, because *tcpdump* (the first filter in Figure 4) outputs these names, which are removed by a downstream Perl filter. Thus it would be trivial for someone to modify our code to log client host and user names. In contrast, *httpdump* is distributed in machine code form only, so it would be difficult for someone to add client name mode.

The uninvertible random mapping used in anonymous client mode in *httpdump* is implemented as follows. A filter examines the four-tuple (client host, client user, server host, server user) for each session that is emitted by a session thread in Figure 5. The filter keeps a table of four-tuples seen so far. Whenever a session thread emits a four-tuple not seen previously, the tuple is added to a table kept in memory. The log file generated uses the index number of entries in the table as the requester number. The mapping from tuple to requester number is based on the order in which the tuples arrived at the network monitor; therefore requester numbers cannot be inverse-mapped back to client host and user names without the table. The table is never written to disk and hence is deleted when the monitor terminates, to prevent someone from inverting requester names.

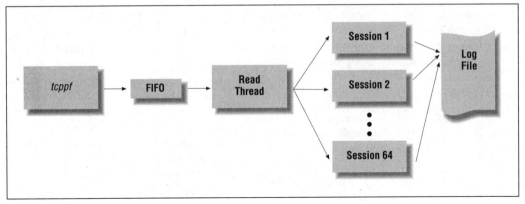

Figure 5   Block diagram of httpdump in its current implementation

What We Can Learn from Network Logs

Network logs reveal information unobtainable from server logs alone. Some examples follow.

- Suppose an advertiser posts an ad on a Web page. What is the "market penetration" of that ad? In other words, can we assign the Web page a rating number that represents what percentage of the total world-wide audience saw the ad? Suppose we define *rating number* of a URL as the ratio of the number of Web browser clients in a population that requested the URL to total number of clients machines in the population. A rating number of 50 for a URL, for instance, means half the clients machines in the population would have seen the URL.

It is impossible to compute this rating number with a traditional Web server log. A server log reveals how many client machines world-wide looked at a particular Web page, but the total population of users worldwide is unknown. Hence a rating number cannot be computed. As an analogy, computing a rating from a server log is like trying to measure market penetration of a magazine by looking only at a list of subscribers to the magazine. The subscriber list tells how many people requested the magazine, but gives no idea of how that number compares to the total number of magazine readers nor to the readership level of other magazines.

In contrast, consider a network log. The network log represents the requests made by a certain population of Web clients, namely the Web clients connected to that network. We can estimate both the numerator and the denominator of a rating number for that population of clients: we know how many clients visited each URL represented in the log, and we know the total number of clients (i.e., by counting the total number of client machines appearing in the log). A network log is analogous to rating magazine circulation by tabulating at a town's post office on how many individuals in the town read each magazine that passes through the post office. Those numbers form the numerators of the rating of each magazine, and the denominator for all ratings is the total number of people in the town that receive magazines. Thus we can tell how many magazine-receiving households would be exposed to an ad in a particular magazine, and how that compares to other magazines. Repeating this for a sample of towns around the world would allow inference of rating numbers world-wide.

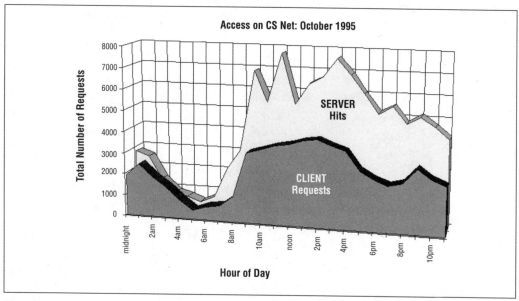

Figure 6   Number of URL accesses per hour averaged over all days in October 1995. Two curves compare results from a network log to a server log

To exemplify network log based ratings, we list the estimated rating numbers of select URLs based on a network log of clients in an undergraduate lab in the *.cs.vt.edu* domain taken during a one month period in Table 1. From the table, *http://www.yahoo.com* has an estimated rating number of 28.57, meaning that an advertisement placed on this page would be seen by more than one quarter of the client browsers in the undergraduate lab in September 1995. Note that the rating number is estimated unless client browsers do not cache documents and the network monitor is fast enough to log all HTTP messages.

- A view of when the peaks and valleys during the day in an organization's use of the Web can be obtained. For example, Figure 6 shows a graph of the number of URL requests made by all clients in the *.cs.vt.edu* domain per hour, averaged over all days in October 1995, obtained from a *network* log. Also shown for comparison is a curve that

would be obtained from a *server* log; in this case it a graph of the number of URL requests made to server *ei.cs.vt.edu* (the most often accessed local server) from anywhere in the Internet, again averaged over all days in October 1995. Comparing the two curves, clients in *.cs.vt.edu* request Web documents at an almost uniform rate between 9 a.m. and 2 p.m., whereas the request rate on server *ei.cs.vt.edu* varies widely in this time period. Few clients start work before 9 a.m., while server *ei.cs.vt.edu* starts its workday of answering hits at 6:30 a.m. (The time difference may be due to use from homes though an ISP that starts earlier in the morning than use from offices.) Also, whereas *ei.cs.vt.edu* experiences a small drop in hits each day from midnight to 1 a.m., and then a sharp drop in hits at 2 a.m., users in offices become busier at 1 a.m., and users appear to go home at a linearly decreasing rate until 5 a.m. before the morning shift arrives.

Table 1 Rating numbers of selected URLs viewed by 70 clients in an undergraduate computer lab in the .cs.vt.edu domain in September 1995. Total HTTP requests in this period was a little over 85,000.

URL	No. Accesses	Rating Number
http://csugrad.cs.vt.edu/index.html	30	42.86
http://infolabwww.kub.nl:2080/calvin_hobbes/new.gif	30	42.86
http://www.cslab.vt.edu/Welcome.html	25	35.71
http://www.vt.edu/index.html	23	32.86
http://www.webcrawler.com/icons/SurferSpidey.gif	23	32.86
http://eewww.eng.ohio-state.edu/~ulug/tsa/people.html	22	31.43
www.cnet.com/Central/Tv/Stories/Murder/Images/altavi320.gif	21	30.00
http://www.ibm.com/images/icons/technology.gif	21	30.00
http://www.yahoo.com	20	28.57
http://home.mcom.com/home/welcome.html	19	27.14
http://ei.cs.vt.edu:80/~cs6704/vtlogo.gif	18	25.71
http://home.netscape.com/home/internet-search.html	18	25.71
http://www.eit.com/web/www.guide/graphics/icon.movie.gif	18	25.71
http://ei.cs.vt.edu:80/~cs5014/fall.95/templates/techreport	17	24.29
http://www.armory.com/~lew/sports/football/49ers/pics/sm_young5.gif	17	24.29
http://ei.cs.vt.edu:80/~cs2504/grades/grades.html	16	22.86
http://home.netscape.com/home/internet-search.html	16	22.86
http://ageinc.com/age/PC.html	15	21.43
http://espnnet.sportszone.com/	15	21.43
http://home.netscape.com/home/internet-search.html	14	20.00
http://necxdirect.necx.com:8002/graphics/bullet.gif	14	20.00
http://www.yahoo.com/Science/Aviation_and_Aeronautics/	14	20.00

Protocol Suggestions to Facilitate Logging

Several changes to the HTTP protocol would facilitate logging and make logs more meaningful to interpret.

First, a standard syntax for the User Agent field of HTTP requests and Server field of HTTP responses would be useful. At present, a logging tool can only write these fields without interpretation into a log file. As mentioned earlier, some

Web browsers include the host machine type in the User Agent field; others do not.

Second, in the normal situation when hosts do not use the ident protocol to identify user names, it is impossible to tell from a server, proxy, or network monitor log whether a URL request from a certain host came from the same user, from multiple users simultaneously (e.g., time-shared hosts), or from multiple users using the host one after another. This could be resolved if a session identifier was added as an HTTP header (naturally a session identifier that could not be mapped back to the actual user identifier). Session identifier standards that maintain a balance between privacy and the need to track individual users have been proposed in [10].

The above two changes would make the *httpdump* and *httpfilt* tools described here more useful. However, some additional changes would help logging in general in the Web:

- To maximize the privacy of Web users, a "non-loggable" bit could be added to HTTP headers. A Web browser might include in its preferences a choice of whether the bit should be set in HTTP messages that the browser generates. If the bit is set, logging agents in the Web could voluntarily restrain from logging information in the packet. An alternate suggestion of client negotiation with a server is described in [2].

- The problem of proxy servers making anonymous the original client host name that requested a file could be solved by extending the session id idea proposed above to include the IP address of the requesting host (`<session-id>@<client IP address>`).

Conclusion and Future Work

"*In theory* online services can collect data on everything a user does," writes Tim Stehel [17]. Logging, because it is autonomous and transparent, gives the illusion of perfect knowledge on what users do. However, in practice, no single logging method—server-based, client-based, proxy-based, and network-based, provides a complete picture. Even if information from all four logging methods were available and were combined, surveying would still be required to complete the picture of demographic information on users. Thus this paper describes one tool—network-based monitoring—that complements others.

The *httpfilt* and *httpdump* tools are available from *http://www.cs.vt.edu/~chitra/www.html*. Also available is *CLFmunge*. *CLFmunge* takes a common log file and generates a new file in the same format with client IP and user fields replaced with unique integers. This allows organizations to exchange log files without compromising individual users. This is also a prerequisite in European Union countries for making log files available for others to use.

In the future, we plan to do the following. First, *httpdump*, which at present runs only on a DECstation using the Ultrix operating system, will be ported to other UNIX systems. We also plan general refinement of our tools to improve their throughput so that they can monitor higher volumes of network traffic. In addition, because *httpdump* sees all of the TCP/IP packets for an HTTP session, it may also be expanded to generate link graphs of accesses based on the links within documents. This would allow more detailed analyses of client behavior. Finally, we intend to support generation of emerging log-file formats (e.g., [9]).

Appendix: Extended Common Log Format

The format of our "Extended Common Log Format" file is a space-separated file with one line per Web document request as follows (numbers denote names of fields):

```
1 2 - [3 4] "5 6 HTTP/1.0" 7 8 9 10
  11 12 13 [14 15] 16 17 18
```

For example, one entry in an extended common log format file might appear as follows (the entry is a single line in the log file, but is displayed as multiple lines below):

```
pc32.cs.zzz.edu ftaylor - [25/Oct/
  1995:18:31:06 -0000]
"GET http://csgrad.cs.vt.edu/
  ~schmidt/cgi-bin/postcards/
  images/upa-staf.jpg"
HTTP/1.0\" 200 4349
  Mozilla:1.1N:16bit:Windows
CERN:v3.0 NCSA:1.4.2
```

```
image/jpeg http://webstation.com/
   ultimate/postcards/
[17/Sep/1995:02:44:58 -0000] 115
   0.087 3.343
```

Items 1–8 are the "Common Log Format" with items 9–18 being the extended information that can be optionally added by our tools. Each numbered item is described below:

Common Log Format portion:

1. (*string/integer*) The client machine. This can be output as the DNS name or as a unique integer.

2. (*string/integer*) The User ID if provided by the `ident` protocol or as an HTTP environment variable. This variable can be output as a string or a unique integer.

3. (*date*) The date and time in the standard format `dd/mmm/yy:hh:mm:ss`.

4. (*integer*) The time zone in the standard format `+/-hhmm` from GMT (Greenwich Mean Time).

5. (*string*) The method: GET, HEAD, POST, PUT, or DELETE.

6. (*string*) The URL that the method is acting on.

7. (*integer*) Server status code.

8. (*integer*) Size of returned URL in bytes (as provided by HTTP `Content-Length` field).

Extended Common Log Format portion:

9. (*string*) Browser information in a ":" separated format   browser-name: browser-version: platform:OS.

10. (*string*) Proxy Gateway information, ":" separated (if available) proxy-server: proxy-server-version.

11. (*string*) Server information, ":" separated
server-name:server-version.

12. (*string*) MIME type of the returned document.

13. (*string*) The "Referer" URL. The URL containing the link to the requested URL.

14. (*date*) The date and time the requested URL was last modified (in GMT).

15. (*integer*) The time zone of the last modified data (always –0000).

16. (*integer*) The milliseconds of the date and time in field 3.
Because *tcpdump* provides greater time resolution we added this field for more accurate records of peak activity and performance.

17. (*float*) Network latency time in seconds. This is the time that elapses between the HTTP GET for the URL and the first packet that the server sends in reply (i.e., T1 in Figure 3).

18. (*float*) File transfer time in seconds. This is the time that elapses between the first packet that the server sends in reply to the HTTP GET for the URL and the disconnection request sent by server to client (i.e., T2 in Figure 3). ∎

References

1. Abrams, M., C. Standridge, G. Abdulla, S. Williams, and E.A. Fox, "Caching Proxies: Limitations and Potentials," *Proc. 4th International World Wide Web Conference*, Cambridge, O'Reilly & Associates, Inc., December 1995, *http://ei.cs.vt.edu/~succeed/WWW4/WWW4.html*.

2. Berman, J., J. Goldman, D.J. Weitzner, and D.K. Mulligan, *Statement of the Center for Democracy and Technology before the Federal Trade Commission Workshop on Consumer Privacy on the Global Information Infrastructure*, June 1996, *http://www.cdt.org/publications/FTC_June96_test.html*.

3. Berners-Lee, T., R. Fielding, and H. Frystyk. "Hypertext transfer protocol—HTTP 1.0," February 1996, *http://www.w3.org/pub/WWW/Protocols/HTTP/1.0/spec.html*

4. Boutell, T., "wusage," *http://www.boutell.com/wusage/*

5. Center for Democracy and Technology, "CDT Privacy Demonstration Page," *http://www.13x.com/cgi-bin/cdt/snoop.pl*

6. Cunha, C.R., A. Bestavros, and M.E. Crovella, "Characteristics of WWW Client Based Traces," TR: BU-CS-95-010, Boston University, July 1995, *ftp:// cs-ftp.bu.edu/techreports/95-010-www-client-traces.ps.Z*

7. Cunha, C.R., A. Bestavros, and M.E. Crovella, "Client Log Traces," *ftp://cs-ftp.bu.edu/techreports/95-010-www-client-traces.tar.gz*

8. Fielding, R. "wwwstat," *http://www.ics.uci.edu/ WebSoft/wwwstat/*

9. Hallam-Baker, P.M., and B. Behlendorf, "Extended Log File Format," World Wide Web Consortium [Working Draft Document], March 1996, *http:// www.w3.org/pub/WWW/TR/WD-logfile.html*

10. Hallam-Baker, Phillip M., and D. Connolly, "Session Identification URL," World Wide Web Consortium [Working Draft Document], February 1996, *http://www.w3.org/pub/WWW/TR/WD-session-id.html*

11. *ISVS HindSite for Netscape Navigator*, ISYS/Odyssey Development, Inc. Englewood, Colorado, *http://www.isysdev.com/hindsite.html*

12. Lawrence Berkeley Laboratory Network Research Group, "tcpdump," *ftp://ftp.ee.lbl.gov/tcp-dump.tar.Z*

13. Long, Q., "gwstat," *http://dis.cs.umass.edu/stats/ gwstat.html*

14. Luotonen, A., and K. Altis, "World-Wide Web Proxies," *Proc. 1st Inter.Conf. on the WWW*, Geneva, May 1994; also appeared in *Computer Networks and ISDN Systems* 27, no. 2, 1994, *http:// www1.cern.ch/PapersWWW94/luotonen.ps*

15. McCanne, S., and V. Jacobson, "The BSD Packet filter: A New Architecture for User-level Packet Capture," *Proc. 1993 Winter USENIX Conference*, January 1993.

16. Stevens, W.R., *TCP/IP Illustrated*, vol. 3, Reading, Addison-Wesley, 1996, p.167.

17. T. Stehle, *Getting Real About Usage Statistics*, Knight-Ridder Inc., *http://www.naa.org/news/ stehle.html*

18. StJohns, M., "Authentication Server," RFC 931, January 1985, *ftp://nic.ddn.mil/rfc/rfc931.txt*

19. Williams, S., M. Abrams, C. Standridge, G. Abdulla, and E.A. Fox, "Removal Policies in Network Caches for World Wide Web Documents," to appear in *Proc. ACM Sigcomm 96*, Stanford, Calif., August 1996, *http://ei.cs.vt.edu/~succeed/96sigcomm/ 96sigcomm.html*

20. World Wide Web Consortium, "The Common Log Format," *http://www.w3.org/pub/WWW/Daemon/User/ Config/Logging.html#common-logfile-format*

Acknowledgments

Roland Wooster and Patrick Brooks helped write *httpdump*, and Ghaleb Abdulla provided comments and suggestions on this paper.

About the Authors

Marc Abrams

Department of Computer Science

Virginia Tech

Blacksburg, VA 24061-0106

abrams@daphne.cs.vt.edu

Marc Abrams is an Associate Professor of Computer Science at Virginia Tech. He received the Ph.D. degree in Computer Science from the University of Maryland at College Park in 1986. His research interests include traffic measurement, modeling, and performance analysis of the Web; design of Web-based tools for visualization, modeling, and statistical analysis of log data; and construction of a system for collaborative learning using the Web.

Stephen Williams

Department of Computer Science

Virginia Tech

Blacksburg, VA 24061-0106

williams@csgrad.cs.vt.edu

Stephen Williams is a Masters student in Computer Science at Virginia Tech. He received his Bachelors degree in Aerospace Engineering from Virginia Tech in 1993. His research interests include network traffic collection and analysis, network video transmission, and graphics. His thesis topic is on methods to reduce transmission of redundant data in the World Wide Web.

WWW Site Measurement

A Collective Interview

Roger Hurwitz, editor

Introduction

The Web's explosive growth and its consequent discovery by advertisers seem to have turned the measurement of individual site use into a frantic numbers game. There are now obvious incentives to boast about "hits" and push to its limits the tracking of users within and across sites. As a result, advertisers have become skeptical about the meaningfulness of the numbers they hear, while users have grown wary about leaving tracks in cyberspace. Such tensions surfaced at the January, 1996 Workshop on Internet Survey Methodology and Web Demographics, where over a third of the participants listed privacy versus data needs as a chief concern. These tensions will haunt future forums until standards for comparing data and assuring privacy are established.

The community of Web developers can speed up the process by looking again at the basic issues in measuring use. Might there not be a small, common set of answers, that satisfy everyone's interests, to questions like: What should we measure? How and why should we do it? How can we reconcile providers' needs for numbers with users' concerns for privacy? What non-invasive methods can overcome problems of counting that come with proxy servers, client-side caches and statelessness?

Developers who specialize in the collection and analysis of site use data are one group that should have practical answers to these questions. They, after all, depend on interest from the provider or sponsor, on one hand, and acceptance by the user public, on the other. So, to start the discussion, we invited "loggers" who presented their systems at the January workshop to a virtual interview, summarized below.

The Loggers

Kent Godfrey, CEO of Andromedia, Inc., *http://www.andromedia.com/*. Andromedia builds systems that provide management information to stakeholders of "stateless" systems. . . . "Consumers of this information include webmasters and other system operators, advertising agencies, and advertisers—each of whom needs different information to make resource allocation decisions."

Paul Grand, Chairman, NetCount LLC., *http://www.netcount.com*. "NetCount is the Web site measurement and research service which measures real users while protecting user privacy, and offers impartial, third party verification of Web site traffic using a method of census-based counting, not sampling."

Ariel Poler, Chairman and Founder of I/PRO (Internet Profiles Corporation), *http://www.ipro.com/*. I/PRO is the "leading provider of Internet-based ratings, research, and performance measurement solutions that enable advertising and marketing professionals to optimize their one-to-one marketing program on the Web."

Neil Smith, Technical Manager of HENSA Unix. "HENSA is an archive of freely available software, for the benefit of the Higher Education community in the U.K. HENSA also operates the U.K. National Academic Web Cache.'

Robert Spielvogel, Senior Scientist, Education Development Center. Developer of Footprints, "a client/server system for use in formative and summative research on Internet use in educational settings. The client consists of a flexible launch pad on users' workstations from which applications of interest, including Web browsers, can be studied."

The Questions and Answers

1. What are the primary reasons for measuring site traffic?

The answers reflected the diverse needs of network managers, site developers, content providers, advertisers, and other sponsors of sites. For **Smith**, measurement is primarily a matter of monitoring how much bandwidth is being used and "not necessarily what it is being used for." The others sounded a common theme of justifying site costs. **Spielvogel** noted the need for "relative comparisons of utilization [of dissemination media] to better adjust resource expenditures. **Godfrey**, **Grand**, and **Poler** mentioned estimating the advertising potential or promotional effectiveness of a site, basing ad rates, and justifying costs of partiuclar technologies, e.g., Java. They also agreed that information on site traffic was a needed input for improving site design.

2. What do you or your customers want to measure at the sites?

The answers to this question ranged from **Smith**'s succinct "cache effectiveness" to extensive agendas of **Poler** and **Grand**.

Poler: "Many things, depending on the customer. For example, the number of visitors by time periods and areas of the site, relative usage of various areas, the domains and demographics of the users, the referring URL and navigational behavior in general, usage trends over time, and comparisons of the site traffic with industry benchmarks."

Grand (in addition to the above): "The optimal locations to place an online advertisement, the number of users seeing a particular online advertisement, and the number responding to (clicking on) it."

3. What are the appropriate units of site use, e.g., pages, visits?

Smith, in line with his focus on cache effectiveness, notes: "We are only interested in the bytes on the wire—making sure that the same bytes don't hit the same wire more than once."

The other loggers agree that number of "hits" is an inadequate unit for measuring interactions with a Web site.

Godfrey: "Users, visits, pages."

Grand: With current technology, the appropriate units of site usage are "pages requested," "pages transferred," and number of "unique hosts." A count of users and visits is only possible if the site is using registration and some form of authentication.

Poler adds, however, that the units depend on the type of activity being measured. "For raw transactional levels, requests and hits are appropriate; for estimating audiences, visitors if there is no registration, and unique individuals if there is some form of registration. Exposure of ads can be measured by how many times they were viewed; effectiveness of the ads can be measured by how many times viewers clicked on them. Pages are an obvious measure of popularity of pages."

4. What sort of demographic data do you think is crucial?

The advertising-oriented loggers (**Godfrey**, **Grand**, and **Poler**) would like to collect data in the usual categories, e.g., age, occupation, gender income, and education, with the exception of unique identifiers such as name and social security number. **Grand** observes that since a browser in a household setting might be shared by several people, data that differentiates the user, like a login name, will be crucial when it is available.

They added that in business-to-business applications, the user's industry, job function, job title, and purchasing authority are crucial data.

5. What are the ethical (or legal) limitations on data collection? How can we reconcile users' demands for privacy and site providers demands for data?

All loggers agree that no unique identifiers should be collected without the users' permission and that users should derive some benefit for providing information about themselves. Beyond that, there are some differences of opinion and practice.

Smith: "We have recently adopted the policy of only keeping summary information. Within these summaries there is no way to identify any individual, or even an individual machine. We are unsure of ethical and legal limitations, especially in Europe, and so have erred on the side of caution."

"A user who wishes to remain entirely anonymous may have to suffer badly directed advertising, and a lot of it. A user who gives up their postal code, age, and occupation will receive more specific information without having identified themselves uniquely. Of course, machine name and IP address are pieces of information that people should choose to keep private or give up. Proxies will be required to ensure that this information remains private."

Poler: "Consumers should be in the driver's seat." More specifically, consumers should control:

- Which sites receive information about them and what level of information they receive

- How the information can be used by each site, e.g., to contact them, for research only, to make them offers

Spielvogel: "Let the user decide if the site's request for data on him or her is a fair exchange for use of particular content." (**Poler** shares this view.)

Grand: "Ethically, the collecting site needs to inform the user what they intend to do with the data collected. A user should not be forced to reveal their identity (name, email address) without this knowledge.

Site providers and advertisers have an economic need to understand the usage of their Web sites, the demographics of their audience, and the response to their advertisements. This data can be delivered through anonymous registration and authentication

Godfrey suggests that, with the exception of unique identifiers, all other data on users can contribute to improving the Web and the user's experience on it. Collection of the data should therefore not be considered an invasion of privacy.

6. What tools are needed to collect the data? Are there scaleable solutions for tracking individual users in large sites and across sites?

Understandably, the loggers referred to their own systems in answering these questions. Godfrey, especially in regard to scalability, and Poler refer readers to information at their Web sites, respectively *http://www.andromedia.com/* and *http://icode.ipro.com.*

For **Spielvogel**, one desirable tool is a client that sits on the user's system and logs history and usage patterns can be used to sample detailed usage.

Grand's collection tools include server-side APIs, registration forms, authentication servers and registration databases. [But] scalability is relative. Referrals are useful. Cookies are useful within sites and domains. Certificates are useful across sites.

Smith wonders how one can keep up with all the data flow. "We are struggling to maintain our summaries on only two million hits a day. What do people like Netscape do with their logs?"

7. What are the best ways of handling problems of measuring site use, e.g., undercounting, created by proxy servers and browser caches?

Everyone agreed that the proxy, on requesting a page, should report the number of times it has delivered that page since the last time it made the request. But there were some differences regarding the adequacy and feasibility of this arrangement."

Smith observes that it unfortunately loses demographic data, and he lists some other options:

- Accept [the problems]—treat the Web as a broadcast medium and determine effectiveness in the market through other measures.

- Report hits with proxy hostname—if the hit counts were accompanied by the name of the proxy, and higher level proxies didn't aggregate these counts, then some rudimentary demographic data would be there. For example, individual institutions would be visible in the data passed back by our national proxy.

- Return full log information.

Poler: "To handle proxy servers, there are two pieces to the solution: cooperation and technology. Maintainers of large proxy caches should cooperate with the sites they are caching and provide them with aggregated usage information. They should do this as a quid-pro-quo for being able to cache (copy) the site's (copyrighted) material. An additional incentive the "cachers" could receive is information from the sites regarding what percentage of that site's traffic they represent. Technology becomes a more important component for smaller proxy caches, for which a seamless and automated way of reporting local usage back to the content sites needs to be developed. This is definitely an area in which the W3C could help a lot."

"Client-side caching is less of a problem since few users view the same pages over and over. Client- side caching is a major challenge to measuring exposure of specific media elements (e.g., *gifs*), which might be repeated in multiple pages. This is the case with advertising banners. To address this, the server can keep track of the pages being used and the relationships that pages have with elements. For dynamically generated elements, the server can keep track of every time an element is selected (even though it might not be requested due to client-side caching)."

Grand supplies a needed element in this last suggestion: "Build a mechanism into the Web browser that transmits cached activity to content owner with the next request."

Finally, **Godfrey** notes that these problems require a standard: "Governing bodies such as W3C should publish standards and endorse the tools that adhere to these standards."

Final Thought

The responses share two characteristics. First, they are restrained, reasonable, and optimistic. They do not anticipate inevitable conflicts either between users and advertisers, between content providers and sponsors, or among site developers. Their apparent confidence in a win-win situation for everyone corresponds to the current state of the Web industry: Explosive growth, plentiful opportunities, low startup costs, no shakeouts yet, and destined to change society. Second, they all emphasize fair exchange as the principle for social interaction on the Web. Even Smith, whose main concern is the adequacy of a public sector proxy server, goes along with this marketplace approach. Users and providers are expected to exchange information (and eventually purchases) for content.

The issue is not whether these assumptions are right or wrong, but how different they are from earlier models of the Web and Internet. For the moment, the broadcast model has all but supplanted the earlier dream of a collaborative tool. Likewise, exchange has replaced the gift as the form of the social bond. So we might expect the problems of measurement to be resolved in a business-like way. ∎

About the Editor

Roger Hurwitz
MIT Artificial Intelligence Lab
545 Technology Square
Cambridge, MA 02139
rhhu@ai.mit.edu

Roger Hurwitz is a research scientist at the M.I.T. Artificial Intelligence Laboratory, an architect of the Open Meeting System, and a contributor to COMLINK Development. His work focuses on the modeling, measurement, and management of collective actions, public communications flows, and organizational intelligence. Hurwitz holds a Ph.D. from M.I.T., has taught at M.I.T. and the Hebrew University (Jerusalem), and has consulted for major communication companies and U.N. agencies.

MODEL-BASED INFERENCE FOR COMPLETE-DATA STATISTICS
FROM VOLUNTARY RESPONSES TO INTERNET SURVEYS

Jeffrey E. Danes

Abstract

This paper presents a statistical method to estimate the complete-data mean and variance from voluntary responses to Web surveys. The inference objective of this paper is to make inferences to the population of visitors who visit a specific Web site such as www.hotbot.com. No attempt is made to infer beyond the boundaries of this specific population. An example is provided. **Keywords:** *Web measurement, metrics, survey methods, sampling, statistics, inference, response bias*

Introduction

Suppose a random selection of visitors to a popular Web site are asked to participate in a market or opinion survey. Further suppose only 1 of 10 voluntarily respond to the survey request. What is one to make of the fact that 90% refused to participate in the survey request? Are there differences between the 10% who responded and the 90% who did not? Does it matter?

This paper presents a statistical model to estimate complete-data statistics from voluntary responses to Web surveys. Those who are asked for feedback but refuse are nonrespondents. A complete-data set refers to a set of data representing both respondents and nonrespondents to Web surveys. The inference objective of this paper is modest. Our goal is only to make inferences to the population of visitors who visit a specific Web site. No attempt is made to infer beyond the boundaries of this specific population. An example population are those who visit *www.hotbot.com* during a specified period of time.

The specific objective of this paper is to estimate the complete-data mean and variance using a model that relates the respondents' mean and variance to the nonrespondents' mean and variance.

Response Propensity, Respondents, and Nonrespondents

There appear to be two general response tendencies in simultaneous operation. When an organism is faced with a stimulus, there is the tendency to respond (approach) and the tendency to avoid responding (avoidance). This is the approach-avoidance paradigm of the behavioral sciences. In the simplest case, an elementary approach-avoidance rule is assumed: If the tendency to approach is greater than the tendency to avoid, then a response occurs; otherwise, there is no response.

In general, there are at least two types of people: those who will and those who will not respond to a survey. In this paper, it is assumed that response propensity is a continuous variable and is normally (Gaussian) distributed in the population. For example, the left tail of the normal distribution represents the hard-core nonrespondent and the right tail represents the zealot. Somewhere in the midsection, there exists a response threshold, a division that separates propensity to respond into the binary outcome, i.e., the respondents and the nonrespondents. Given the appropriate context, incentives, and motivation, a nonrespondent in one setting may be a respondent in different setting.

Model Assumptions

The proposed model makes the following assumptions:

- Web metrics and other measurements can provide an indicator of response propensity.

- Response propensity is normally distributed over the population.

- Response propensity and variables of interest are bivariate normally distributed.

The bivariate normal distribution implies that the regression line of y, the variable of interest, on to response propensity will exhibit equal variance over the regression line (homoscedasticity). It is this fact that enables the prediction of complete-data statistics from only respondent data, as is explained below.

The Approach and Notation

The Superpopulation modeling approach is used to make inferences to the population from voluntary responses to Web questionnaires; see [1] and [3]. In the Superpopulation approach to survey sampling, the elements in the population are not fixed, as they are in the traditional approach, but rather they are treated as random variables. If one assumes a normal (Gaussian) distribution then, for example, all elements in the population are normally distributed with mean and variance, $y_i \sim G(\mu_k, \sigma_k^2)$, where μ_k is a realization of the Superpopulation distribution ξ.

The population mean may be expressed as $\mu = q\mu_1 + p\mu_0$, where μ_1 is the mean for the respondents μ_0 is the population mean for the nonrespondents, p = the proportion of nonrespondents and $(1-p) = q$ = the proportion or respondents. Let y_i = quantitative response variable such as the age of a Web site visitor. The elements of y for the nonrespondents are denoted by $y_0 = (y_{10}, y_{20}, y_{30}, ...y_{n_0})$, and the elements of y for the respondents is denoted by $y_1 = (y_{11}, y_{21}, y_{31}, ... y_{n_1})$.

The unobserved complete-data vector for y is $n_0 + n_1 = n$ and is denoted $y = (y_0, y_1)$.

The two sample sizes are not necessarily equal; in fact, it is likely that n_0 will be substantially larger than n_1. The total, theoretical sample size is $n = n_0 + n_1$; however, as is noted below, the operative sample size is n_1.

The vector of unknown response propensities for the nonrespondents is denoted, $\varphi_0 = (\varphi_{10}, \varphi_{20}, \varphi_{30}, ... \varphi_{n_0})$.

And the vector of known response propensities for the volunteer respondents is denoted $\varphi_1 = (\varphi_{11}, \varphi_{21}, \varphi_{31}, ...\varphi_{n_1})$.

The unobserved complete-data vector of response propensity is $n_0 + n_1 = n$ and is denoted $\varphi = (\varphi_0, \varphi_1)$.

Let S_i be a realization of response propensity, a binary variable indicating those who responded and those who did not (a selection indicator).

$$S_i = \begin{cases} = 1, i \in \varphi_1 \\ = 0, i \in \varphi_0 \end{cases}$$

Development of the Model

Suppose N people visit a Web site (over some period of time) and using a randomization mechanism, n are requested to respond to a survey. Of these, n_1 of these respond to a survey while n_0 refuse. What is the mean and variance of the response variables for the entire population of N Web site visitors?

The objective of the model is to predict complete-data statistics from the data obtained from voluntary responses to Web surveys. This section presents the highlights of the model proposed in this paper. The goal of the model is to predict the mean μ_y and variance σ_y^2 of y from the data obtained by voluntary responses to Web surveys. For this purpose, let us begin with the population regression model, (c.f., [2]), for the linear regression of the y on response propensity, φ.

$$E(y_i|\varphi_i)(-\mu_y) = \rho(\rho_y/\rho_\varphi)(\varphi_i - \mu_\varphi) \qquad [1]$$

where ρ is the population correlation between y and response propensity φ. As noted above, it is desirable to dichotomize the normally distributed response propensity into $S_1 = 1$ and $S_0 = 0$ and write the linear regression as:

$$E(y_i|S) - \mu_y = \rho(\sigma_y/\sigma_\varphi)(E(\varphi_i|S) - \mu_\varphi) \qquad [2]$$

In terms of mean regression, there are three means for y and three means for φ (respondent, nonrespondent, and complete-data). Using the complete-data mean in both cases, two regression equations may be written, one for the respondents:

$$E(y_i|S_i) - \mu_y = \rho(\sigma_y/\sigma_\varphi)(E(\varphi_i|S_i) - \mu_\varphi) \qquad [3]$$

and one for the nonrespondents:

$$E(y_i|S_0) - \mu_y = \rho(\sigma_y/\sigma_\varphi)(E(\varphi_i|S_0) - \mu_\varphi) \qquad [4]$$

The coefficient ρ, as noted above, is the correlation between y and response propensity φ. Following the structure of Pearson's biserial correlation coefficient [5], the prediction of μ_y may be derived from [3] as $\mu_y = E(y_i|S_i) - \rho(\sigma_y h/q)$ and since $\mu_1 = E(y_i|S_i)$,

$$\mu_y = \mu_1 - \rho(\sigma_y h/q) \qquad [5]$$

The symbol h is the height or ordinate of the normal (Gaussian) curve at the point of dichotomy defined by the proportions q and p, the proportions of respondents and nonrespondents.

Estimation of Model Parameters

A model-based complete-data value y_i may be written following equation 5 as

$$y_i = y_{i,1} - \rho(\sigma_y^2 h/q) \qquad [6]$$

where $y_{i,1}$ is the observed data value for the i-th respondent. Equation 6 shows the proposed model to be a simple linear adjustment of the observed data value, that is, the observed value is shifted to account for the influence of nonre-

sponse. The variance of y may therefore be expressed as,

$$\sigma_y^2 = \sigma_{y_1}^2 + \sigma_\rho^2[\sigma_y^2 h/q]^2$$

or by,

$$\sigma_y^2 = (q^2 \sigma_{y_1}^2)/(q^2 - \sigma_\rho^2 h^2) \qquad [7]$$

where q is the proportion of respondents, h is the height of the normal curve at the dichotomy defined by p and q, and σ_ρ^2 is the variance of the unobserved complete-data propensity correlation, ρ.

$$\sigma_\rho^2 = (1 - \rho^2)^2/n$$

The unobserved complete-data correlation between the response variable y and propensity may be expressed as:

$$\rho = [1 - (\sigma_e^2/\sigma_y^2)]^{1/2} \qquad [8]$$

where σ_e^2 is the unobserved residual mean square of the regression of y on φ and σ_y^2 is the unobserved complete-data variance of y. An estimate σ_e^2 may be found from observed data as s_e^2, the residual variance of the observed regression of y_1 on to φ_1. The assumption of bivariate normality implies that the residual variance of y conditioned at different levels of response propensity is equal (homoscedasticity). Therefore, the residual variance at any one level (respondents) may be used as an estimate of variance at any other level (nonrespondents). In other words, $\sigma_{e_1}^2 = \sigma_{e_0}^2 = \sigma_e^2$.

Estimation of σ_y^2 and ρ

As noted above, the observed sample size is n_1, but the theoretical complete-data sample size is $n = n_0 + n_1$. How does one determine the operative sample size?

What is the sample size for, say, the computation of a standard error of the mean?

Inspection of equation 6 shows the predicted value to be a simple shift, by an additive constant, of the observed value. Therefore, the operative sample size should be the observed sample size, n_1, not the theoretical sample size n.

From the two equations 7 and 8, the two unknown quantities σ_y^2 and ρ may be found. An algebraic solution for the variance σ_y^2 is given below:

$$\sigma_y^2 = (\sigma_{y_1}^2/2) \qquad [9]$$
$$+ [nq^2\sigma_{y_1}^4 + 4\sigma_e^4 h^2]^{1/2}/(2q[n]^{1/2})$$

As estimate of the complete-data variance for y is given as s_y^2

$$s_y^2 = (s_{y_1}^2/2) \qquad [10]$$
$$+ [(n_1 - 1)q^2 s_{y_1}^4 + 4s_e^4 h^2]^{1/2}$$
$$/(2q[n_1 - 1]^{1/2})$$

where $s_{y_1}^2$ is the observed variance for the respondents, n_1 is the observed sample size, and s_e^2 is the observed residual mean square variance for the regression of the observed y_1 on to the observed response propensities, φ_1. The estimate of the complete-data propensity correlation ρ is given by r.

$$r = \left[1 - (s_e^2/s_y^2)\right]^{1/2} \qquad [11]$$

Example Application

Below is a worked (hypothetical) example designed to clarify the process and steps needed to estimate the complete-data mean and variance from voluntary responses to Web surveys. (This paper makes no attempt to define the concepts of "hit," "page," "visit," or "visitor." These definitions are handled elsewhere in this volume.) Suppose a popular Web site routinely conducts surveys of its visitors; suppose a different survey is run each week. Also, suppose that Web measurements accurately record the survey respondent, each time they participate in the survey. If such measurements are not possible, then verbal questions could be used to ask the survey respondent if they had participated in previous surveys, and if so, how many in the past six weeks? A combination of these two methods could be used to produce an index of response propensity, φ_1.

Suppose on the last week of a six-week period, a short survey is run to determine, among other things, the age of the visitor, y_1. The results of the age survey from the q=10% who responded produces the following summary of mean age by level of survey participation shown in Table 1.

The observed $\bar{y}_1$ is 27.158, the observed s_{y_1} is 8, and the operative sample size n_1 = 2,500 respondents. The mean ages in the table shows a negative correlation between age and response propensity. The observed Pearson product-moment correlation coefficient for y_1 and φ_1 is r_1 = -.13. This number is used to estimate the residual standard error of the linear regression of y_1 on to φ_1 by the formula $s_e = s_{y_1}\sqrt{(1 - r_1^2)}$, which is 7.932.

The above paragraphs contain all of the information necessary to apply equations 10 and 11 to estimate σ_y^2 and ρ. The complete-data variance for age is s_y^2 = 64.0783 and the complete-data propensity correlation is r = −.13445.

As can be seen from equation 5, the prediction of μ_y requires the height of the normal curve at the point of dichotomy defined by p and q, which is readily found from tabled values presented, for example, in Owen [4]. The height of the normal distribution, h, for q = 10% is .178. As noted, the estimate of μ_1 is given by $\bar{y}_1$, and the estimate

Table 1 Results by Mean Age and Levels of Participation

Number of Times Respondent Participated in a Survey	one	two	three	four	five	six
Proportion of Respondents	0.44	0.11	0.18	0.13	0.09	0.05
Mean Age	27.7	27.3	26.8	26.7	26.3	26.1

of σ_1 is given by s_1. The predicted, complete-data mean μ_y is 29.075 years of age.

Are there differences between the 10% who responded and the 90% who did not? Does it matter? For the above example, the answer is yes to both of the questions. There is a difference and it does matter! The mean age for the respondents is 27.158 and the predicted mean age for the complete-data set is 29.075. What is the mean age of the nonrespondents? Simple algebra shows this to be $(\bar{y} - q\bar{y}_1)/p = \bar{y}_0 = 29.228$ years of age.

Summary

This paper presented a statistical method to estimate complete-data mean and standard deviation from voluntary responses to Web surveys The inference objective of this paper is to make inferences only to the population of visitors who visit a specific Web site. The complete-data statistics are estimated from a model that relates the respondents' mean and variance to the nonrespondents' mean and variance. The model makes two key assumptions: (1) response propensity can be measured via Web measures, metrics, and questions, and (2) response propensity and the outcome variable, y, are bivariate normally distributed. ∎

References

1. Cassel, Claes-Magnus, Carl-Erik Sarndal, and Jan Hakan Wretman, *Foundations of Inference in Survey Sampling*, New York, John Wiley and Sons, 1977.

2. Hoel, Paul G., *Introduction to Mathematical Statistics*, New York, John Wiley and Sons, 1971.

3. Little, Roderick, J.A., "Models of Nonresponse in Sample Surveys," *Journal of the American Statistical Association*, vol. 77, 1983, pp. 237–250.

4. Owen, D.B., *Handbook of Statistical Tables*, Reading, Addison-Wesley, 1962.

5. Pearson, Karl, "On a New Method for Determining Correlation Between a Measured Character A and a Character B of Which Only the Percentage of Cases Wherein B Exceeds (of falls short of) a Given Intensity is Recorded for Each Grade of A," *Biometrika*, vol. 7, 1909, pp. 96-106.

About the Author

Jeffrey E. Danes is Professor of Marketing in the College of Business at Cal Poly, San Luis Obispo, California, and is a Senior Statistician and Research Scientist at Marketruler Corporation (*http://www.marketruler.com/network/*). He may be reached at *network@marketruler.com* or *jdanes@oboe.aix.calpoly.edu*.

POLLS, SURVEYS, AND CHOICE PROCESSOR TECHNOLOGY ON THE WORLD WIDE WEB

Arnold B. Urken

1. Introduction

Normally, information about voter preferences, priorities, and judgments is collected and processed as if interpreting it were straightforward. In reality, there is an underlying complexity associated with voting processes that, if properly understood, can be used to provide guidance by *accurately* identifying what groups think and feel. Although voting or "social choice theory [1] [2] [4] provides a basis for finding out if a voting system does not produce accurate results, the Web environment makes it imperative to have a tool that can guide analysis of voting input dynamically—even as votes are being cast. Using the Web as a superadding machine to make data collection rapid and inexpensive is not sufficient for answering questions about marketing products or services.

This paper describes a system for creating polls and surveys on the Web based on an analysis-centric approach adopted by SmartChoice Technologies Corporation (SCTC). SCTC's choice processor[*] tools for the Web employ technology that uses "social choice" analysis to provide instant insight into the interpretation of collective choice processes and outcomes. This technology can be used for marketing applications, but it is also applicable for Web-based group decisions that are made from interfaces in which the Web is the desktop.

For marketing applications, SCTC's choice processor technology is designed to enable users who are not experts in voting theory to analyze

data. This design is based on an awareness of the limitations of randomization techniques when dealing with populations in which the parameters of respondent preferences, priorities, and judgments are not well understood. In such cases, standard techniques for generating a random sample may be irrelevant and misleading.

Web-based choice processing makes it possible to collect granular information that can be used to learn about respondents. Without the Web, marketing analysts must spend much time and money collecting intensity-of-preference data and comment data. If we move away from the habitual practice and limiting perspective of using electronic communication for delivering and collecting survey instruments directly prepared on paper, we can create significant opportunities for avoiding distortions and gathering more reliable results.

SCTC is committed to promoting an open standards, client-server approach to creating such opportunities. Our non-proprietary, public data structure standard for choice transactions, the ChoiceObject,[†] enables analysis to be carried out in any computer-mediated process. This means that "surveys" or "polls" can be conducted from within any type of application (e.g., CAD/CAM, video-on-demand, group editors) as long as there is a Web connection.

Figure 1 outlines the relationship between inputs and outputs in the architecture of a choice processor. Any computer-mediated input/output device such as a fax, set-top box, phone (mobile

---

[*] Choice Processor, patent-pending, is a trademark of SmartChoice Technologies Corporation.
[†] ChoiceObject is a trademark of SmartChoice Technologies Corporation. Information on the ChoiceObject standard can be obtained by sending electronic mail to *info@smartchoice.com* with ChoiceObject as the subject.

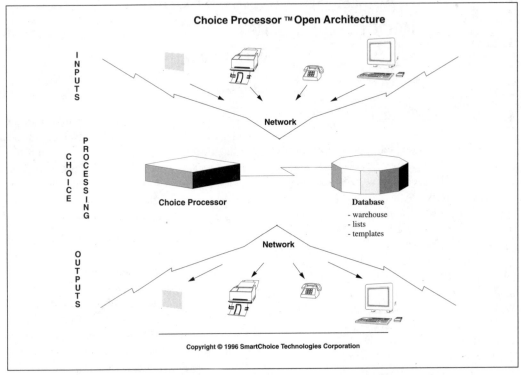

Figure 1   The relationship between inputs and outputs of a choice processor

or wired), or Personal Digital Assistant can be used. This means that survey data collection and dissemination can be digitally diverse. Respondents can be notified about a survey by electronic mail. Alternatively, a distributed daemon might check a server to detect waiting surveys. Either way, redundant communication can be used to contact respondents who are mobile.

For example, imagine a marketing manager who needs to collect estimates from twelve people during a four-hour interval between meetings that involves a car or plane trip. Choice processing makes it possible to initiate a poll by calling a template and disseminating it to respondents via the Internet. This system allows respondents to be reached via computer on the Web as well on gateways for other devices. For messages that involve multimedia or multipurpose information, MIME-compliant mail can be used as a transport

medium as well. SCTC has prototyped both of these systems for implementing choice processing.

The same choice processor technology can turn the Web into an environment for making group decisions about a wide range of tasks. Such decisions are not limited to occasions when a group decides to use computer-mediated communication to reach a formal consensus. They also involve supporting individuals who want to pool information from colleagues or customers to gain help in rendering individual decisions. For both types of group decisions, typical decision-making tasks include choosing a vendor, picking a restaurant, scheduling a meeting, and many other everyday tasks. In these situations, even though the membership of the group may be fixed and known, its voting patterns may be complex and variable. If group decision-making software is not supported by a tool that enables users to analyze these patterns, collective decision-making outcomes may be distorted without being detected. As a result, computer supported cooperative work will be less efficient than it can be or should be.

Since the Web is rapidly becoming part of an open systems desktop to the world, a working distinction between "polls" and "surveys" may be useful in highlighting the scope of choice processor applications:

> A *poll* involves questioning each member of a group to reach a conclusion.

> A *survey* entails analyzing a situation in more detail to answer a question.

In practice, this distinction may not be apparent because "poll" and "survey" are used interchangeably in contemporary discourse, yet these terms are also used idiomatically to connote a difference in the level of analysis.[*] Certainly, polling a distributed workgroup to select a restaurant for an upcoming meeting involves analysis at the level of counting heads.[†] In contrast, surveying a randomly selected group of restaurant goers to find, say, the best Chinese restaurant in a city requires a different sort of counting. The art and science of random selection are differentiated by the level of knowledge about the population that guides a sampling strategy. [3] [6] To explain how the choice processing methodology underlying our choice processor technology can enhance knowledge about randomly selected or non-random populations, Section 2 presents a hypothetical voting situation to show how the control of the voting system can provide insight into the interpretation of the outcome of a group deci-

sion. Sections 3 and 4, respectively, discuss how this methodology can be used to gain insight into longitudinal survey data as well as specific group decisions. Section 5 concludes with a description of our vision of the evolving role of polls and surveys on the World Wide Web.

2. Why Voting Systems Matter

This section aims to show why understanding voting systems matters when data from computer-mediated group decisions is being pooled. The point is not that voting systems are more likely to break down or produce undesirable outcomes in computer-mediated environments than they are in face-to-face situations. (In fact, it is normal for voting systems to fail and malfunction under all conditions.) The point is that computer-mediated decision making on the Web gives us an opportunity to prevent or detect and correct breakdowns so that humans control voting systems rather than being controlled by them.

In a Web environment, precautions can be taken to avoid making the results an artifact of the survey or polling system.[‡] In every voting situation, the underlying set of respondent preferences must be represented or described via a collective choice process. The objective of this section, however, is to show that voting systems used in this process may distort our understanding of the respondent preference set, but that potential distortion can be controlled through proper planning.

To see this point, let us consider two cases. In Case 1, suppose that a Web survey is used to find out how Web customers of Corporation X want to be billed. Moreover, let us also assume that the

---

[*] The history of the terms in other languages is consistent with this distinction. In classical Greek and Roman institutions, collective decisions by jurors, administrators, and voters (in elections) seem to have been regarded as polls where randomness was used in an ad hoc way to create fair procedures (Stavely, 1982). And although early French has a word for survey in a very general sense, specific technical terms for survey techniques such as sondage were developed as early as the eighteenth century to identify more rigorous methodologies. The absence of such special terms in English aggravates the ambiguity and ambivalence associated with polls and surveys.

[†] In fact, the etymology of poll suggests a root meaning of head counting using a voting or scoring method.

[‡] For instance, questions can be randomized to preclude order-of-presentation effects and questions can be asked without impeding respondents from communicating the complexity of their thoughts and feelings.

	Academic Users	Business Users	Government Users
First Place Choice	Flat Billing	Functional Billing	Hourly Billing
Second Place Choice	Functional Billing	Hourly Billing	Functional Billing
Third Place Choice	Hourly Billing	Flat Billing	Flat Billing

degree of randomness associated with selecting participants is not a factor—an assumption to be revisited below. In this scenario, three billing choices are being evaluated: flat, hourly, and functional billing. Each respondent is asked to rank these choices and to indicate which one(s) of the three options would be acceptable. Respondents can be categorized into academic, business, and government groupings. For simplicity, suppose that 200 users are in each group, giving us a total of 600 voters. Table 1 shows the rank-orderings of each grouping.

If a Web survey yields the ranking data shown above, what conclusion can we reach about what customers want? Table 2 shows a representation of the data in Table 1 filtered through a one-person, one-vote system.

If the choice data are processed this way, the collective outcome would be a three-way tie with each choice receiving 200 votes. What does this signify? Does it mean that voters intensely support all of the choices, or does it indicate that respondents are indifferent to the entire agenda of choices and might prefer some other options? The one-person, one-vote analysis does not help us answer these questions.

However, the same data can be interpreted under different voting systems to clarify these questions. As an example of another voting system, we might ask what would happen under approval voting, where voters can communicate by casting one vote for each approved choice? If we assume, for simplicity, that voters approve of their first and second place choices,[*] the resulting vote allocations are shown in Table 3.

Based on these data, the totals for the options are given below:

Flat Billing	200 votes
Functional Billing	600 votes
Hourly Billing	400 votes

Under this approval voting interpretation of the survey data, customers are not indifferent about the choices: each of the 600 respondents approves functional billing! Moreover, this approval voting interpretation of the data is based on a system that voting theorists regard as being efficient in identifying the strongest choice(s) in a collective choice outcome. One of

Table 2   Vote Allocations of 600 Respondents to a Corporation X Survey on Billing Options under a One-Person, One-Vote System

	Academic Users	Business Users	Government Users
Flat Billing	200	0	0
Functional Billing	0	200	0
Hourly Billing	0	0	200

---

[*] Empirical studies of approval voting show that voters typically cast two approval votes, regardless of the number of choices.

Table 3   Vote Allocations of 600 Respondents to a Corporation X Survey on Billing Options under an Approval Voting System

	Academic Users	Business Users	Government Users
Flat Billing	200	0	0
Functional Billing	200	200	200
Hourly Billing	0	200	200

the nice properties of the approval system is that it allows for ties if a majority or all of the respondents approve of all the choices, thus allowing the articulation of intensely-tied collective outcomes. This granularity can occur because voters do not have to cast all three of their approval votes.

For instance, in the context of Corporation X's survey, this means that it would be possible to determine if a majority of the respondents or all of the respondents strongly approved (or disapproved) of the billing options. Extremely strong approval for all three options would be indicated by maximum allocations of approval votes (unanimous approval), generating 1800 total votes cast. Less extreme support would be communicated if each billing option received a majority of respondent approval in each category (101 votes), producing a total of 303 votes cast.

Now let us consider Case 2: suppose that the ranking data collected from Corporation X's survey were instead initially ordered as shown in Table 4.

In this scenario, there seems to be majority support for Functional Billing when ranking data are filtered through a one-person, one-vote system, as shown in Table 5.

Although Functional Billing seems to have a decisive majority of 400 votes to 200 for Hourly Billing, Table 6, which processes the same initial

preference information from Table 4 through an approval voting system, presents a different picture.

These allocations produce the following collective outcome:

Flat Billing	200 votes
Functional Billing	400 votes
Hourly Billing	600 votes

According to these data, Functional Billing's one-person, one-vote majority is displaced by a more granular display of unanimous support for Hourly Billing as gauged under approval voting.

These simple illustrations show how collective decision analysis can provide insight into the meaning of collective outcomes. In Case 1, a decisive consensus was detected from data that seemed to indicate an indecisive outcome, while in Case 2, analysis of an ostensibly decisive choice indicated a decisive reversal in favor of another option. These examples highlight the importance of taking account of voting systems in scoring the results of any group decision. Most voting scenarios are much more intricate and dynamic, and the complexities of the collective choice process cannot be seen or controlled without an analysis provided by a choice processor.

Table 4   Preference Orderings of 600 Respondents to a Corporation X Survey on Billing Options

	Academic Users	Business Users	Government Users
First Place Choice	Functional Billing	Functional Billing	Hourly Billing
Second Place Choice	Hourly Billing	Hourly Billing	Flat Billing
Third Place Choice	Flat Billing	Flat Billing	Functional Billing

Table 5 Vote Allocations of 600 Respondents to a Corporation X Survey on Billing Options under a One-Person, One-Vote System

	Academic Users	*Business Users*	*Government Users*
Flat Billing	0	0	0
Functional Billing	200	200	0
Hourly Billing	0	0	200

3. Reliability and Distortions in Web Surveys

One of the challenges of conducting surveys over the Web is defining a target population. Since there is no well-defined population of potential respondents with "persistent identification," classical procedures for randomly selecting respondents are not appropriate without preliminary analysis. Choice processing is an enabling technology that allows us to build a granular, analytical picture of respondents over time by designing a survey strategy that builds a database of information about what customers, Web-site visitors, and others like and dislike. As this picture takes shape, it provides a basis for using increasingly rigorous sampling methodologies that are suitable for the survey or polling task.

For example, the need to extend hit-rate and related log analyses as measures of site use can be satisfied by collecting this type of survey data. Assuming that potential respondents identify themselves or can be identified adequately for a task, interactive surveys can collect data about what respondents have used, seen, played with, purchased, or returned. These surveys can be generated on-the-fly to learn from visitors or customers. If surveys allow branching, respondents may not all see or answer the same questions, but each person can be provided a customized question. Flexible surveys enable us to learn more. For instance, we can direct customers with extremely favorable or negative reactions to answer questions designed to obtain an explanation for such behavior. Appropriately designed branching questions provide a means of learning about respondents and either constructing follow-up surveys or immediately directing branchers to other polls. Collecting this type of data and processing it with collective choice analysis can immediately generate insight. For instance, it is not sufficient to know that some visitors to a Web site come more frequently than others. What choice processing can deliver are answers to questions about what frequent visitors like the most and least (including their reasons) and what would bring infrequent Web visitors back.

As responses to questions are collected longitudinally, the types of choice processing insights illustrated in section 2 can be provided to help create a sensitive baseline reference for understanding trends. For if specific collective decisions are not properly analyzed, the direction or magnitude of changes in respondent opinion may be misinterpreted or not noticed at all.

Once this baseline is established, we could identify the distinguishing characteristics of real and nominal groups to gather more data interactively about respondents. This type of data analysis would allow us to go beyond simply identifying

Table 6 Vote Allocations of 600 Respondents to a Corporation X Survey on Billing Options under an Approval Voting System

	Academic Users	*Business Users*	*Government Users*
Flat Billing	0	0	200
Functional Billing	200	200	0
Hourly Billing	200	200	200

lists of things that real or nominal groups say they intend to buy to finding out the rank-orderings of the characteristics embedded in these lists based on the pages that have been visited and the files that have been downloaded. These derived insights will enable us to use collective decision analysis to determine which groups have the same or consistent rank-orderings.

Combined with background log analysis of potential respondents, real or nominal groupings of respondents will provide an opportunity to launch flexible, branching surveys to gather rich data. These data will be enhanced by dynamic analysis of the collective decision-making implications of patterns of response.

The development of interactive polling and collective decision analysis can also improve reliability and reduce distortion in Web surveys by providing a methodology and technology for identifying the complex public repositories of information that can be used for evolving analogs of standard randomization protocols such as callbacks. [3] [6]. Adapting a technique from the use of phone surveys, we can follow up to verify that participants fit into a randomly selected nominal group. For instance, if a randomly selected group is composed on the basis of responding at a particular time of day or visiting a Web page with a particular frequency, the validity of the randomness assumption can be tested by repeatedly identifying the presumed pattern of behavior. Such techniques will enable surveys on the Web to be conducted according to more rigorous analytical standards.

This evolution can be expedited by the creation of new Web standards and institutions. For example, data collection in HTML forms can be modified to allow any object to be defined as a selector as long as it complies with open standards. Even if Java applets provide such flexibility as well as offer sliders and comment buttons (that require less real estate than boxes), there will still be a need to create a common data standard for processing information. Our ChoiceObject data model provides a public domain basis for sharing data archives and promoting a better understanding of the relationship between Web demographics and respondent preferences and judgments.

New institutions such as anonymous or trusted survey servers will normalize and legitimize Web surveys. This type of server can set high standards for security that simultaneously assure respondents that they will not be deluged with junk mail while they enable survey publishers to collect valuable data based on persistent identification. The value of the data involves not only gaining answers to questions, but having access to aggregated data analysis derived from all of the respondents who use the server. To protect individual privacy and maintain professional standards, aggregations will not include names or addresses of respondents.

4. Web Polling as an Interface Tool

As the Web evolves into another desktop interface as well as a window for home information services and entertainment, there will be opportunities for polling applications that offer a different set of challenges. When someone polls his or her colleagues in a project about when to have a project meeting, when a workgroup chooses what conference to attend, or when groups make any number of everyday decisions using their Web interfaces, the need for collective decision analysis in support of the task becomes strikingly evident.

The open client-server choice processor architecture makes it possible to create task-specific templates for group decision making from within any application. As long the data conform to the ChoiceObject model, instant analysis can be provided.

This type of functionality will not only support groups working on the Internet or Intranet, it will also support an individual's need to reach out to collect information to guide their own decisions. Instead of playing telephone tag or relying on the rigid and awkward process of collecting and analyzing data via normal electronic mail, individuals can use a tool that simplifies the processing of choices and integrates instant analysis tailored to the task.

5. Our Vision of Choice Processing

The future of the Web is one in which the use of a choice processor for making group decisions or for using data about collective preferences and priorities will become as ubiquitous as the use of a word processor for preparing documents is now.

Ultimately, this evolution will even have an impact on how people think about voting systems and their level of sophistication in dealing with such systems including the interpretation of their results [5]. Consequently, we foresee a world in which political surveys—and even elections—will be expected to operate in different ways.

For example, imagine a networked world in which the Internet is the backbone for voting from home. Assuming that security is managed by smart cards or similar encryption technology, suppose that elections last a week, not a day, and that citizens can change their votes. In such a world, the incentives for interacting with candidates would change. Now candidates and parties do everything they can to engineer a winning coalition through surveys and advertising by targeting a specific, irreversible decision in which voters cast a single, categorical vote. Obfuscation, ambiguity, and lies are used to achieve this objective. But in extended elections, candidates and parties would have incentives to respond to public debate if more complex expressions of voter preferences could be communicated. For instance, if voters could approve of more than one choice, the dynamics of coalition formation (and reformation) would enable citizens to take a more active role in the dissemination of information.

Obviously this type of system requires more analysis and testing, but the point is that having an integrated system for processing choices will make it possible to reengineer social institutions to meet the requirements of an advanced social system instead of relying on practices that may be intolerably inefficient and ineffective. ■

References

1. McLean, Ian, and Arnold B. Urken, *Classics of Social Choice*, Ann Arbor: University of Michigan Press, 1995.

2. Mueller, Dennis C., *Public Choice II*, New York: Cambridge University Press, 1989.

3. Roll, Charles W., and Albert H. Cantril, *Polls: Their Use and Misuse in Politics*, New York: Basic Books, 1972.

4. Urken, Arnold B., "Social Choice Theory and Distributed Decision Making," in R. Allen (ed.) *Proceedings of the IEEE/ACM Conference on Office Information Systems*, Palo Alto, 1988.

5. Urken, Arnold B., "The Social Impact of Computer-Mediated Voting," in W. Maner and T. Bynum (eds.), *Proceedings of the National Conference on Computers and Values*, New Haven, 1991.

6. Williams, Bill, *A Sampler on Sampling*, New York: John Wiley & Sons, 1978.

Acknowledgments

I would like to thank Roger Hurwitz for his criticism and suggestions.

About the Author

Arnold B. Urken, President
SmartChoice Technologies Corporation
610 River Street Hoboken, NJ 07030
aurken@smartchoice.com
http://copeland.smartchoice.com

President and co-founder of SmartChoice Technologies Corporation, Dr. Urken is an expert on voting systems. His work includes studies of the adoption and use of voting systems in organizations as well as theoretical and empirical analysis of system properties.

MEASURING THE WEB

Tim Bray

Abstract

"When you can measure what you are speaking about, and express it in numbers, you know something about it; but when you cannot express it in numbers, your knowledge is of a meager and unsatisfactory kind; it may be the beginning of knowledge, but you have scarcely in your thoughts advanced to the state of science." —Lord Kelvin

This paper presents some difficult qualitative questions concerning the Web and attempts to provide some partial quantitative answers to them. It uses the numbers in these answers to drive some 3-D visualizations of localities in the Web.

The Questions

History

Since the first robot was launched on Saint Valentine's Day 1995, the Open Text Index software has examined millions of pages and maintained an ever-growing inventory of information about them.

This effort has been, from the outset, marketing-driven. Open Text is a long-time vendor of search and retrieval technology, and the WWW became, during the course of 1994, the world's largest and most visible retrieval problem. Failing to have attacked it would have been a vote of no confidence in our own technology.

As a business exercise, it has been successful. Open Text's Livelink Search and Livelink Spider are leaders in the fast-growing market for Web site indexers. Considered as an intellectual effort, it has been less than satisfying. We advertise our work as an index of the WWW—and yet it covers much less than the whole. Our difficulty is similar to that of the cartographers of centuries past, struggling with the task of mapping territories that are still largely unknown. Observe, for example, *Terra Australis Incognita* in Figure 1.

Questions Without Answer

- How big is the Web?

- What is the "average page" like?

- How richly connected is it?

- What are the biggest and most visible sites?

- What data formats are being used?

- What does the WWW look like?

This paper uses the resources of the Open Text Index to derive some approximations to the answers.

The Answers

The Sample

The information on which this report is based was extracted in November 1995, when the Open Text Index covered the content of about 1.5 million textual objects retrieved from the WWW. Today, the sample would be much larger. To keep things simple, we'll call these objects "pages." The pages were identified and retrieved as follows:

- *Initialization.* We started in late 1994 with a bootstrap list of some 40,000 URLs alleged to be those of "home pages"; nobody can remember where this originally came from. We retrieved as many as possible of these (about 20,000) and formed the initial index.

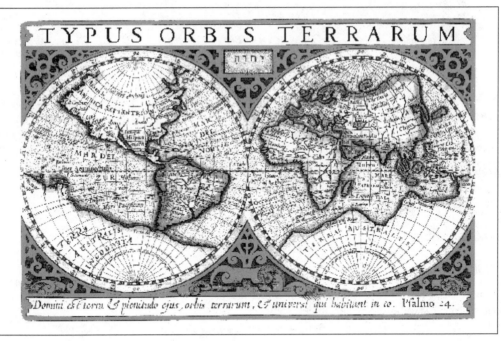

Figure 1   1601 Mercator-Hondius

- *Page Refresh*. For each indexed page, we maintain a time-stamp indicating the last time it was visited. Our initial page refresh strategy simply involved sorting the total inventory of pages oldest-first and dedicating fixed periods of time to revisiting them in that order. Revisiting a page has three possible results: the page is gone, the page is there but has changed, or the page is unchanged.

  We have since become more sophisticated in our processes for selecting pages to revisit, but the possible outcomes are the same.

- *Enlargement*. Each time we copy in the contents of a page, we extract from it all *http*, *gopher*, and *ftp* style anchors. Those that are not duplicates of already indexed pages are queued for addition to the Index.

- *"Good" pages are over-represented*. Other sources of new pages are voluntary submissions to the Index and well-known Internet announcement venues.

Nobody can say how good a sample this is of the whole Web. However, the basic statistics presented below for page size and contents have not changed much since we started measuring them, during which time the Index has grown by more than an order of magnitude. Thus, while there is probably systematic bias in these numbers, it does not seem a function of the sample size.

The following are personal intuitions, which should be taken as speculation rather than *ex cathedra* wisdom, about the sample:

- "Home pages" are over-represented (we acknowledge that there is no formal definition of this term)

- HTML pages are over-represented

- Asian language pages are under-represented

- "Good" pages are over-represented

- Long-lived pages are over-represented

How Big is the Web?

Bear in mind, once again, that these numbers are the result of a snapshot taken in November 1995; recent estimates are in excess of 50 million.

Number of unique URLs: 11,366,121

Number of unique servers: 223,851

This includes only URLs that begin with *http*, *ftp*, or *gopher*. To find duplicates, we apply the following heuristics:

- Strip redundant port numbers (80 for *http*, 70 for *gopher*)

- Convert hostnames to IP addresses

- Strip trailing slashes (this is sometimes [very rarely] wrong)

- Remove Unix filesystem no-ops; for example both `/a/./b/./c` and `/a/d/../b/e/../c` are converted to `/a/b/c`

The servers are counted simply by syntactic processing of URLs; there is no guarantee (or expectation) that all of them are actually valid.

What is a "Site"?

Should the two terms *Web site* and *Web server* mean the same thing? Clearly, *www.berkeley.edu* and *web.mit.edu* are two different sites. But are Berkeley's Academic Achievement Division on server *www.aad.berkeley.edu* and Academic Preparation and Articulation on *ub4.apa.berkeley.edu* different? At Open Text, the search engine and the main corporate site have different webmasters, run on different computers, and exist to serve quite different purposes.

Formalizing the notion of a "site" causes some information loss but allows us to develop some useful statistics. The current formalization (implemented in perl) may be summarized as:

- *<anything>* (*.edu* or *.com* or *.gov* or *.net*)

- *<anything>* (*.co* or *.com*).*<country-digraph>*

- *<anything>* (*.ac* or *.edu*).*<country-digraph>*

- *<anything>* (*.army.mil*, *.af.mil*, or *.navy.mil*)

- *<anything-else>.mil*

- *<anything>.<country-digraph>*

- and a bunch of ad-hoc rules to help with the *.k12*, *<state-digraph>.us*, and *<province-digraph>.ca* sites

Thus, *ucla.edu*, *ox.ac.uk*, *sun.com*, *cern.ch*, and *arl.army.mil* are all "sites."

These rules clearly underestimate the number of independently operated "sites"; for example, they make no distinction, at the "site" named UIUC, between the University of Illinois Press and NCSA. However, they also usefully conflate many superficially different aliases and capture something close enough to the human conception of a "site" to be useful, so we shall use them as the basis for quite a number of statistics.

Number of unique "sites": 89,271

What is the "Average Page" Like?

The size of the average page has consistently been between 6K and 7K bytes during the entire lifetime of the Index. The size has fallen slightly as the sample size has grown, from just under 7000 to about 6500 at the time of writing. This amounts to about 1050 "words," depending, of course, on how one defines a word—we use an indexable token beginning with an alphabetic character. Figure 2 illustrates the clustering in this

Table 1 Page size statistics

Mean	6518
Median	2021
Standard Deviation	31678

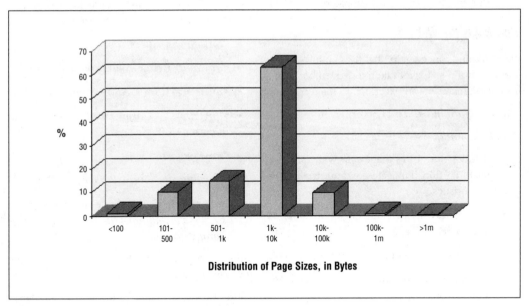

Figure 2   Distribution of page sizes, in bytes

distribution and the presence of a significant number of very large pages.

The page sizes are highly variable, as illustrated in Table 1, which covers one snapshot of 1.524 million pages.

The Web is quite graphically rich. Figure 3 shows that just over 50% of all pages contain at least one image reference. It is interesting to note that about 15% of pages contain exactly one image. Quite likely, for many of the pages that contain large numbers of images, those images are in fact typographical marks *reddot.gif* variety.

How Richly Connected is It?

Outbound Connections

As Figure 4 shows, a large majority (just under 75%) of all pages contain at least one URL. Note that this includes local (#-prefixed) URLs; still, it is fair to conclude that pure "leaf" pages are in the minority. It is fairly uncommon (less than 10%) for a page to contain exactly one URL.

Inbound Connections and Off-Site Links. A one point in the history of the Open Text Index, we built a search function that would, for any URL, retrieve all pages that contained references to that URL. This was easy to implement simply by doing a full-text search for the page's URL, but the results were disappointing. The vast majority of pages proved to have no incoming links at all. We realized quickly that the problem is that most WWW links are relative rather than absolute. What we had discovered, in fact, is that most pages are pointed to only by other pages at the same site.

When we think of Web connectivity, we are more interested in inter-*site* linkages. Our analysis, summarized in Figure 5, reveals some surprising facts.

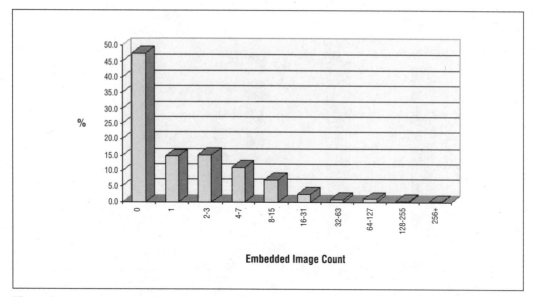

Figure 3   Distribution of embedded image counts

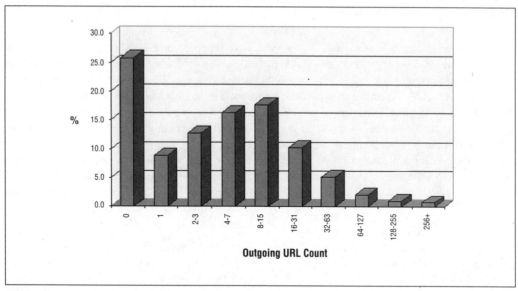

Figure 4   Distribution of embedded URL counts

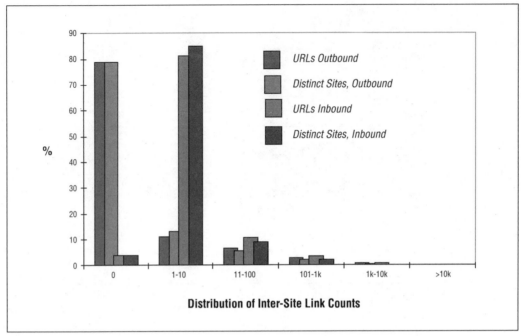

Figure 5   Inter-site link count distribution

First, a large majority of sites (over 80%) are pointed to by "a few" (between one and ten) other sites. Some sites are extremely "visible," with tens of thousands of other sites pointing to them. But a few (just less than 5%), oddly enough, have *no* other sites pointing to them. Presumably, these are sites that have been placed in the Index via the submission process but are not, in one important sense, truly "connected" to the Web

Second, Web sites in general do a poor job of providing linkage to other Web sites. Almost 80% of sites contain *no* off-site URLs. Clearly, a small proportion of Web sites are carrying most of the load of hypertext navigation.

What are the Biggest and Most Visible Sites?

The observation that there are sites with thousands (even tens of thousands) of incoming URLs is interesting. These sites, highlighted in Figure 6, must be deemed unusually "visible." They are, in some sense, at the center of the Web. Perhaps not surprisingly, UIUC leads the list, illustrated in Figure 6, of such sites. The ordering is somewhat different depending on whether it is done by number of incoming off-site URLs, or the number of sites they come from. For example, the European Molecular Biology Laboratory in Heidelberg and the Geneva University Hospital both make the top-URL list by virtue of thousands of off-site pointers from sites such as Argonne National Labs.

With these exceptions, the top sites are a list of well-known universities, organizations (CERN and the World Wide Web Consortium), and a few companies. The only commercial sites that make the top 10 list ranked by number of other sites are Yahoo!, number 3, and Netscape, number 5.

Reversing this statistic, we next rank Web sites by the number of *outgoing* URLs, and number of

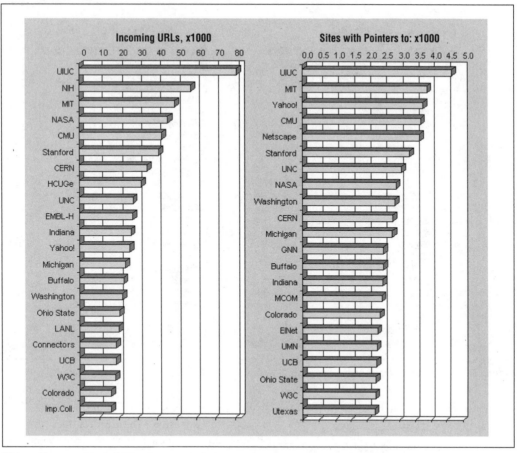

Figure 6   Most visible sites

other sites they point to. At the top of the list are the relatively few sites who, as noted above, carry most of the Web's navigational workload. This statistic, illustrated in Figure 7, is somewhat flawed. A small number of sites, not listed here, contain more off-site pointers than all of these combined. These would be the Web indexers such as Open Text, Lycos, and Infoseek. Not surprisingly, the list, whether ranked by URL count or number of sites pointed to, has Yahoo! in position 1. There are a few other surprises here; but in general, we think that all the sites on this list deserve respect; they provide the silken strands that hold the Web together.

What Formats are Being Used?

HTML is said to be the language of the Web. However, its most important underlying protocol, HTTP, can be used to transport anything. Unfortunately, the Open Text Index does not capture the MIME Content-Type that is associated with each page by its server. Thus, we can only use heuristics to approximate the measurements of data formats. The Open Text Index explicitly excludes data formats that are largely non-textual (graphics, PostScript, WP documents). Over the universe of textual pages on the Web, we think the following are fair:

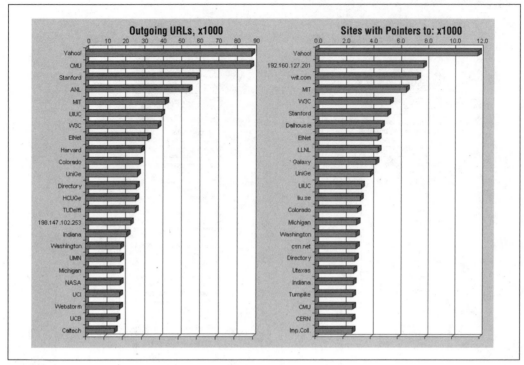

Figure 7   Most luminous sites

- If it doesn't contain <TITLE>, it's not even trying to be HTML.

- If it *does* contain <TITLE>, it is making at least some effort to be HTML.

- If it contains <!DOCTYPE HTML>, it's really trying hard to be HTML.

Based on this heuristic, the analysis, summarized in Figure 8, shows that a large majority of pages (over 87%) are making some effort to present themselves as HTML. A pleasing 5% have gone so far as to include an SGML declaration—of course this is no guarantee that they are actually validated against any particular DTD. About one-eighth of all pages are either raw text or are making no effort whatsoever to be HTML

There is one other source of information about data types: the file extension. Over 80% of all Web pages are likely HTML because they carry

no file extension or are explicitly identified as such by extension. The 18% of files that are explicitly identified by extension as something other than HTML is, amusingly, larger than the proportion of pages that contain no <TITLE> tag.

Figures 9 and 10 show which other file extensions most often appear in URLs. Not surprisingly, GIF graphics and text files are the most popular, each at about 2.5%. PostScript, JPEG, and HQX files all hover just over 1%. All other formats are below 1%.

What Does It Look Like?

The Web, when you're in it, feels like a place. It manifests, however, as a sequence of panels marching across your screen. This leads to an absence of perspective, of context, and finally, of comfort. Most of us who have worked with the Web, in particular, those who have read Gibson

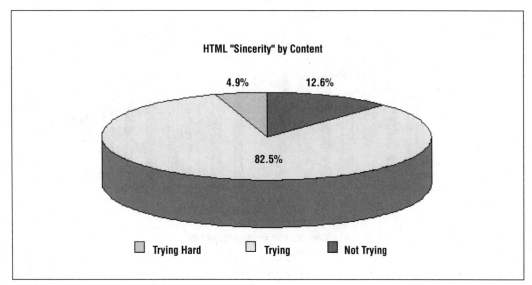

Figure 8 HTML sincerity

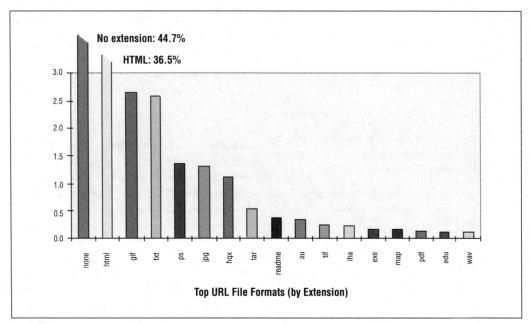

Figure 9 Popular file formats, by extension

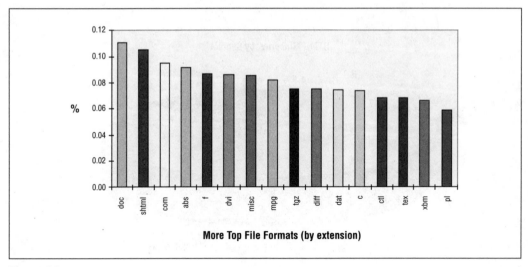

Figure 10   More popular file formats, by extension

or Stephenson, want to see where we are. "Visualizing the Web" is a perennial on the program of these conferences.

The database behind the Open Text Index, and behind the statistics in this paper, can be used to drive Web visualization. Some of the principles we adopt are:

- The "site" is the appropriate unit of display.

- The appearance of a site should reflect its *visibility*, as measured by the number of other sites that have pointers to it.

- The appearance of a site should reflect its *size*, as measured by the number of pages it contains.

- The appearance of a site should reflect its *luminosity*, as measured by the number of pointers with which it casts navigational light off-site.

- The appearance of a site should reflect the information encoded in its Internet domain address.

- The appearance of a site should reflect any information about its subject category coverage that may be deduced heuristically from its textual content and from connectivity to other well-categorized sites.

- Sites should be distributed in space in a fashion that reflects the strength of their connectivity.

Let us examine some database-driven visualizations. The graphics are captured from VRML representations generated dynamically from the Open Text Index database, viewed with Paper Software's WebFX plug-in (now appearing as Netscape's Live3D). We represent sites as ziggurats crowned with globes: the diameter expresses the number of pages, the height the visibility, the size of a globe floating overhead the luminosity, and the color the site's domain. We distribute sites in space based on the strength of the linkages between them.

Figure 11 tells us that UIUC (including NCSA, of course) is the Web's most visible site. Neither

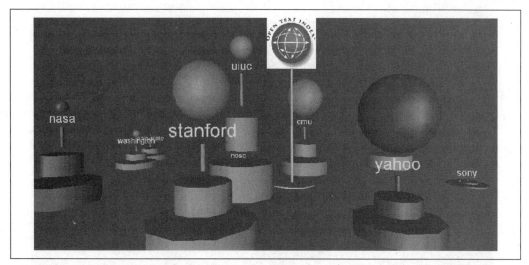

Figure 11   Some well-known sites

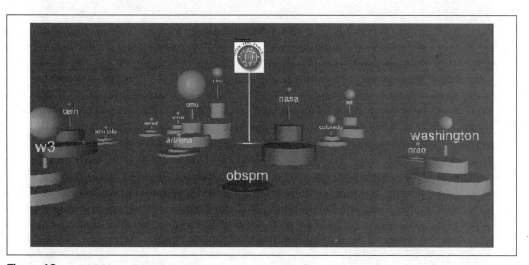

Figure 12   NASA's neighborhood

Stanford nor CMU is quite as visible, but both cast more light on the Web. Yahoo! is most luminous of all.

The sites most closely linked to NASA, shown in Figure 12, are a mixed bag; government sites are red, academic sites green, and nonprofit organizations golden. CMU's navigational strength is obvious once again, as is that of the Web Consor-

tium site. NASA itself provides relatively little navigational help.

Figure 13 shows the four most visible sites on the Web. The tiny red dot above the "i" in "nih" reveals that very visible site's poverty in outgoing links. UIUC's visibility and CMU's luminosity are obvious.

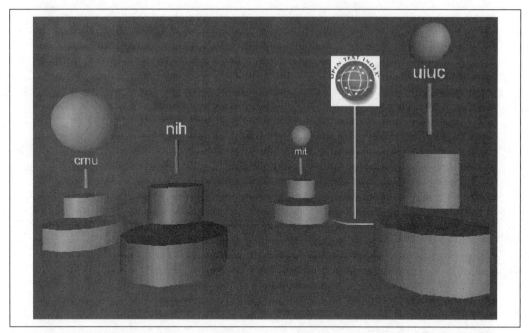

Figure 13   At the very center

Figure 14   A wider view

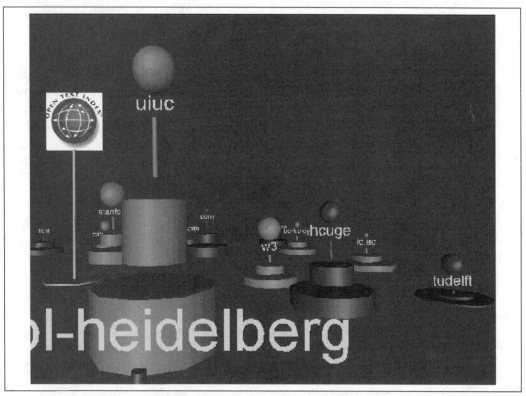

Figure 15   The Web is world-wide, after all

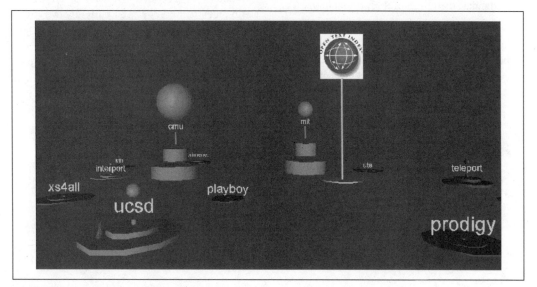

Figure 16   Friends of *Playboy*

The scene in Figure 14 starts to give a feeling for the Web's chaos. Commercial sites are rendered in blue and network infrastructure in cyan. The navigational strength of Yahoo! and Einet is obvious.

Figure 15's view, spiraling out from UIUC, has a European slant. Particularly interesting is the fact that the highly illuminated European Molecular Biology Laboratory in Heidelberg casts almost no light; the tiny dot representing its Web-luminosity may be visible in some viewers above and to the left of the "i" in "heidelberg."

The sites that are most closely linked to the Playboy site, illustrated in Figure 16, provide an interesting study in contrast. CMU, MIT, and UCSD seem to have about the same number of pages. However, CMU leads MIT and then UCSD in both visibility and luminosity.

Conclusion

At the moment, we don't know very much about the Web. The statistical lore in this paper may be generated straightforwardly (at the cost of considerable computation) from a properly structured Web index. We would like to devise a way to automate the generation of these statistics and, in particular, their graphical representations.

Techniques for presenting this information automatically, dynamically, compactly, and three-dimensionally are a significant subgoal of the larger campaign to build a working cyberspace.

That in itself is sufficient motivation for further work on the problem. ∎

Acknowledgments

None of this would have been possible without the data gathered via the superhuman efforts of the Web Index team.

Thanks are also due to Tamara Munzner for provoking thought and to Lilly Buchwitz for polishing language. Thanks also to James Hess and the Heritage Map Museum for the use of the "Typis Orbis Terrarum" map.

About the Author

Tim Bray
Senior Vice President of Technology
Open Text Corporation
1965 West Fourth Avenue
Vancouver, B.C.
tbray@opentext.com

A Canadian, who was raised mostly in Lebanon, Tim graduated from the University of Guelph in 1981. After on-the-job training from Digital and GTE, he became manager of the *New Oxford English Dictionary* Project in 1986. Tim co-founded Open Text in 1989, using as a basis the New OED technology. He currently serves as Senior Vice President of Technology for Open Text. Tim invented and implemented the Open Text Index, starting in January 1995. He has published on the subjects of computer science, high-end audio, and philology.

THE U.K. NATIONAL WEB CACHE
A STATE OF THE ART REPORT

Neil G. Smith

Abstract

Two years after its introduction at the First International World Wide Web Conference at CERN, Geneva, the use of caching technology to improve the efficiency of network utilization has become a hot topic. With relatively poor international connectivity, it was through necessity that U.K. academia was one of the first communities to make widespread use of this technology on a large scale. The implementation of a national strategy proposed by HENSA Unix in June 1995 has led an experimental project to become what is probably the most mature caching facility in the world today. In this paper we present a brief history of the project, a discussion of the evolution of the hardware, software, and networking systems involved, and take a look to the future of the project within the framework of the U.K.'s networking strategy. It is hoped that some of our experiences may be of use to other large bodies of users who are tired of waiting for their Web pages to arrive. **Keywords**: *World Wide Web, proxy, caches*

Introduction

The World Wide Web has long suffered as a result of its own popularity. The combination of the ease with which large video and audio data types can be incorporated into documents, and the model of a single publisher serving countless clients places great demands on bandwidth. While this may not present a problem on a local area network, or even within a national context, as soon as information passes across international networks the lack of bandwidth and the resulting congestion is immediately apparent. (This problem is very obvious in the U.K. Nationally we have good connectivity with a 150Mbps backbone, but our international links are relatively slow: 4Mbps to the United States, 4Mbps to Europe, and 2Mbps to Scandinavia.) The problem was already recognized by the time of the First International World Wide Web Conference [1] in May 1994 and has received a steady stream of attention since then. The consensus of opinion suggests that distributing the publication responsibility through the deployment of Web proxy caches gives us the quickest route to a medium term solution. In the future, more sophisticated schemes may allow for more flexible publication mechanisms that avoid some of the problems

that proxies introduce. However, for the moment they are all that we have and their role is now central in many users' access to the Web. This means that all new protocol developments must take account of these intermediate servers and work with them. This makes protocol development more complicated, but the impact that proxy caches can have is so great that we cannot afford to ignore them.

System Evolution

The evolution of the systems in use at HENSA Unix has been forced by the great demand on the service. Until recently this demand always out-stripped the resources available. At points in the services history the demand has been so great that queues on the servers resulted in using the cache actually being slower than going direct. Figure 1 shows how the service has grown (December's dip is, of course, the seasonal norm).

Lagoon-CERN-Netscape

In November 1993, after initial experiments confirmed that the wholesale mirroring of Web pages was not an effective way to reduce the

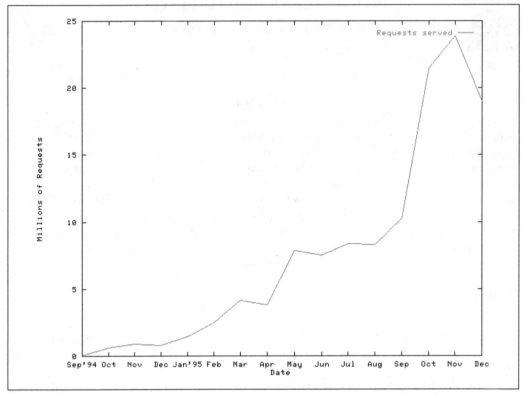

Figure 1   Service growth

latency seen on the networks, HENSA Unix adopted Lagoon [2] as an experimental proxy cache. At the time, the necessary protocol extensions to support proxying were not in place and early versions of Lagoon had to make use of a CGI script that rewrote HTML on the fly in order to direct clients back to the cache for each subsequent page that they retrieved. Despite some innovative features (cache cooperation was already being discussed), this HTML rewriting and other performance-related problems meant that the client base being supported by HENSA Unix was becoming too large for Lagoon.

At about the time of the First International Conference, a proxy mechanism was introduced into the CERN HTTP server [3]. New versions of Mosaic made the use of this facility transparent to the user, and proxying started to become a viable proposition. HENSA Unix continued to use the CERN server for almost a year, but with the increasing popularity of the cache, the forking process model used by the CERN server started to place a higher and higher load on our hardware. At this point the caching service was still experimental and not receiving its own funding.

It was because the CERN server forked for each connection it received that the service eventually started to fail. The incoming connections could not be accepted fast enough, and users were being turned away. Hacks to increase the priority of the parent process while decreasing that of the child processes only helped for a very short time.

At the beginning of 1995 Netscape started beta testing their own proxy server, and HENSA Unix was asked to act as a test site. The Netscape server [4] relies on a non-forking process model and thereby places a significantly lower strain on the hardware. The Netscape proxy server is still used to provide the main caching service; a service currently responding to over 1,100,000 requests every day.

Alternative Servers

While the evolution from Lagoon to the CERN server and finally to the Netscape proxy server represents a considerable improvement in stability, configurability, and performance, the fundamental principles involved have not changed a great deal. Each of these servers still merely acts as a simple proxy with a cache of pages to improve performance. Other projects have developed proxy servers that attempt to go further. The most notable of these being the Harvest Object Cache [5].

Harvest allows a single cache to interact with neighbor and parent caches in a cooperating hierarchy. These neighbors will normally be on networks that the cache has good access to. This model improves performance in the case of a cache miss by allowing other close-by caches to say whether they have the requested page. If another local cache has the page, then it will be retrieved from that cache rather than the remote site. This means that any cache that is part of a large cooperative hierarchy benefits from the pages stored in all the other caches in that hierarchy.

While Harvest's approach goes one better than other simpler proxies, it unfortunately relies on a single process model. This process uses non-blocking I/O, and this results in relatively good performance. However, the question remains as to whether this model can ever be fast enough to serve the size of community currently using HENSA Unix. This community currently averages 28 connections a second at peak times in the afternoons, with peaks in activity of more than 100 connections per second.

Hardware Demands

For the first eighteen months of service, the HENSA Unix cache was placed on the same single processor Sparc 10 serving the HENSA Unix FTP archive. As the popularity of both services increased, an upgrade was required, and a Silicon Graphics Challenge S was deployed. It was anticipated that the cache would remain on the Sparc 10 while the FTP archive moved to the Silicon Graphics machine. Unfortunately the demand on the service increased to fill all the spare capacity on the Sparc, and with the Challenge S being the fastest machine available, both the FTP and the Web caching service were moved to this machine.

The very high connection rate being experienced on this server and on other conventional HTTP servers at other sites, stressed operating systems in ways in which they had never been stressed before. Now it was not the hardware that was insufficient, but bugs in TCP code implementations that made the service unstable. With the obvious demand for fixes from all quarters of the community, the vendors were quick to patch up the problems, and demand could continue to grow. At this point another problem struck the HENSA Unix service. The Silicon Graphics machine had always been intended to support the FTP archive, and as a result, it was ordered with a small number of very large disks (three 9GB disks). Even with the cached files spread across three disks, the I/O bottleneck was great enough to mean that in some cases going via the cache was actually slower than going to a site directly. The impact this had on the FTP archive (the service for which we received our funding) was that FTP users were unable to connect to the machine at all. At this point, the cache was serving about 300,000 requests each day.

The solution to the problem came when an emergency equipment purchase expanded the service with a dual processor Silicon Graphics Challenge DM. This machine was ordered with six 2GB disks to ensure that bandwidth within the machine would not be a constraint on the service. The service was migrated to this machine in June 1995. The start of the U.K. academic year in October 1995 saw this machine responding to over 900,000 requests each day. Once again, the demand had expanded to fill the available capacity.

A proposal by HENSA Unix to take the experience gained through operating this experimental service and deploy a scalable and reliable national service was accepted in July 1995 and, for the first time ever, enabled us to invest in equipment that would be capable of keeping up with the demand. In order to provide resilience in the case of hardware failure, a number of machines would be used. Based on previous experience, each of these machines would have the optimum balance of processor power, disk bandwidth, and system memory.

Hardware Resource Balancing

A busy Web cache tests all the sub-systems in a machine. Surprisingly, network bandwidth is not always the most important concern or the first bottleneck hit. This reflects the disparity between transfer rates on local and on international networks. Instead, a lack of disk bandwidth, processor speed, or real memory can bring a cache server to a grinding halt.

In the case of the Netscape Proxy server, it is the combination of the speed of the processor and the amount of real memory that determines how many concurrent users you may support. Each of our 175MHz R4400–based servers, with 128MB of memory, can support approximately 650 concurrent connections.

Disk bandwidth is a more serious concern than disk space once a minimum level has been passed. Simulations based on real cache activity show the hit-rates being achieved by larger and larger caches stabilizing at approximately 55%. The growth in hit-rate is quite rapid, and with very large disk drives now available at a fraction of their cost even two years ago, there is no rea-son why all caches could not achieve this hit-rate. While the size of the disk determines the hit-rate, bandwidth to the disks is most likely to be the first bottleneck after the international networks. Making use of a large number of disks, and distributing the cache data across these disks is a facility now offered by both Harvest and the Netscape

It remains to be seen whether the continual growth of both server and client populations on the Web makes a significant difference to the hit-rates attained by, and the disk space demanded by, caching proxies. It is true to say that with more servers there will be more potentially cachable data, but on the other hand, with more clients there are a greater number of hits on the popular pages. This may lead to caches that are as effective without any increase in disk capacity.

Networking and Machine Load Balancing

Throughout the first two years of service, the network structure surrounding the HENSA Unix cache did not change. It was only with the acceptance of the proposal for a national strategy that changes were made to the operation of the cache on the network.

Having multiple machines provides resilience in the case of hardware failure. If these machines are distributed across several sites, then resilience against network failure is also gained. Currently the HENSA Unix cache is implemented with machines at two sites, the University of Kent and the University of Leeds. This distribution also ensures that the bandwidth into or, more importantly, as the caches are bandwidth magnifiers, out of any particular site does not become the bottleneck in the whole scheme.

In order to evenly distribute the load across the machines supporting the cache, we anticipated having to modify a DNS name server to return the name of the most lightly loaded machine. In fact, this proved unnecessary as more recent versions of BIND provide a round-robin facility that rotates the list of addresses corresponding to a single name. With a five minute time-to-live on the name, this is sufficient to ensure that, over a 24 hour period, the load across all six machines is even. It also gives us the ability to quickly reconfigure the group of machines supporting the service in the event of a hardware failure.

Further distribution of the caching facility is envisaged in the U.K.'s overall strategy. This distribution consists of local caches operated by an institution or even a department within an institution. We are encouraging these local caches to then make use of the national cache to minimize redundant transfers across the international network links. Simulations based on the log files collected at HENSA Unix show us that an institution, even with only a relatively small cache, 500MB of disk, can reduce the load placed on the national facility by as much as 40%. Institutions without the specialist knowledge to operate a WWW proxy cache are being encouraged to approach their closest metropolitan area network to make use of a cache at this point.

Through the study of server log files from sites outside the U.K., a number of institutions were found who were not making use of the national caching facility. When questioned, the most common response was that they intended to install a local cache and did not want to have to go through the user education procedure twice; first they would be telling their users to make use of the national cache at HENSA and, shortly afterward, redirecting them to the local cache.

We are sympathetic to their problem as educating a population that is increasingly unaware that it is even using a cache is exceedingly difficult. In order to provide a solution and encourage the early use of the caches available the "virtual local cache" was created. This technique allows an institution to give its users the impression that they already have a local cache. The education program can start without investment in hardware, software, or time. The technique makes use of the DNS to direct clients to the national cache through the use of a canonical name (an alias for another machine). Once a local cache

has been installed, this canonical name can be changed to point at the new machine without the users seeing a break in service.

The Users

As the service offered by the HENSA Unix cache has evolved, so has the user community that it serves. In 1993 and 1994 virtually all of the users were conscious of the fact that they were using a cache, and all of them understood the function that it served. With the wider use of institutional caches installed by computing service departments, a larger population is now making unconscious use of caching technology.

These users are obviously aware of the congestion on the international network links; they experience it every day. Unfortunately, they are not aware of the techniques that can be used to maximize throughput on a congested link, and they are not prepared to accept these techniques when they are forced upon them.

The Netscape proxy server's process model allows a cache administrator to exactly specify the number of simultaneous connections that the proxy can hold open at one time. At HENSA Unix, this fact was used to restrict the number of connections to between 400 and 600 in a vain hope that this restriction would reduce network congestion and result in better throughput. In order to ensure that all the processes in the process pool were not in use at the same time, which would result in users being turned away, the timeout placed on each connection was kept deliberately short, 90 seconds.

Unfortunately, this scheme did not prove popular. The cache administrator had not understood the way in which the vast majority of clients use the Web—that is, in batch fashion. The author had assumed that a user who had not received their page within 90 seconds would probably have given up and moved on. In reality it seems that large numbers of users are prepared to wait much longer for their pages. Often this waiting time is spent doing other things, with the client visiting their browser every so often to see how much longer the transfer is estimated to take. In order to accommodate these users the timeout on cache connections was increased to 15 minutes. This is not 15 minutes for the complete transfer, but rather 15 minutes between individual packets. It is probably safe to assume that if packets are more than 15 minutes apart the network is not worth using.

This significantly increased timeout means that a much larger proportion of the Netscape proxy server processes are in use simply waiting for packets. These processes are no longer available to other users. In order to ensure that users are not turned away, a much larger number of processes must be made available. Currently each of the servers in use at HENSA Unix runs 650 processes, meaning that the whole cache can support nearly 4,000 simultaneous connections.

This very large number of connections almost certainly results in far greater congestion on the international links. However, at least the users never have to wait for a process to become available, and they never see a time out as a result of the cache. Perversely, throughput is down, but the customers are happy.

Future Developments

In terms of efficiency, and as a method of saving bandwidth, caching has a lot of potential still to be developed. Stable, and well understood cache cooperation is one goal, client resilience in the event of cache or network failure another. These issues are currently under development, while others, such as "missed hit" reporting (reporting hits that a server would have seen if the cache had not been there) and user identification on the far side of a cache, or chain of caches, receive less coverage. For a cache to be totally acceptable, its use has to be completely transparent to both clients and servers. There is still some way to go, but some of the most recent developments representing the state of the art are discussed here.

Proxy Auto-configuration

The problems of user education and resilience are addressed by version 2 of the Netscape Navigator, currently available in a beta test version. This client has the ability to run arbitrary pieces of Javascript to determine which proxy or proxies it should use. This script can be downloaded from anywhere on the Web, thereby giving cache maintainers or site administrators a single point at which they can define the configuration of all their users' clients.

In addition to choosing whether or not to use a cache, or which cache to use, this Javascript can return a list of caches that should be tried. In the event of one proxy becoming unavailable, the next in the list is tried. If no proxy responds to the client, then the final option is for a direct connection. In the worst case the client will simply behave as if it were not configured to use a proxy at all.

By encouraging users of the national cache to upgrade to a client that understands this proxy auto-configuration [6], it is hoped that we will be able to make significantly more efficient use of the caches. Currently each of the six cache machines operates independently, and as a result, the caches have a large number of pages in common. Disk space is wasted with duplicated pages and can result in a client having to wait for a remote transfer when another cache may already have the page locally.

By using proxy auto-configuration we hope to dedicate each of the cache machines to a specific list of domains. These domains would be chosen to balance the load across all the machines and would result in the same machine always being used for pages from a specific domain. This should result in higher hit-rates as fewer duplicate pages will give more efficient use of disk space, and every client accessing a particular domain will use the same cache.

Cache Cooperation

As far as cache cooperation is concerned, Harvest is leading the field. Unfortunately this cooperation is limited to networks of Harvest caches as no other server currently understands the inter-cache communication protocol used. In order to make cache cooperation the norm rather than the exception, it is necessary to extend and standardize this protocol.

Currently the protocol talks in terms of cache hits or cache misses. Both the CERN server and the Netscape proxy server have an additional state, which is a cache hit based on the result of a conditional request to the remote server. This means that the CERN or Netscape server may physically have the appropriate file in its cache, but before releasing it, the server would like to ensure that the file is up to date. This up-to-date check consists of a conditional request to the remote server. If the cache's copy is still up to date, then no further transfer is required. If the cached copy has gone out of date, then the remote server sends a fresh copy. In any case, a conditional request will take significantly longer than a pure cache hit. However, in the case where a transfer of the whole file does not occur, the conditional request will very often be significantly faster than a cache miss.

Ultimately, what is required is a server with the cooperative model implemented by Harvest and the speed, ease of configuration, and administrative features of Netscape.

Networks for Caches

The Web caching service at HENSA Unix provides real benefits. However, these benefits are only appreciated in the case of a cache hit. Cache misses, or checks to ensure that documents are up to date, have to make use of the same shared and highly congested bandwidth as all other international traffic. While this shared bandwidth is soon to be augmented, past experience has shown that demand will quickly rise to fill that capacity, and we will quickly return to the same congested situation. With the cache's relatively low demand for and extremely efficient use of bandwidth, it would make sense to provide dedicated international network links for use by caches alone. In this case, cache hits are as fast as they always were, but cache misses are accelerated to a point where they are significantly better than if the shared bandwidth were used. It is with this property that the cache starts to become a very much more attractive service. As the U.K.'s shared international links are upgraded, it is hoped that the old, now redundant, links will become dedicated to the caching service. With hit-rates at their current levels, a dedicated 4Mbps link could mean the cache delivering as much as a conventional, shared 10Mbps link.

In order to demonstrate the effectiveness of the cache in a situation where there is spare bandwidth, HENSA Unix asked for help from Lulea University in Sweden. The U.K. has a 2Mbps connection to Scandinavia, which typically runs at 50% capacity. Scandinavia has a 34Mbps link to the U.S., which is running at well below full capacity. By directing the HENSA Unix cache to make use of another proxy at Lulea University, we were able to test its performance with, what was virtually, a dedicated 1Mbps line. In order not to place too great a load on the Lulea server, and in order to be able to compare the two routes, direct and via Sweden, only two out of the five machines operating the cache at HENSA Unix were configured to go via Sweden. In addition, it was only the .gov domain that would be fetched by that route. This resulted in about 17,000 requests to the Swedish proxy over a two-day period. The results are clear from Figure 2, which shows the percentage of all requests that have been successfully serviced within a specific number of seconds.

New HTTP Protocols

Dedicated bandwidth will offer the U.K. National Cache a lot more than just faster access to pages in the U.S. Extensions to, or developments of, the HTTP protocol, such as Keep-Alive [7] and HTTP-

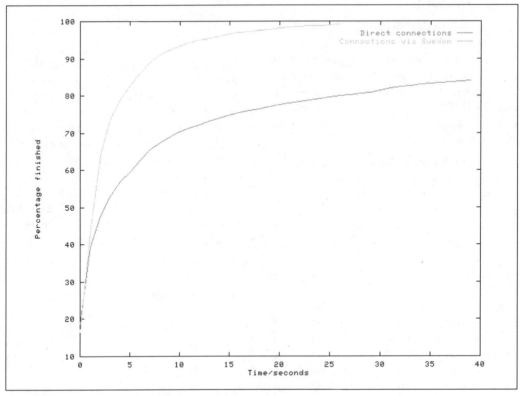

Figure 2   Successfully serviced requests

NG [7], will make use of connections persistent across many URL requests.

On a congested line, these protocols are liable to result in poorer performance as the TCP protocol slows down the transfer rates as the connection ages in order to attempt to reduce the congestion. This effect can be clearly seen when retrieving large files across congested network. The transfer rate starts relatively high but gradually degrades as the connection ages.

On a non-congested link, the cache will be able to take full advantage of these protocols. This advantage can be gained whether or not the user's browser makes use of the new protocols, as the cache will be able to translate from plain HTTP to the new protocols and back again.

It is possible to imagine a situation where a particularly busy cache holds open a connection to a popular server permanently. This would completely eliminate the costs associated with making a new connection for every URL requested.

Conclusion

"Necessity is the mother of invention." In the summer of 1993, it was clear that the bandwidth demands placed on the Internet by the World Wide Web made the dream of global hypermedia communication very difficult to achieve. The problems faced by the U.K. (good national bandwidth allowing individuals easy access to very limited international bandwidth) will sooner or later be faced by all other countries as they embrace the revolution. We hope that the description of the problems that we have faced and overcome will help these other communities deploy bandwidth-saving measures that are also "state of the art." ∎

References

1. The First International World Wide Web Conference, *http://www.elsevier.nl/cgi-bin/ID/WWW94*;
   Luotonen, Art, and Kevin Altis, "World Wide Web Proxies," CERN, CH;
   Glassman, Steve, "A Caching Relay for the World Wide Web," SRC, DEC, US;
   Smith, Neil, "What can Archives offer the World Wide Web," Unix Hensa, University of Kent at Canterbury, U.K.

2. Lagoon, *http://www.win.tue.nl/lagoon/*

3. CERN Server, *http://www.w3.org/pub/WWW/Daemon/*

4. Netscape Proxy Server, *http://home.netscape.com/comprod/proxy_server.html*

5. Harvest Object Cache, *http://excalibur.usc.edu/*

6. Netscape's Proxy Auto-Config, *http://home.netscape.com/eng/mozilla/2.0/relnotes/demo/proxy-live.html*

7. Keep-Alive and HTTP-NG, *http://www.w3.org/hypertext/WWW/Protocols/*

About the Author

Neil G. Smith
HENSA Unix
The University of Kent at Canterbury
ngs@unix.hensa.ac.uk

Since graduating from the University of Kent in 1992, Neil Smith has worked as the technical manager of the HENSA Unix Archive. Provoked by a disappointment with the performance of the World Wide Web, his early work on proxy caching has, two years later, led to the creation of a U.K. national caching facility under his direction. Most of his work now involves improving and promoting this service and striving to improve the performance of the Web wherever possible.

THE HARVEST OBJECT CACHE IN NEW ZEALAND

Donald Neal

Abstract

No New Zealand government funding has ever been directed towards Internet development. The Internet in New Zealand has always been funded at least in part by charges to users. This, combined with the high cost of bandwidth to and from New Zealand, has triggered more rapid and widespread adoption of World Wide Web caching than has been seen in most countries.

This paper gives a brief history of the development of the Internet in New Zealand. It describes the use of WWW caching in New Zealand between 1993 and January 1996, concentrating particularly on the deployment of the Harvest Cache software. This software entered production use in October 1995, and less than four months later, a single server using it processes the equivalent of around 5% of all Internet traffic between New Zealand and the rest of the world.

The deployment of Harvest Cache software in a number of other countries is briefly described. The results of a survey of New Zealand WWW cache users are presented, indicating that priorities are different for identifiable types of user organization.

Issues raised by the commercialization of international bandwidth provision are discussed, and expected development of the Harvest software is outlined. ***Keywords:*** *Harvest, New Zealand, World Wide Web, WWW, caching*

Introduction

"The uncomfortable reality that a free good can invite essentially unlimited demand has slowly dawned on system administrators around the world" [2].

New Zealand is a technologically developed country with a population of less than four million located in the southwest Pacific. Its considerable distance from even its nearest neighbors has influenced the way in which the Internet has developed in New Zealand, as has the highly deregulated telecommunications environment that has existed here in recent years.

The high cost of bandwidth between New Zealand and the major Internet exchanges of the United States west coast has lead New Zealand universities to use WWW caching more heavily than has been the case in most countries, and this lead has been followed by other New

Zealand organizations. Distributed caching using the Harvest Cache software seems now to be increasing the cost savings and performance improvement delivered in the past by stand-alone use of the CERN WWW server software.

This paper is divided into four parts. The first provides background information, giving a very brief history of the Internet and the use of the CERN software in New Zealand, then describing the workings of the Harvest Cache software as they relate to communication between caches. The second part describes the use of the Harvest software in New Zealand to date and describes the growth of an international network of communicating Harvest Cache servers. The third presents the results of a survey of New Zealand WWW cache users, indicating among other conclusions that universities are substantially more cost-conscious than are commercial Internet Service Providers (ISPs) who use WWW caching. The fourth part considers the effect on distributed caching of the competitive provision of international bandwidth and vice versa and describes expected development of the Harvest software.

Background

A Very Short History of the Internet in New Zealand

New Zealand's first link to the Internet entered service in April 1989. This was a 9600bps leased circuit between the University of Waikato in Hamilton and the University of Hawaii, running on an undersea analog cable. The New Zealand end half circuit was paid for by six New Zealand universities, with the U.S. end half circuit paid for by NASA as part of the Pacific Communications program (PACCOM).

The Kawaihiko network began operation in April 1990, using 9600bps leased lines to provide TCP/IP communication among all of the country's seven universities. By 1992, most of these lines had been upgraded to 48kbps.

In early 1992 New Zealand had three research and education networks. DSIRnet was a leased-line network linking sites in the Department of Scientific and Industrial Research (DSIR). MAFnet was a private X.25 network linking Ministry of Agriculture and Fisheries sites. These were interlinked with the universities' Kawaihiko, providing a single TCP/IP network known as Tuia.

In 1992 the government restructured the DSIR and MAF, creating eleven partly independent Crown Research Institutes (CRIs). In that year a new Tuia network was built, linking all of the country's universities, the CRIs, the National Library, and the Ministry of Research, Science, and Technology. This new network was built around a frame relay backbone, with digital leased-line links to smaller sites. The increased capacity provided by these changes was reflected in increased traffic through New Zealand's Internet link to the outside world, by this time pro-

vided by a 128kbps satellite circuit to NASA Ames research center in California.

By the end of 1995, the highest-capacity connection within the Tuia network was the 512kbps link between the University of Waikato and Victoria University of Wellington. Most links, however, were at 64kbps or 128 kbps.

Work began in 1994 on links between New Zealand and major commercial backbone providers, with NSFnet routing ending on 25 April 1995. While a small amount of commercial traffic was carried on New Zealand's international links early in 1995, the volumes involved only became significant from May of that year. By the end of 1995 research and educational institutions accounted for only half of New Zealand's international Internet traffic. Commercial international traffic was divided roughly equally between the Tuia network and the other links to the Hamilton gateway.

A major reason for the volume of commercial traffic on the Tuia network is that most universities have in the past acted as commercial ISPs. (The University of Waikato has never had such a role—as gateway and exchange operator it has sought to avoid competing with its customers.) Another reason is geography. New Zealand is a long, thin country, with universities located so that links between them form a logical national backbone. While some ISPs operate long-distance links between particular cities, there is no apparent advantage to the construction of a separate commercial backbone to mirror the Tuia network.

A few ISPs operate their own international links, but in early 1996 the overwhelming majority of traffic to and from New Zealand continues to flow through the Hamilton gateway, now the New Zealand Internet Exchange (NZIX).

Paying for the Internet in New Zealand

When New Zealand's first international Internet link was established in 1989, New Zealand's share of the costs was divided equally among six universities. There has never been any central government subsidy for Internet development or operation.

Bandwidth across the Pacific has always been far more expensive than bandwidth within New Zealand. This means that the relative costs of the international bandwidth consumed by different organizations can be highly disproportionate to the relative capacity of their links to the gateway site. To ensure that each of the participating universities felt it was getting value for money, the universities adopted a system of charging for international bandwidth based on the volume of traffic to and from each university. Volume charging began in late 1990 [1].

In the interests of predictability, charges were made on the basis of bands of traffic use. A site using, say, between 200MB and 300MB of international traffic per month would pay a given monthly fee so long as their traffic remained in that band. If their traffic consumption exceeded 300MB for a single month only, no additional charge would be made. If their traffic consumption exceeded 300MB for a second consecutive month, they would from then on be taken to be operating in that higher use band and would be charged a higher monthly fee accordingly. This system was subsequently revised and elaborated, but it remained the case that each university, and later each of the three distinct research and education networks, paid a share of the cost of international bandwidth closely related to its use of that bandwidth.

With income closely related to costs, available international bandwidth could rapidly be increased, as shown in Figure 1.

NASA ceased to fund the U.S. end half circuit at the end of 1993. By that time revenue to the gateway's operators was sufficient that no change in service needed to be made as a result of the loss of NASA funding. And because each customer of

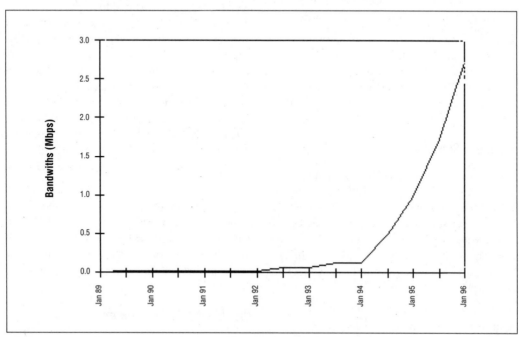

Figure 1   Total capacity of international links operated by the University of Waikato

the international service paid its own way, there was no difficulty later in adding commercial users, who were treated in exactly the same way as educational or research customers (indeed, as was noted earlier, the two groups are not always distinguishable).

A model in which users pay for the traffic they generate might be expected to cause less use to be made of the Internet than would have been the case had services been provided without charge to the end user. The only attempt made in New Zealand to determine the extent of this effect [2] failed to find consistent evidence from total traffic figures that the effect even existed. It is interesting to conjecture to what extent demand might have been constrained by restricted performance resulting from limited availability of funds for capacity increases.

In an environment where more efficient use of available bandwidth will produce a direct financial reward to the user, it is to be expected that significant interest will be shown in means of providing such efficiency. Certainly such interest has been shown in WWW caching software.

It is also important that where customers are used to paying by traffic flow, it is easy to establish a basis for charging for the use of a caching server, and hence for the provision of WWW caching as a self-supporting or even potentially profitable service.

The CERN Server in Practice

WWW caching software was first adopted in New Zealand by Victoria and Waikato universities in 1993. Both used what is still usually called the CERN server software, recently renamed by the World Wide Web Consortium as the W3C server [16]. The CERN software acts as an orthodox WWW page server and can also act as a proxy server with or without caching.

By August 1995 the CERN software was being used in New Zealand to provide WWW caching by at least six universities, a polytechnic, five ISPs, the National Library, a state research organi-

zation, and one private company whose primary business is not Internet-related.

A CERN server may be configured to use another server as its proxy, referring requests not satisfied by hits on its own cache to that other server. Using this feature, a tree of servers may be constructed, offering the potential of greater savings than could be achieved solely by placing unconnected caches at individual sites.

From May 1995, the University of Waikato made available a CERN caching server, separate from the CERN caching servers used directly by staff and students within the university, to act solely as a parent for caching servers operated by the university's international bandwidth customers. This is known as the "NZGate cache," NZGate being the name under which the university operated international Internet links. This service continued to use the CERN software until November 1995, returning moderate savings in bandwidth to the three universities that used it.

A major weakness of the CERN server is that once it has been configured to use another cache as proxy, it will forward requests to that other cache with no attempt to verify whether the other cache is still functioning. Also, the choice of other cache to be used can only be on the basis of the protocol used to retrieve the object— gopher, HTTP, news or FTP. So while a cache can have separate parents for, say, HTTP and FTP requests, it can have only one parent for HTTP requests. This makes the server at the root of any tree a single point of failure for the entire tree.

It became clear during 1995 that no further development was being undertaken on the CERN software. Since the University of Waikato saw WWW caching as a service of strategic importance to its role as an Internet exchange, alternative software was sought.

The Harvest Cache Software

The Harvest Cache software [3] is part of a suite "designed and built by the Internet Research

Task Force Research Group on Resource Discovery"[16]. The bulk of the Harvest software is concerned with the extraction and distribution of WWW index information.

Unlike the CERN server, the Harvest Cache software is intended solely as a caching server. It offers high-performance WWW proxy caching, supporting FTP, gopher, and HTTP objects. The software is freely available in both binary and source forms and is substantially faster than the CERN server software, dramatically so when returning an object as a result of a cache hit. The large difference in speed is due to the fact that while the CERN software forks a new process for each incoming request, a Harvest server forks only for FTP transfers. The Harvest Cache software is implemented with non-blocking I/O, caches DNS lookups, supports non-blocking DNS lookups, and implements negative caching both of objects and DNS lookups.

The Harvest Cache software consists of a main server program, *cached*, a DNS lookup caching server program, *dnsserver*, a program for retrieving data via FTP, *ftpget*, and some management and client tools.

On starting up, *cached* spawns a configurable number of *dnsserver* processes, each of which can perform a single, blocking, DNS lookup. This reduces the time spent by the server in waiting for DNS lookups. (For a more detailed description of aspects of the software's design, implementation and performance, see [4]. For a description of its internals, see [14].)

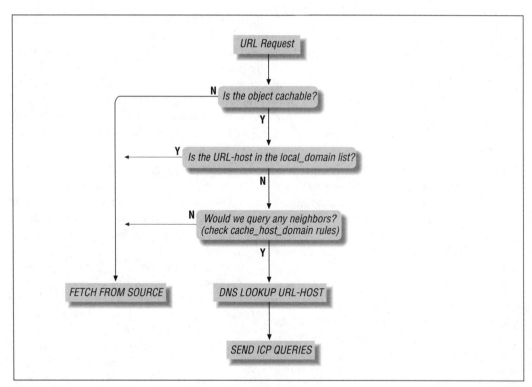

Figure 2   General process for selecting server for retrieval

A Harvest server may be configured with an arbitrary number of parents and neighbors. The selection of a server from which an object is to be retrieved is based in large part on round-trip times. The usual process is shown in Figure 2, omitting the case where the server is behind a firewall.

A server may retrieve an object directly in four cases. First, if the URL requested matches any entry in a stop list in its configuration file. This stop list contains patterns that match objects not to be held in cache. For example, the default configuration file included in the harvest distribution will cause any object whose URL contains the string "cgi-bin" to be treated as uncacheable, and hence not to be requested from any other cache.

Second, if the host identified in the URL is a member of a domain in the configuration file's `local_domain` list.

Third, the configuration file may contain `cache_host_domain` records, specifying the domains for whose URLs a parent or neighbor cache is, or is not, to be queried. If due to these restrictions no parent or neighbor is to be queried for the particular URL in question, the object will be retrieved from the source.

If at least one other cache is to be queried, a DNS lookup is performed on the hostname specified in the URL. This is done to ensure the hostname is valid, and because after querying other caches the object may be retrieved from its original host. After this lookup is completed, the process described in Figure 3 is begun.

An Internet Cache Protocol (ICP) query packet is sent to each neighbor or parent permitted by the `cache_host_domain` restrictions. As many replies are expected as queries sent. If the cache is configured with `source_ping on`, it also bounces a HIT reply off the original host's UDP echo port.

ICP reply packets are received until all have arrived or the `neighbor_timeout` occurs. The object is immediately fetched from the source of the first HIT reply received. Any parent not using the Harvest software will always return a HIT.

If no HIT is received before the timeout occurs, the object is fetched from the first parent from which a MISS reply was received. If no parent reply was received, whether due to network packet loss or `cache_host_domain` restrictions, the object will then be retrieved from the host identified in the URL. The query/reply process minimizes the risk that requests will be sent to unreachable or non-operational caches.

Note that the terms *parent* and *neighbor* can be misleading, as they imply a hierarchical structure to intercache relationships which is not necessarily present. The only difference between a parent and a neighbor is that a cache miss will not be resolved through a neighbor.

One use of neighbor relationships is to prevent caching loops, in which cache A seeks to retrieve an object through cache B, which in turn tries to retrieve it through cache A. But neighbor relationships can be one-way only. Cache A might use cache B as a neighbor rather than a parent if cache A's administrator felt that using cache B would only be preferable to direct retrieval in the case of a cache hit.

The `cache_host_domain` restrictions were first seen in a beta release of version 1.3. They were added in response to the undesirable behavior of a server under test at the University of Waikato, with a server at San Diego Supercomputer Center as its only parent. Because round-trip times between Hamilton and San Diego were much lower than round-trip times between Hamilton and some smaller towns in New Zealand, the Harvest server in Hamilton would attempt to retrieve material from those smaller towns via San Diego. It is by means of `cache_host_domain` entries that traffic patterns in the international Harvest network now in use are controlled.

In September 1995, version 1.3 of the Harvest Cache software was released. Harvest had previ-

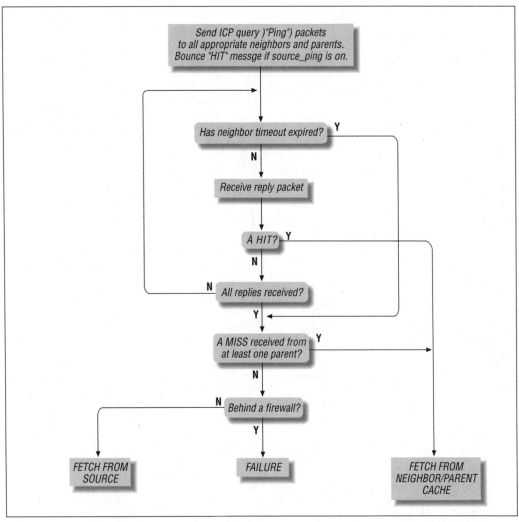

Figure 3   Process of querying neighbor and parent caches

ously possessed advantages over the CERN software; most important was the fact that it was designed to operate in a network of cooperating caches and the much higher speed with which it returned objects, but it was at this time that features were added to Harvest, which made it a feasible alternative to CERN.

Unlike the CERN software, a Harvest caching server holds cache metadata (the name of the cache file holding the object, the time when the

object expired or will expire) in memory. Version 1.3 was the first release to write that metadata to a log held on disk, allowing a Harvest cache to retain its contents when the server is restarted.

There was also an improvement the server's logging, which made billing by volume served to clients possible, as was then being done from the logs produced by the CERN software.

And it was in version 1.3 that it first became possible to restrict from which clients a Harvest server would accept requests, allowing a cache's administrator to dictate to whom that cache would provide service.

The Harvest Cache Network Today

New Zealand

The University of Waikato transferred its main WWW caching server from CERN to Harvest Cache software on 4 October 1995. This was the first production use of the Harvest cache outside American universities (though this was not known in New Zealand) at the time, and the highest-volume use to that date.

On 7 November 1995, CERN software was replaced on the NZGate caching server by Harvest Cache version 1.4 beta. Like the CERN cache before it, this cache resides on a Digital AXP 4000 model 710 server, with 128MB of memory. By January 1996, 10GB of disk was available to the cache, though only about half of that was being used.

Canterbury and Massey universities continued to use CERN servers as children to the cache as they had to its CERN predecessor. During November,

Otago and Victoria universities also set their CERN servers to use this cache as a parent, while the Internet Company of New Zealand, an ISP, set up a Harvest server with the NZGate cache as its parent.

Through November and December, problems were experienced with the software's reliability, which resulted in the loss of some of the CERN users as customers. An important factor in perception of Harvest's reliability was the fact that, unlike the CERN server, the Harvest software loads cache metadata into memory at startup. This meant that any software crash was followed by an automatic restart process taking up to an hour. While other Harvest servers would detect that the parent was not serving requests, CERN servers would simply continue to forward requests. Restart times have been substantially reduced in later versions of the software, but this remains a problem where a Harvest server acts as parent to a CERN server.

During November and December, the software underwent considerable revision as one beta version after another proved insufficiently reliable. Version 1.4 beta 23 and the subsequent produc-

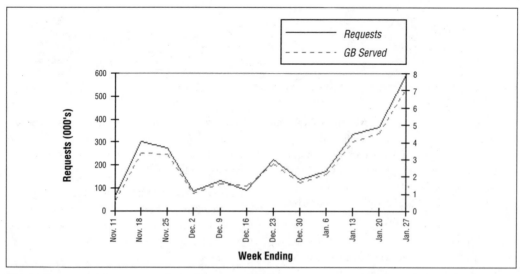

Figure 4   NZGate cache traffic to 27 January 1996

tion release version 1.4 patch level 0 have proved stable. Beta 23 was installed on the NZGate cache server on 27 December 1995, and by mid-January all those who had ceased to use the service had returned to using it.

Among influences on the traffic levels shown in Figure 4 is the fact that New Zealand's undergraduate teaching year runs roughly from March to November, with relatively few university or other employees at work in late December and early January. Even so, it seems safe to interpret the pattern of use seen as showing an initial willingness to try using the NZGate Harvest Cache as a parent, then a period of disillusionment as reliability problems continued, with increasing confidence in 1996 that stability has been achieved.

Objects served by the NZGate cache to parents or neighbors in the U.S. and Australia account for only a negligible proportion of total traffic.

Figure 5 shows the traffic saving achieved by the NZGate cache as calculated from its logs. The proportion of requests identified in Figure 5 as "non-cacheable" are objects whose URL identifies

them to the Harvest server as not to be cached—for example, URLs containing a question mark. CERN children forward requests for these to their Harvest parent, where Harvest children do not. One result of this is that the overall NZGate cache hit rate is depressed by the use of CERN rather than Harvest software on child servers.

During January the proportion of the NZGate cache's children made up of Harvest servers has fallen, which may be why the increase in the number of children shown in Figure 6 is not associated with consistent improvement in cache hit rate.

A further large cache is to be added as a child of the NZGate cache before the end of January 1996. Even without that addition, the traffic served to child caches by the NZGate cache in late January 1996 was the equivalent of approximately 6% of all traffic across the links from Hamilton to the U.S. and Australia, and hence was likely to amount to over 5% of all Internet traffic to and from New Zealand.

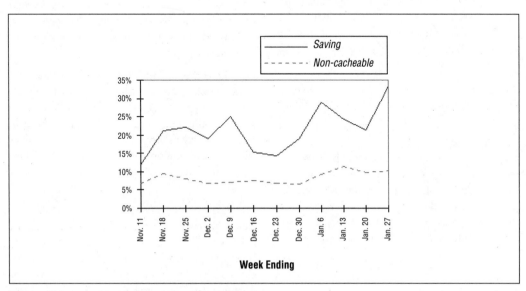

Figure 5   NZGate cache traffic characteristics

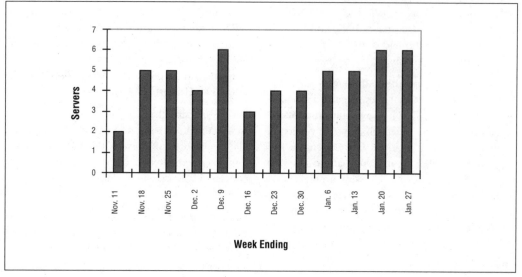

Figure 6   NZ servers using NZGate cache

NLANR

In the U.S., the National Laboratory for Applied Network Research (NLANR) has established what they see as a prototype caching system, with the aim of experimenting with scalable hierarchical caching architectures [12]. Their initial testbed consists of six cache servers at locations across the U.S., which are listed in Table 1.

Each of these servers is a Digital UNIX machine with a 266MHz Alpha CPU, 128MB of memory, 10GB of disk, and FDDI and Ethernet interfaces.

Each acts as parent to the others for particular domains. For example, any request for a file in the *nz* domain (New Zealand) will be forwarded to the Silicon Valley server, which is parent to the others for that domain. In turn, the NZGate cache is parent to the Silicon Valley server for the *nz* domain. The assignment of domains to servers reflects the underlying structure of the Internet.

In a similar way, objects are requested of NLANR servers by other Harvest servers outside the U.S. For example, the Silicon Valley and San Diego servers are parents for the NZGate cache for all objects outside the *aq*, *au*, *fj*, and *nz*

domains (Antarctica, Australia, Fiji, and New Zealand). So a cachable object from, say, the *uk* domain requested by a client using the NZGate cache is likely to be retrieved through *cache1.nzgate.net.nz*, *sv.cache.nlanr.net*, *pb.cache.nlanr.net*, and *wwwcache.doc.ic.ac.uk* in London, if that last server responds more quickly to the Pittsburgh server than does the original site.

On the other hand, the NZGate cache will retrieve objects from Australia itself or through a neighbor in Australia, since it is as near in terms of round-trip time to Australia's major international gateway as any other Harvest server. While Harvest's application has tended to be described as hierarchical [3] [12], the reality is a little more complex.

The vast bulk of traffic recorded in NLANR's published analysis of their servers' logs [12] comes from outside the U.S. The largest user to date has been the NZGate cache, though the NLANR caches also have relationships with servers in Australia, Germany, Poland, South Africa, and the U.K. as well as some education and research sites in the U.S. The low level of interest from U.S.

Table 1   Locations of NLANR testbed servers

Server	Location
bo.cache.nlanr.net	National Center for Atmospheric Research, Boulder, Colorado
it.cache.nlanr.net	Cornell Theory Center, Ithaca, New York
pb.cache.nlanr.net	Pittsburgh Supercomputing Center, Pittsburgh, Pennsylvania
sd.cache.nlanr.net	San Diego Supercomputer Center, San Diego, California
sv.cache.nlanr.net	FIX West, Silicon Valley, California
uc.cache.nlanr.net	National Center for Supercomputing Applications, Urbana-Champaign, Illinois

Internet users and providers may be due to the relatively high availability (or low cost) of bandwidth within the U.S. Some telecommunications service providers may also be concerned about a U.S. regulatory framework that prevents them from offering "value-added services."

However, "NLANR is supportive of having international clients seed the system, provide the benefit of their domestic experiences, cooperatively develop, deploy and test the performance of mechanisms to encourage efficient and high performance caching. [5]"

The Wider World

Because no site other than the NZGate and NLANR caches publishes traffic figures, comparison of the progress made in different countries is difficult.

Poland

In Poland, work is under way on a national caching structure, with upper tier caches operated by educational and research organizations. Mutual parent relationships also exist with an NLANR server (in the same way as the NZGate cache) as well as servers in France, Germany, and the U.K. A national root server is in use, along with seven metropolitan servers and a number of servers used only by specific institutions. The project aims to "officially start to serve [the] whole Polish Internet community" in July 1996 [15].

It has been stated that all of the national and metropolitan servers "are to be stable installations,

based on adequate hardware platforms" [15]. However, where the NZGate cache's primary source of funding is charges to users and NLANR and JANET (see next section) caching work is funded by government, the Polish project's source of funding is unclear. It is currently "using hardware platforms kindly lent by hosting institutions, but these are both used for other purposes and scarce in disk space" [15].

It is difficult to see how a rapid increase in traffic such as that now being experienced by the NZGate cache (see Figure 4) could be sustained solely by the use of borrowed equipment. That many New Zealand customers, especially commercial customers, would prefer higher performance to lower price (see below) seems to raise a further question about the advisability of attempting to construct a national infrastructure

The United Kingdom—JANET

The U.K.'s Joint Academic Network (JANET), is built on top of British Telecom's Switched Multi-Megabit Data Service (SMDS), with most sites' connections having bandwidths between 4Mbps and 34Mbps. JANET is connected to the rest of the Internet by two 2Mbps trans-Atlantic lines to the University of London and a 4Mbps link to EuropaNET. Bandwidth within JANET is seen as plentiful, while "trans-atlantic bandwidth is in a dire state" [10].

A number of JANET sites operate WWW caches, and a few make these publicly available—for example, SunSITE Northern Europe at Imperial College and HENSA at the University of Kent [10].

HENSA has received funding to provide a caching service to higher educational institutions.

A survey of JANET sites in progress at the time of writing appeared to show that "around half of the JANET sites run a cache server . . . (mostly the CERN or Harvest packages), and that most of these local servers are configured to chain requests on to one of the regional/national servers" [8]. It found also that most of the sites not operating a cache "would like to deploy one, but were unable to devote the necessary human or computing resources to this task" [8].

JANET is unusual in that being built on SMDS, its underlying structure is hidden from IP routing protocols [9], and round-trip times between sites tend to be more or less uniform. This makes a tree structure less necessary within JANET than, say, within New Zealand. However, "a configuration which seems to work well in practice with the Harvest software is for an individual site to have several neighbors . . . and to make one or two of the national/regional servers into parents for non-U.K. domains" [9], with servers retrieving material from within the U.K. directly. Cache hit rates of up to 60% are reported.

Where high international bandwidth costs have driven the use of caching by universities in New Zealand, it is the poor performance delivered by a system in which there is no separate charge for international traffic that has driven the use of caching by U.K. universities.

A potentially important aspect of U.K. Internet topology is that all JANET traffic to and from continental Europe passes across the London Internet Exchange (LINX), which is also an interconnection point for U.K. ISPs. It seems odd that no cache has been located at the LINX.

Elsewhere

Another two countries where progress in the use of Harvest will be interesting to observe are Australia and South Africa. Australia faces cost considerations similar to those seen in New Zealand, but where New Zealand's international gateway has been opened to competing international bandwidth providers, that used by Australian education and research institutions is operated by Telecom Australia, commonly called Telstra. Telstra customers pay what is in effect a charge per megabyte, with no differentiation between regional and international traffic. This pricing structure appears unfavorable to cache operation.

South Africa also communicates with most of the Internet over very long distances, but the South African user of Harvest, which has a mutual-parent relationship with an NLANR server, is not a university but a commercial ISP, Pipex Internet Africa. It is too early yet to say what difference if any this will make to the development of WWW caching in South Africa.

New Zealand Customers

In January 1996, brief questionnaires were sent to all WWW cache administrators known to the author and to all those identified by replies to requests placed in relevant Usenet groups. This section summarizes and draws conclusions from responses to that questionnaire.

Responses are categorized by the type of organization employing each administrator:

Tertiary ITS
> Information Technology Services or Computer Services divisions of tertiary education institutions that operate caches for the whole institution.

Other University
> Teaching departments or larger units within universities who operate their own cache or caches.

ISP
> Retail Internet Service Providers.

Others
> The Horticulture and Food Research Institute of New Zealand, the National Library of New Zealand, and two private companies whose primary business is not Internet services.

Table 2 Numbers of questionnaires sent and replies received

	Tertiary ITS	Other University	ISP	Others	Total
Questionnaires Sent	7	3	5	5	20
Replies Received	6	3	4	4	17

Table 2 shows the numbers of questionnaires sent and replies received.

Adoption of WWW Caching

Table 3 addresses when organizations started using caching software and why.

Many respondents gave more than one answer to this latter question. Both tertiary ITS divisions who gave improved performance as a reason for adopting caching stated that this was secondary to saving money, while a third who adopted caching to save money noted that performance had improved. One "other" company to give saving money as a reason stated that this was secondary to performance improvement.

One ISP that originally adopted caching to save money has continued to use it for performance reasons.

All respondents except one felt that their adoption of WWW caching had been successful. Three ISPs qualified this, expressing concern over specific difficulties in the operation of the CERN software. One administrator for a non-Internet based company felt that his company's allocation of insufficient disk space adversely affected cache hit rate. The administrator who felt adoption had not been successful did not know what hit rate had been achieved by the cache he administered.

Respondents were asked whether they would elect reduced cost or increased performance given the choice now. Their replies are summarized in Table 4.

Two tertiary ITS administrators gave cost as the preference of their managers, with performance as their or their users' preference. One university division stated that they preferred performance because they expected improved performance to discourage end users from bypassing the caching system. Another division stated that they preferred performance because their level of use and hence traffic costs were very low.

Table 3 When organizations started using caching software and why

	Tertiary ITS	Other University	ISP	Others
Question: When did your organization start using WWW caching software?				
1993	2			
1994	4	1	2	1
1995		2	2	3
Question: Why?				
Save Money	5	3	2	3
Improve Performance	2		2	2
Research	2		1	
Preserve Bandwidth for Other Traffic	1			
As Part of a Firewall	1		1	
Monitor WWW Use/User-level Accounting	1			1

Table 4   Reduced cost or increased performance given as response

	Tertiary ITS	Other University	ISP	Others
Performance	2	3	4	1
Cost	4			3

It seems reasonable to conclude that universities have led the adoption of caching in New Zealand partly from a greater desire to experiment with new software than is shown by most other users, and partly due to greater sensitivity to cost. This sensitivity seems likely to derive from the relatively large total traffic consumption and hence relatively large traffic bills of universities.

Communication with Other Caches

As shown in Table 5, respondents were also asked whether their caching server was using the NZGate cache as a parent or not, and what reasons there were for that decision. The NZGate cache has only been made available directly to organizations already buying international bandwidth directly from NZGate rather than through an intermediary. (All three university divisions who replied use a university cache as a parent to reduce their costs, with one doing so for performance reasons also.)

A number of respondents gave more than one answer. The ISP unwilling to use the NZGate cache as a parent stated that once they were able to use Harvest software themselves they would try using the NZGate cache. The university not now using the cache intends to start using it before the end of January 1996.

Glen Eustace, systems manager for Massey University, replied that "Our experience with a cache clearly showed it to be worthwhile. I suppose I was interested to see whether a hierarchy of caches would be also. Budgetary issues are making it worth considering anything that gives both improved performance and a lower operational cost." This appears to sum up the appeal of networking caches—universities have led because they wish to find out how well it works, and because it offers reduced cost without performance loss, or performance improvement without financial cost, or some compromise between the two.

Table 5   Number of respondents who used the NZGate cache as a parent and reasons given by those who did not

Question: If you use the NZGate cache as a parent, why? If not, why not?	Tertiary ITS	ISP	Others
Yes, to reduce cost	3		
Yes, to improve performance	2	1	
Yes, because the project is worthwhile	2		
Yes, to see how well a hierarchy works	2		
No, haven't got around to it	1		1
No, from fear of reduced performance		1	
Number able to use service	5	2	1

The Software

As shown in Table 6, all respondents except one began by using the CERN server software, and most still use it.

The university and both ISPs using Harvest do so in the belief that it provides faster response and handles communication between caches better than CERN. One of these ISPs also described it as reliable and stated that the code was easier to understand and modify than that for CERN or Spinner. The university using Harvest and one university moving to it expressed concern at the lack of new development of the CERN software.

The university division using Harvest saw it as more reliable than CERN, referring to the fact that the Harvest software will automatically restart the cached daemon on failure.

Two ISPs referred to the CERN server's practice of continuing to load an object after the requested client has aborted the request. This can result in a "server push" graphic being transferred continuously to a CERN server for a theoretically unlimited time, with a severe adverse effect on a cache operator's traffic bill. Clearly the one-line code modification needed to prevent the CERN server from doing this is not as widely known as it could be.

In some cases, CERN is retained because of features it has which Harvest lacks. One university keep the CERN software because they have written a large number of patches for it, and because it allows them to restrict client access to particular Web sites, as the current version of Harvest does not. Another university uses CERN's ability to get and log a user's login name for each request received from a multi-user computer to bill according to use of the service in a more precise way than would be possible by billing by machine.

One ISP continues to use CERN rather than Harvest because they set up their retail customers' browsers to read the ISP's home page on startup. Harvest Cache version 1.4 does not support an If-Modified-Since GET, which means that the whole of this page is transferred to each retail user every time their browser starts up, even if their browser already holds a current copy in its local cache. In this situation, Harvest delivers much poorer performance than does the CERN software. This ISP is trialing Spinner [11] at present but has found it insufficiently stable for production use.

Another ISP continues to use the CERN server because they are unwilling to bear the cost of throwing away the contents of their CERN cache.

The company using Spinner chose it for its speed and for the high speed with which bugs in it are fixed. The company using Purveyor selected it because they wished to run a cache using Windows NT rather than UNIX.

It seems safe to conclude that visible use of a WWW caching product within New Zealand is an important factor in subsequent choices to adopt particular software. While only one organization stated that it adopted CERN at the recommendation of someone at another site, another mentioned as a reason for using the CERN software a lack of "staff resource to put into investigating alternatives," and as late as June 1995 one organization adopted CERN in the belief that it was the only WWW caching software available.

The Future

Competition on the Backbone

The author knows of no comment published to date on the relationship between WWW cache operators and large-scale Internet bandwidth providers. Yet there are important issues to be considered.

Big Caches as Big Customers

As was described in the opening section of this paper, until the end of 1995, the overwhelming bulk of Internet traffic to and from New Zealand traveled over lines operated by the University of Waikato. The building in which those interna-

Table 6   Caching software currently in use

	Tertiary ITS	Other University	ISP	Others
Question: What caching software are you using now?				
Harvest	1	1	2	
CERN 3.0, but moving to Harvest	3			
CERN 3.0, but planning to move to Harvest				1
CERN 3.0 or 3.0 pre-release	2	2	2	1
Purveyor				1
Spinner			1	

tional links terminate also houses the New-Zealand Internet Exchange (NZIX), across which flows traffic among ISPs, universities, and a variety of other organizations within New Zealand as well as to and from the international links.

Various transitional measures are now in place as the operation of international links to NZIX becomes the business of competing telecommunications companies. Two companies announced in November 1995 that they would be providing international links to and from NZIX by February 1996. Organizations connected to NZIX are now being asked to choose between international service providers.

Yet the NZGate cache now makes up around 6% of total traffic across the exchange, a proportion that seems likely to increase over the coming weeks. The potential exists for the operator of a very large cache to wield considerable power in a bandwidth market, to the disadvantage of bandwidth vendors from whom the cache operator chose not to buy.

It is possible that a cache operator might be able to operate on the basis of purchasing from all bandwidth providers, using route-arbitration software that might be added to Harvest or might operate separately from it. But it seems reasonable to assume that bandwidth providers would seek to compete with such a service by providing their own caches.

Another option is for there not to be a single large cache at such an exchange. Instead, each international bandwidth provider might provide a cache from which customers could choose to take traffic. Harvest Cache software would allow such caches to cooperate as neighbors if the companies operating them chose to work in that way.

Big Caches and Backbone Pricing

As has already been observed, the use of volume-based charging in New Zealand has promoted the growth of WWW caching services, as universities in particular sought to reduce their costs. But the exact method used to charge for volume has the potential to greatly affect the attractiveness of caching.

Consider three different charging models. The pricing models offered to customers by international bandwidth providers to NZIX are confidential, so it is necessary to use hypothetical cases to illustrate this point.

In the first model, traffic is charged at a flat rate per, say, megabyte. The return to a cache's users (ignoring hardware and administration costs) is therefore the traffic saving they achieve.

In the second model, traffic is charged at a fixed rate per megabyte during a peak period and a lower fixed rate during an off-peak rate. Under such a regime, a cache operator may be able to increase the savings achieved beyond those available with the first model by "cache priming," bringing into the cache during the off-peak period objects that are expected to be read during the peak period.

In a third model, charging is not per unit traffic but is based in some way on peak traffic load. A cache operator will be able to generate very large savings in this case if their cache serves children or end users with very different load patterns when viewed over time. Taking a very simple example, consider a cache that has only two children. The first child is a cache for an organization that consumes the bulk of its traffic during the day, while the second is for an organization that consumes the bulk of its traffic at night. In this case the peak load and hence traffic cost for both together may be only slightly greater than for each separately.

The greater the saving that cache administrators can make by manipulating traffic profiles, the more attractive operation of a cache will be.

Big Caches and Big Exchanges

Another factor for backbone and exchange operators to consider is the likelihood that the presence of a large cache or set of caches at an exchange will add to the advantage gained, and seen to be gained, by customers who connect to that exchange. It is to be hoped that this effect will encourage multiple bandwidth providers at a single exchange to have their caches there cooperate, with a view to improving the performance seen by end users whose Web traffic uses that exchange and thus increasing the total bandwidth through that exchange point.

In New Zealand at least, these are matters for a future that is weeks rather than years away, but how the introduction of competition to international backbone services and the large-scale use of caching will interact in practice is not yet entirely clear.

Charging for the NZGate Cache

A further question facing the NZGate cache's operators is how to respond to requests for access to the cache by organizations which connect to the NZIX through an intermediate service provider. At the time of writing, only one such request has been received from a large organization, and in that case, the intermediate provider seems willing to set up a Harvest cache themselves.

The NZGate cache will not be made available simply to any New Zealand organization wishing to use it. This is partly to ensure that a developing caching network has a structure appropriately related to that of the underlying links. It is also to avoid the administrative work and the complication of relationships with the NZIX's direct customers, which would result from direct use of the NZGate cache by a large number of customer organizations.

The Harvest Software

All discussion of the Harvest software up to this point has related to the free software now available. There are two distinct efforts to develop future versions of Harvest cache software. One is to be carried out under the auspices of the NLANR. This effort is non-commercial, aiming to continue the practice of making the source code produced freely available. However, while a list of planned improvements to the software has been published [17], no completion date has been announced for any change.

Harvest Cache Version 2.0

Work is also under way on Harvest Object Cache version 2.0. This is intended to be a supported piece of software, subject to license fees and distributed in binary form only.

A beta release of this commercial release is claimed [6] to have improvements over version 1.4, which are of major interest to New Zealand users:

- If-modified-since retrievals are supported.

- It is possible to restrict access for particular clients to particular URLs.

- It is possible to restart the server without service to clients being suspended for a significant period. This will be of particular interest to operators of large Harvest caches serving CERN child caches.

These three improvements would remove all but one of the shortcomings that have lead some New Zealand cache administrators not to adopt version 1.4. The even wider adoption of the Harvest software may follow rapidly on a reliable version 2.0 becoming available, though no research has been carried out in New Zealand on the prices organizations may be willing to pay for the software. The author knows of no computer in New Zealand today running WWW caching software that has been paid for.

Performance improvements are claimed for version 2.0, but the author suspects that line speeds within New Zealand are still low enough that most New Zealand users would not see a significant performance improvement as a result of a change solely in server throughput.

The Longer Term

In the short term, it seems likely that both NLANR and commercial Harvest development will concentrate on incremental improvements to their respective existing code.

It is planned that HTTP 1.1 will be integrated into a later release of the commercial code, after the draft standard "is accepted or at least settles down a bit" [7]. Implementation of HTTP 1.1 is also among the "general areas" [17] on which NLANR will focus.

Future Harvest software may use a more intelligent mechanism for avoiding cache loops— encapsulating cache signatures in the messages sent between caches. But the existing approach using "manual configuration should suffice for a few more months until there is a more dynamic interface to configure cache resolution." [5]

An issue of increasing importance as the international Harvest network grows is that of determining with what other caches a new server should have parent or neighbor relationships. From version 1.4 patch level 1 on, the Harvest Cache software allows an administrator to have a computer running the Harvest Cache software report back to an NLANR server its latitude and longitude, as well as arbitrary other comments on the caching server's role or relationship to other caching servers. This information is collected and made publicly available at the NLANR Caching project's Web site [13]. NLANR intends to release maps generated from this information.

It is intended that in future the information provided by the caching server will be more tightly defined, following templates issued by NLANR or some other coordinating body. In future versions of the software, it is intended that it will be possible for each server to transmit the information to more than one

In the longer term, however, it will be necessary to replace cache selection based on DNS domains with a means more closely related to the underlying structure of the Internet. While simply replacing DNS domains with IP address ranges in a manual configuration scheme has been proposed as a short-term measure, this will most likely be achieved by the direct use of IP routing protocols. However, using network and transport-layer logic in application-layer code may pose its own problems. And the fact that cache operators may wish for commercial reasons to exercise additional control over cache selection is likely to add further complexity.

Conclusion

The use of WWW caching software has gained wider acceptance in New Zealand than in most other countries, and cached WWW traffic accounts for a higher proportion of international traffic in New Zealand than anywhere else. This has come about in large part because of the visible production use of the software by universities, who in turn have adopted it largely as a cost-saving measure. This has happened to a greater extent in New Zealand than elsewhere because in New Zealand, the true and, by the standards of the developed world, high cost of international bandwidth is seen by those able to employ means of making more efficient use of that bandwidth.

The relatively small size of the country may also have contributed, with information about successful use of WWW caching spreading more quickly than would have been the case among a larger population of network administrators and managers.

A similar pattern seems to be being followed in the adoption of distributed caching using the Harvest Cache software.

It is interesting that while cost considerations drove all but one of the university implementations of caching, cost was not the dominant factor in use of caching by other organizations. It is therefore possible that publicity for the use of Harvest in New Zealand and elsewhere may lead to the wider adoption of caching in countries where traffic-based charging is not employed.

New Zealand's history of cost-based pricing has fueled rapid Internet growth in this country and has encouraged the deployment of WWW caching as a technology to make more efficient use of a resource not perceived as free. New Zealand is now making the transition to competitive provision of international bandwidth at a national exchange after self-funding WWW caching has already become a significant factor in the operation of the Internet here. Even for countries that do not share New Zealand's geographical isolation, much is still to be learned from New Zealand's rapidly changing Internet environment.

The Harvest Cache software has proved itself as a fast, reliable, reasonably easy to install means of constructing large-scale caching networks, at a time when no other software with similar functionality exists. So far as anything can be predicted in the Internet of 1996, its future seems assured.

Possibly the real test of WWW caching's implementers will be one of changing perceptions. We shall have succeeded if in New Zealand and other countries where caching is now being introduced, WWW caching is seen not as a service entirely separate from the provision of bandwidth, but as an upper layer in a more intelligent and hence efficient mechanism for the provision of information than has existed before. ∎

References

1. Brownlee, Nevil, "New Zealand Experiences with Network Traffic Charging," *ConneXions* 8, 12, December 1994, *http://www.auckland.ac.nz/net/Accounting/nze.html*

2. Carter, M., and G. Guthrie, "Pricing Internet: The New Zealand Experience," Discussion Paper 9501, Department of Economics, University of Canterbury, January 1996, *ftp://ftp.econ.lsa.umich.edu/pub/Archive/nz-internet-pricing.ps.Z*

3. Chankhunthod, Anawat, "The Harvest Cache and Httpd-Accelerator," *http://excalibur.usc.edu/*

4. Chankhunthod, A., et al, "A Hierarchical Internet Object Cache," *Proceedings of USENIX 1996 Annual Technical Conference*, pp. 153–163, *http://excalibur.usc.edu/cache-html/cache.html* or *http://catarina.usc.edu/danzig/cache.ps*

5. Claffy, Kimberly, NLANR, private email to the author, 26 January 1996.

6. Danzig, Peter, "Harvest Object Cache: Cached-2.0," *http://www.netcache.com/*

7. Danzig, Peter, private email to the author, 12 March 1996.

8. Hamilton, Martin, University of Loughborough, private email to the author, 27 January 1996.

9. Hamilton, Martin, "WWW Caching on JANET," 1996, *http://wwwcache.lut.ac.uk/caching/janet/*

10. HENSA, "The U.K. National Web Cache at HENSA Unix," *http://www.hensa.ac.uk/wwwcache/*

11. Informations Vävarna AB, "The Spinner WWW-Server," 1995, *http://spinner.infovav.se/*

12. National Laboratory for Applied Network Research, "A Distributed Testbed for National Information Provisioning," 1996, *http://www.nlanr.net/Cache/*

13. National Laboratory for Applied Networking Research, 1996, *http://www.nlanr.net/Cache/Tracker/caches/*

14. Schuster, John, "Harvest Cache Server Description," unpublished technical report for the University of Southern California, 1995, *http://netweb.usc.edu/danzig/cache-description/harvest_desc.html*

15. Sylwestrzak, Wojtek, "WWW Cache in Poland," 1995, *http://w3cache.icm.edu.pl/*

16. Wessels, Duane, "The Harvest Information Discovery and Access System," *http://rd.cs.colorado.edu/harvest/*

17. Wessels, Duane, untitled, *http://www.nlanr.net/~wessels/NLANR-cached.html*

18. World Wide Web Consortium, W3C httpd, *http://www.w3.org/pub/WWW/Daemon/*

Acknowledgments

This paper's description of the Harvest Cache software both present and future owes much to Kimberly Claffy of San Diego Supercomputer Center, one of those coordinating the NLANR caching project, and to Duane Wessels of the University of Colorado. Duane Wessels also kindly provided Figures 2 and 3.

Martin Hamilton of Loughborough University was most helpful in describing caching on JANET.

Thanks are also due to John Houlker of Information and Technology Services, the University of Waikato, for his comments on the history of the Internet in New Zealand and for the information presented in Figure 1.

About the Author

Donald Neal
Information & Technology Services
University of Waikato
d.neal@waikato.ac.nz

Donald Neal received his BSc in Computer Science from the University of Waikato in 1987 and his MSc in 1990. Since December 1993 he has been a Systems Programmer/Analyst in that university's Information and Technology Services Division's Networks and Systems Group. His work is primarily with on-line services, in particular the deployment and administration of World-Wide Web serving and caching software, and directory services. He is the administrator of the NZIX cache described in this paper. Since 1995 he has been a member of the council of the Internet Society of New Zealand and current serves that society as Secretary.

Performance Engineering of the World Wide Web
Application to Dimensioning and Cache Design

Jean-Chrysostome Bolot, Philipp Hoschka

Abstract

The quality of the service provided by the World Wide Web, namely convenient access to a tremendous amount of information in remote locations, depends in an important way on the time required to retrieve this information. This time in turn depends on a number of parameters, in particular the load at the server and on the network. Overloads are avoided by carefully dimensioning the server (so that it has enough resources such as CPU power and disk space to handle expected requests) and the network (so that it has enough resources such as bandwidth and buffers to transport requests and replies), and by using mechanisms such as caching that minimize the resource requirements of user requests. In this paper, we consider performance issues related to dimensioning and caching.

Our contribution is twofold. Regarding dimensioning, we advocate the use of time series analysis techniques for Web traffic modeling and forecasting. We show using experimental data that quantities of interest such as the number of Web requests handled by a server, or the amount of data retrieved per hour by a server, can be accurately modeled with time series such as seasonal ARIMA models. We then use these models to make medium-term predictions of client requests characteristics (number of such requests and size of document retrieved), which in turn can be used as a basis for dimensioning decisions. Regarding caching, we advocate the use of novel cache replacement algorithms that explicitly take document size and network load into account so as to minimize the retrieval time perceived by clients. **Keywords:** *Web traffic, network and server dimensioning, caching*

1. Introduction

The World Wide Web provides a service of access to vast amounts of geographically distributed information. Clearly, the quality of the service depends on the quality of the access to the data. This quality in turn depends on a number of parameters, some of which are difficult to quantify. However, it appears that Web users rate access time to remote data as an essential component of quality. Thus, they tend to avoid overloaded servers and pages that take a long time to retrieve.

Access time to remote data (which we refer to in the paper as *retrieval time* or *Web latency*) is made up of many components, which include:

1. The time for the client request to reach the server

2. The time at the server to process the data

3. The time for the reply to reach the client from the server

4. The time at the client to process the reply

Times 1 and 4 depend on the hardware configurations at the client and at the server, on the type of client request, and on the load at the server. To avoid long delays, it is important to have enough client and server resources (CPU, disk size and disk access time, and memory size) to support the anticipated load. Times 2 and 3 together add up to what is referred to as the roundtrip delay between client and server. This delay is the sum of the delays experienced at each intermediate router between client and server. Each such delay in turn consists of two components, a fixed component that includes the transmission delay at a router and the propagation delay on the link to the next router, and a variable component that includes the processing and queueing delays at the router. (Note that packets may be rejected at the intermediate nodes because of buffer overflow, causing packet loss.) To avoid large roundtrip delays, it is important to have enough network resources (bandwidth and buffer sizes at the routers) to support the anticipated load and to control the amount of data that is sent into the network. This latter control can be done in many different ways, one of which being to minimize the number of client requests sent to distant servers, which is typically done with caching.

Thus, it is clear that the quality of the service provided by the Web depends on the careful match of network and server resources to anticipated demand and on the careful design of caching schemes. The art of matching resources to anticipated demand is referred to as *resource/capacity planning*, or *dimensioning*. We use the term *dimensioning* in the paper. Thus, dimensioning and cache design are the focus of this paper.

In Section 2, we consider issues related to dimensioning. Specifically, we use time series analysis to model the number of client requests arriving at a Web server and the amount of data sent by a Web server back to its clients. We show using experimental trace data that the above quantities can be accurately modeled with so-called seasonal autoregressive integrated moving average (seasonal ARIMA) models. These models are then used to make short and medium term predictions of client requests characteristics (number of such request and size of document retrieved), which in turn can be used as a basis for dimensioning decisions. ARIMA models have been used in many different areas to make reasonable medium- and sometimes even long-term predictions. Thus, they hold great promise as a tool for Web traffic forecasting and hence for Web server dimensioning.

In Section 3, we consider issues related to cache design, in particular, proxy cache design. A client request for a document that is not present in the cache may require that one or more cached documents be replaced by the requested (and newly fetched) document. Which documents are replaced is determined by a so-called cache replacement algorithm. Most recently proposed such algorithms use the frequency of reference, and sometimes the size, of the documents requested by clients to replace documents. Surprisingly, they do not explicitly take retrieval time into account, even though their goal is precisely to minimize, or at least to reduce, the retrieval time perceived by clients. We introduce a very general class of cache algorithms that do take retrieval time and other relevant parameters into account. We show, using experimental data collected at INRIA, that these algorithms outperform commonly used algorithms. Section 4 concludes the paper.

2. Using Time Series Analysis for Web Dimensioning

Measurements at a connection endpoint such as a Web client/server site on the Internet can be obtained in a passive or active fashion. Passive measurements typically involve collecting request and/or reply information at client or server sites. Active measurements typically involve collecting information, such as delay and loss distribution, about the connection between client and server.

With the passive method, we obtain measures such as the number of requests req_n to a Web server during the nth measurement interval. With the active method, we obtain measures such as the roundtrip delay rtt_n of packet n. If packet n is a HTML client request, then rtt_n measures the retrieval time associated with this request. Trace data obtained with the passive method is shown later in Figures 2 and 3. Trace data obtained with the active method is shown in Figure 1. Figure 1

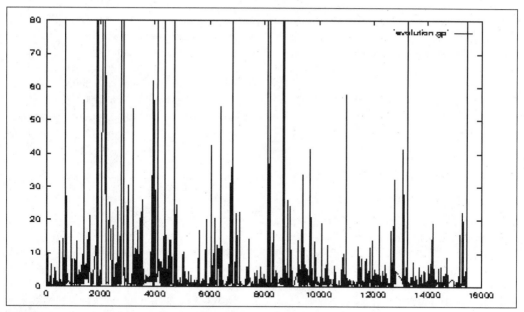

Figure 1   Evolution of rtt_n (in seconds) vs. n

shows the evolutions of rtt_n as a function of n in the range $0 <= n <= 15000$ obtained from a trace collected at Boston University [5].

The evolutions of rtt_n in Figure 1 are an example of a time series plot, by which is meant a finite set of observations of a random process in which the parameter is time. A large body of principles and techniques referred to as *time series analysis* has been developed to analyze time series, the goal being to infer as much as possible about the whole process from the observations [11]. It is thus natural to investigate whether and how well these techniques can be applied to Web data. The most important problems in time series analysis are the model fitting problem and the prediction problem. In the first problem, the goal is to obtain a statistical model that fits the observations. In the second problem, the goal is to predict a future value of a process given a record of past observations. We describe the model fitting problem next.

2.1 Time Series Modeling

Constructing a time series model involves expressing rtt_n in terms of previous observations rtt_{n-i} and of noise processes *en* that typically represent external events. The noise processes are generally assumed to be uncorrelated white noise processes with zero mean and finite variance. These are the simplest processes, and they correspond to processes that have "no memory" in the sense that the value of a noise process at time n is uncorrelated with all past values up to time $n-1$. Thus, for $n>0$, we express rtt_n as follows:

$rtt_n = f(\{_{n-i}\}, \{e_{n-i}\}, i>0)$

We now need to take a closer look at how to define the function f. Most models described in the literature are linear models, the most well-known being the so-called AR (autoregressive), MA (moving average), and ARMA (auto regressive and moving average) models. An autoregressive p (denoted by *AR(p)*) describes the current value rtt_n using the weighted sum of p previous values $rtt_{n-1}, ..., rtt_{n-p}$, plus one noise term e_n. A moving average of order q (denoted by $MA(q)$) describes the current value rtt_n using the weighted sum of q noise terms. An ARMA model of order (p,q) combines the above models and describes the current value rtt_n using p previous values of rtt and q noise terms. Specifically

$$rtt_n = x1 rtt_{n-1} + \ldots + x_p rtt_{n-p}$$
$$- y0 e_n - y1 rtt_{n-1} - 1 - \ldots - y_p e_{n-p} \quad [1]$$

where $x1 \ldots x_p$ and $y1 \ldots y_q$ are constant values.

This equation is typically rewritten as

$$X(B) rtt_n = Y(B) e_n \quad [2]$$

where B is a lag operator defined as $B rtt_n = rtt_{n-1}$, and X and Y are polynomial operators defined as $X(B) = 1 - x1 B - x2 B^{**}2 - \ldots - xp B^{**}p$ and $Y(B) = -y0 - y1 B - y2 B^{**}2 - \ldots - yq B^{**}q$. In these equations and for the rest of this paper, $A^{**}B$ stands for "A to the power of B."

ARMA models have been widely used to analyze time series in many different areas. For example, they have been used to describe video traffic call requests in telephone networks [8], and memory references in software [9]. However, they have been comparatively rarely applied in computer networking.

Fitting an ARMA model to time series data is done in three steps, which are:

1. Identification (i.e., determine the values of p and q in Equation 1)

2. Estimation (i.e., estimate the constants $x1 \ldots x_p$, $y1 \ldots y_q$)

3. Evaluation or diagnostic checking (i.e., check how well the fitted model conforms to the data, and suggest how the model should be changed in case of a lack of good fit)

Once a good model has been obtained with this method, it can be used, for example, to make forecasts (predictions) of the future behavior of the system.

The ARMA model fitting procedure assumes the data to be stationary. Specific approaches have

been developed if the time series shows variations that violate this stationarity assumption. The more commonly used approach is to use two models, one for the nonstationary part of the process, the other for the "residual" part, which remains after the nonstationary effects have been removed. If the nonstationary part is a polynomial function of time, then the overall process can be modeled with integrated models (p, d, q) is an ARMA (p, q) model that has been differenced d times. Thus it has the form:

$$((1 - B)^{**}d) X(B) rtt_n = Y(B) e_n \quad [3]$$

where $X(B)$ and $Y(B)$ are the same as in Equation 2.

Unfortunately, many "real-life" time series include non-polynomial non-stationarities that cannot be removed simply by differencing. The most common such non-stationarities are seasonal trends. For example, the data for a particular hour in a month-long trace is typically correlated with the hours preceding it as well as with the same hours in preceding days. Seasonal trends can be taken into account in seasonal ARIMA models, which are referred to as ARIMA $(p,d,q) \times (P,D,Q)_s$ models. The idea in these models is to carry out two separate ARMA analyses, one for the entire series, and another one only for data points that are s units apart in the series. In practice, the original series is first differenced by the length of the period s. The resulting series is analyzed according to order (P,D,Q) while the original series is analyzed to order (p,d,q).

2.2 Application to Web Data Analysis

We have used the techniques above to analyze trace data collected at one of INRIA's Web servers. The data includes the number of requests handled by the server and the size (i.e., the number of bytes) of the corresponding replies. The data was collected between December 1, 1994, and July 31, 1995. We are interested in the hourly variations of the data. To simplify data analysis, we consider averages over a period of one

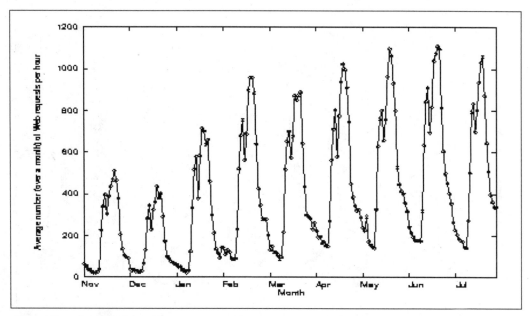

Figure 2   Evolutions of the average number (over a month) of Web requests-per-hour

month. Figure 2 shows the average number of requests (computed over a month) received every hour. The hours are numbered 0 to 23, with 0 corresponding to midnight. Thus, the first data point in the figure represents the average number of requests received during November 1994 between midnight and 1:00 a.m. The second data point represents the average number of requests received between 1:00 and 2:00 a.m., etc. Thus, Figure 2 can be thought of as showing the evolutions of the number of requests in a typical day in November, December, etc.

As expected, we observe strong seasonal variations that correspond to daily cycles. The number of Web requests is smallest at night between 8:00 p.m. and 6:00 a.m. We also observe a slight dip around noon. This strong daily cycle suggests that most requests to this server originate in France, or at least in countries with little time difference with France. Indeed, more than 60% of the requests originate in the *.fr*, *.uk*, and *.de* domains (corresponding to France, the U.K., and Germany, respectively), while requests originat-

ing in the *.edu*, *.gov*, *.mil*, and *.jp* domains account for less than 15% of the total.

In addition to daily cycles, we observe a trend that reflects the growing number of requests handled by the server over the past year. We have used differencing to remove the trend. Although most of the non-stationarity is removed by the first differencing, we observe an additional effect when differencing $d = 2$. Clearly, the seasonal period is $s = 24$. Model identification then proceeds using standard identification techniques [11] implemented in Matlab. (Matlab is a trademark of The MathWorks, Inc.) We have found that the seasonal ARIMA model $(2,2,1) \times (3,2,0)_{24}$ provides a good fit to the data.

We have carried out a similar identification procedure for the number of Mbytes requested from the server.

Figure 3 shows the average number of bytes (computed over a month) sent every hour by the server. Not surprisingly, we observe the same strong daily cycles as in Figure 2. However, the overall trend that reflects the growing number of

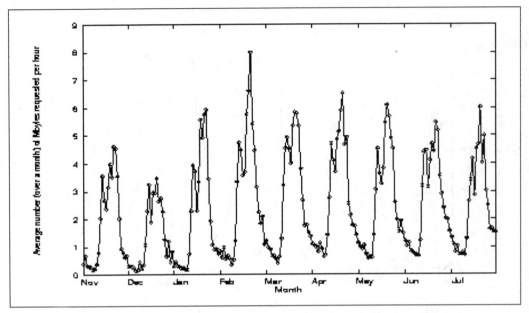

Figure 3   Evolutions of the average number (over a month) of bytes sent by the server per hour

bytes transferred in Figure 2 is not as clear as that found in Figure 3.

We have used the seasonal models developed above for forecasting purposes. Forecasting the number of requests is useful to dimension and plan upgrades to the server. Forecasting the number of bytes transferred is useful to dimension the networks over which these bytes are transferred. (In our specific case, these include INRIA's own network as well as the regional network for southeastern France.) The forecasting n (such as the number of requests $\{req_n\}$), predict the value of req at some specific time in the future, say req_{n+k}, that minimizes some prediction error, which we take here to be the mean square prediction error. With ARIMA (p,d,q) model such as that of Equation 3 and its seasonal extension, the minimum square error forecast for req_{n+k} which we denote by $req_{n+k}\sim$, is given by [11]:

$$req_{n+k}\sim = sum(i=1,p)\ x_i\ req_{n+k-i}\sim - sum(j=1,q)$$
$$xi\ yj\ 0e_{n+k-j} \tag{4}$$

where $0\ e_{n+j} = e_{n+j}$ if $j <= 0$ and $0e_{n+tj} = 0$, otherwise. Note that we assume above that the parameters x_i, y_i, p, and q of the ARIMA model are known. In practice, they are, of course, estimated from trace data as shown earlier.

We have found that ARIMA-based forecasting does provide reasonably accurate short- and medium-term predictions. Table 1 shows the predicted and actual values of the average number of Web requests-per-hour for the month of October 1995. We have used the above ARIMA predictor to forecast the number of requests from the trace data shown in Figure 2 (i.e., using data from November 1994 to July 1995).

We observe that the predicted values do reflect the daily variations observed in the data. However, they are in general lower than the actual values by 10 to 30%. Our ability to make reasonable medium- and long-term forecasts is limited at present because the amount of trace data available is quite limited. In particular, we do not have enough data for the ARIMA model to capture the long-term growth data of Web traffic and

Table 1   Actual and predicted values of requests for the month of November

Hour	0	1	2	3	4	5	6	7	8	9	10	11
Actual	316	282	278	264	209	210	170	201	441	913	1193	1271
Predicted	320	275	250	245	200	202	185	185	295	680	870	980
Hour	12	13	14	15	16	17	18	19	20	21	22	23
Actual	1043	1320	1439	1577	1609	1420	1096	689	550	470	495	426

to capture yearly cycles. Yet both factors obviously have an important impact. For example, Figure 2 clearly shows dips for the months of December and July that reflect decreased activity caused by Christmas and summer vacations.

3. Designing Efficient Cache Replacement Algorithms for Web Proxy Servers

The adequate dimensioning of network and server resources is important to avoid overloads and their consequences, such as excessive retrieval times. Another way to avoid overloads is to control the amount of data sent into the network, and thus to control the resource requirements of Web users. This latter control can be done in many different ways, for example, by minimizing the number of client requests sent to distant servers, which is typically done with caching. In this paper, we consider in particular proxy caching.

Measurements have shown that proxy caching can significantly reduce network load [1]. This is because a proxy server returns the locally cached copy of a document named in a URL from a previous client request if this document is requested again. However, proxy caching decreases the network load as well as the retrieval time perceived by the client only if client requests exhibit a sufficiently high degree of what is referred to in the literature as *temporal locality*. Temporal locality is a bit of a misnomer, and *temporal proximity* (as suggested by a reviewer) would be more appropriate. Temporal locality implies that identical requests (possibly from different clients) follow each other closely in time with high proba-

bility. The property of temporal locality has been observed in many situations, including program execution [10], file and database access [14], and network addresses in data packets [6] [7].

A hit is said to occur in the cache when a document named in a URL from a previous request is already in the cache. A fault or miss is said to occur when the document is not found in the cache. On a cache miss, one of the entries in the cache must be replaced to bring in the missing document. Several replacement algorithms have been described in the literature, the more notable of which is the Least Recently Used (LRU) algorithm and its many derivatives [1]. The LRU algorithm orders cache entries in a stack. On a cache miss, the LRU algorithm moves the missed name to the top of the stack and discards the entry at the bottom of the stack. The algorithm attempts to approximate an "optimal" algorithm, which would replace the entry that will be referenced furthest in the future. This algorithm requires to look ahead in the trace, and hence it cannot be implemented in a real system.

We compare the performance of replacement algorithms using two measures, namely the miss ratio and the normalized resolution time. The miss ratio or miss probability is defined as the probability that a requested document is not already in the cache. Clearly, the lower the miss ratio, the lower the network resource requirements of the client requests. However, the client is not so much interested in the miss ratio as in the decrease in perceived retrieval time made possible by the use of the cache. Thus, we quantify the performance improvements gained by using the cache via the normalized resolution time t, which is equal to the ratio of the average name resolution time with and without the cache. The lower t is, the higher the performance increase gained with proxy caching.

Let p denote the miss probability, T_c denote the average time to access an entry in the cache, and T_{nc} denote the average time to retrieve a document that is not in the cache. Then

$$t = (T_c + pT_{nc})/T_{nc} \quad\quad\quad [5]$$

Assuming that T_{nc} is much bigger than T_c, t is about equal to p. Therefore, t is minimized if p is minimized.

This seems to argue for as large a cache as possible. However, the cache size is limited in practice. Furthermore, the miss ratio is in general a function of the size of the documents in the cache. Indeed, for a given cache size, the number of cached documents, and hence the hit ratio, decrease with the average document size. Also, experimental evidence suggests that smaller documents are more often requested by clients [5]. This has led to the introduction of cache replacement algorithms that do not depend on temporal locality only, but on document size as well [1].

Surprisingly, however, no Web cache algorithm we are aware of takes as input parameter the time it took to retrieve a remote document (and insert it in the cache). Yet it seems natural that a decision to discard from the cache a document retrieved from a far out (in terms of network latency) site should be taken with greater care than the decision to discard a document retrieved from a closer site, all the more so since the time required to retrieve documents from different sites can be considerably different one from the other as illustrated in Figure 1. Thus, we argue that Web cache replacement algorithms should take into account the retrieval time associated with each document in the cache. One way to do this is to assign a weight to each item in the cache and to use a weight-based replacement algorithm that replaces the item with the lowest current weight [12]). In general, the weight could be a function of the time to last reference of the item, the time it took to retrieve the item, the

expected time-to-live of the item, the size of the document, etc. Such weight-based algorithms have been advocated for distributed database systems [13].

In general, the problem of selecting an algorithm for replacing documents in a cache is a function that, given a state s for the cache (defined below), and a newly retrieved document i, decides:

1. If document i should be cached

2. In case answer to question 1 is positive but there is not enough free space in the cache to include the document, which other document(s) should be discarded to free the space needed

We define the state of the cache to be:

1. The set of documents stored in the cache

2. For each document a set of state variables that typically include statistical information associated with the document

Examples of state variables associated with document i include:

t_i The time since the document was last referenced

S_i The size of the document

rtt_i The time it took to retrieve the document

ttl_i The time to live of the document (i.e., the expected time until the document will be updated at the remote site, which is also the time interval until the cached document becomes stale)

We assign a weight to each cached document i that is a function of the state variables associated with document i. We denote the weight function by $W_i = W(t_i, S_i, rtt_i, ttl_i)$. Observe that this general weight function can be specialized to yield commonly used algorithms. For example, with the function $W(t_i, S_i, rtt_i, ttl_i) = 1/t_i$, documents are replaced according to the time of last reference. This models the LRU algorithm. With $W(t_i, S_i, rtt_i, ttl_i) = Si$, documents are cached on the basis of size only. The general form of the weight function depends on the application and, more specifically, on the types of requests and replies expected in the system. For Web proxy caching, we suggest the following function:

$$W(t_i, S_i, rtt_i, ttl_i) =$$
$$(w_1 rtt_i + w_2 S_i)/ttl_i + (w_3 + w_4)/t_i \ t \qquad [6]$$

where w_1, w_2, w_3, and w_4 have constant value. The second term on the right-hand side captures the temporal locality. The first term captures the cost associated with retrieving documents (waiting cost, storage cost in the cache), while the multiplying factor $1/ttl_i$ indicates that the cost associated with retrieving a document increases as the useful lifetime of the document decreases.

It is not clear yet how to best handle the cache coherence problem in the Web. Recent work suggests that hierarchical invalidation schemes are not as attractive as might have been expected. Instead, remote sites exporting time-critical documents should associate adequate expiration times (i.e., ttl_i values) to these documents [3] [2]. Our model above is geared toward such schemes. However, few sites already implement these schemes. Thus, it is difficult to practice to obtain a value for the state variable ttl_i. Therefore, we do not consider it in the rest of the paper. In this case, Equation 6 becomes:

$$W(t_i, S_i, rtt_i, ttl_i) = w_1 rtt_i + w_2 S_i + (w_3 + w_4 S_i)/t_i$$

There remains to define parameters w_i. Not surprisingly, the choice of adequate values for w_i depends on the goal of the caching algorithm. This goal might be to maximize the hit ratio, or to minimize the perceived retrieval time for a random user, or to minimize the cache size for a given hit ratio, etc. Each goal can be expressed as a standard optimization problem and solved using variants of the Lagrange multiplier technique. We do not describe these optimization problems here (to save space and because they

do not add much insight into the design of the algorithms). Instead, we use trace-driven simulation to compare the performance of various schemes. A trace-driven simulation requires a trace of requests sent to remote servers and a model of the cache being simulated. The cache model can be altered to simulate a cache of any size with any type of replacement algorithm, and the simulation can be repeated on the same trace data.

We consider two different cache replacement algorithms, namely the LRU algorithm and an algorithm that takes all state variables into account. We refer to these algorithms as algorithm 1 and 2, respectively. They are defined as follows:

- Algorithm 1: $W(t_i, S_i, rtt_i, ttl_i) = w_3/t_i$

- Algorithm 2: $W(t_i, S_i, rtt_i, ttl_i) = w_1 rtt_i + w_2 S_i + (w_3 + w_4 S_i)/t_i$

We express $W(t_i, S_i, rtt_i, ttl_i)$ in terms of bytes, and we take in all cases w_1 =5000 b/s, w_2 = 1000, w_3 = 10000 bs, and w_4 = 10 s.

The performance measures we consider are the miss ratio, and a weighted miss ratio defined as the probability that a requested document is not already in the cache multiplied by the weight associated with that document. In the same way, we define a weighted miss history that records the number of misses, multiplied by the weight associated with a miss, versus the number of documents that have been processed by the simulator. Figure 4 shows the weighted miss history for both algorithms.

It turns out that the miss ratio for algorithm 1 is slightly lower than that for algorithm 2. However, the weighted miss ratio, and hence the perceived retrieval time, is much lower for algorithm 2. This clearly shows the benefits of using cache replacement algorithms that take retrieval time into account.

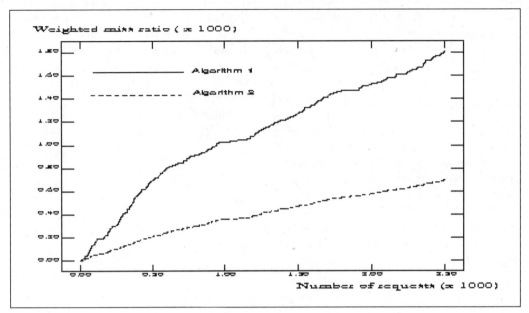

Figure 4   Weighted miss histories for algorithms 1 and 2

4. Conclusion

Our contributions in the paper can be summarized as follows:

- It is reasonable to use time series analysis techniques to model Web traffic and forecast Web server load.

- Cache replacement algorithms should be a function of variables other than simply time to last reference and document size.

The results we have presented to support these claims are preliminary. However, they are very encouraging. We are now working on precisely quantifying the gains associated with the techniques we have advocated here. ∎

References

1. Abrams, M., et al., "Caching Proxies: Limitations and Potentials," *Proc. 4th WWW Conference*, Boston, December 1995, pp. 119–133.

2. Bowman, C.M., et al., "The Harvest Information Discovery and Access System," *Proc. 2nd WWW Conference*, October 1994, pp. 763–771.

3. Chankhunthod, A., et al., "A Hierarchical Internet Object Cache," in *http://excalibur.usc.edu/cache-html/cache.html*

4. Crovella, M., and A. Bestavros, "Self-Similarity in World Wide Web Traffic: Evidence and Possible Causes," *Proc. ACM Sigmetrics '96*, Philadelphia, May 1996.

5. Cunha, C., A. Bestavros, and M. Crovella, "Characteristics of WWW Client-based Traces," Technical Report TR-95-010, Boston University, April 1995.

6. Estrin, D., and D.J. Mitzel, "An Assessment of State and Lookup Overhead in Routers," *Proc. INFO-COM '92*, Florence, May 1992, pp. 2332–2342.

7. Feldmeier, D., "Improving Gateway Performance with a Routing Table Cache," *Proc. INFOCOM '88*, March 1988, pp. 298–307.

8. Filipiak, J., and P. Chemouil, "Time-Series Analysis of Traffic Updates in Loss Systems," *Applied Stochastic Models and Data Analysis*, 6, 1, January 1990, pp. 1–11.

9. Haikala, I.J., "ARMA Models of Program Behavior," *Proc. ACM Sigmetrics'86*, Washington, D.C., May 1986, pp. 170–179.

10. Madison, A., and A. Batson, "Characteristics of Program Localities," *Comm. ACM* 19, 5, May 1976.

11. Priestly, M.B., *Spectral Analysis and Time Series*, Academic Press, 1981.

12. Robinson, J.T., and M.V. Devarakonda, "Data Cache Management Using Frequency-based Replacement" *Proc. ACM SIGMETRICS '90*, Boulder, May 1990, pp. 134–142.

13. Sellis, T. "Intelligent Caching and Indexing Techniques for Relational Database Systems," *Information Systems*, 13, 2, 1988, pp. 175–185.

14. Smith, A.J., "Optimization of I/O Systems by Cache Disks and File Migration: A Survey," *Perf. Evaluation* 1, 4, November 1981, pp. 249–262.

Acknowledgments

Many thanks to the anonymous reviewers for carefully reading the paper and for useful comments.

About the Authors

Jean-Chrysostome Bolot
INRIA
B. P. 93
06902
Sophia-Antipolis Cedex
France
bolot@sophia.inria.fr

Jean-Chrysotome Bolot received his M.S. and Ph.D. from the Unersity of Maryland in 1988 and 1991, respectively. Since 1991, he has been working at INRIA in Sophia Antipolis in Southern France in the high-speed networking research group. His research interests include the design (with an emphasis on error and flow control mechanisms for real-time applications in the Internet) and measurement and analysis of network traffic.

Philipp Hoschka
World Wide Web Consortium.
INRIA
B. P. 93
06902
Sophia-Antipolis Cedex
France
hoschka@sophia.inria.fr

Philipp works on the integration of real-time data transmission (audio, video) into the Web. He organized a Birds of a Feather session on this subject at the WWW4 conference in December 1995.

Before joining the W3C in January 1996, Philipp was a member of the high speed networking research group at INRIA (directed by Christian Huitema, member and former president of the Internet Activities Board). This group is one of the leading research groups world-wide in the area of transmission of real-time data over the Internet. Philipp received a Ph.D. in Computer Science for his work on automatic code optimization of marshalling code. He also holds a Master's in Computer Science from the University of Karlsruhe, Germany.

This paper was supported in part by a grant from France Telecom-CNET.

REAL-TIME GEOGRAPHIC VISUALIZATION OF WORLD WIDE WEB TRAFFIC

Stephen E. Lamm, Daniel A. Reed, Will H. Scullin

Abstract

The rapid growth of the World Wide Web (WWW) is well documented, with WWW sites now advertised in magazines, newspapers, and television commercials. Given current use of the WWW for scientific and educational information sharing and its emerging use for electronic commerce, studying access patterns is an important first step in understanding network implications and in designing future generations of WWW servers that can accommodate new media types and interaction modes.

Due in large part to early development of the Mosaic WWW browser by the National Center for Supercomputing Applications (NCSA), the access load on the NCSA WWW server remains extremely high. Using the NCSA WWW server as a high load testbed, we describe Avatar, a virtual reality system for real-time analysis and mapping of WWW server accesses to their points of geographic origin on various projections of the Earth. As HTTP protocols expand to demographic data, Avatar architecture can be extended to correlate this data as well. **Keywords:** *Virtual reality, demographics, access pattern analysis, performance analysis, information mining*

Introduction

Within the past few years, the profile of the Internet has changed from that of a network connecting a modest number of research institutions to the backbone connecting individuals, government agencies, and corporations in an emerging information infrastructure. Much of this change can be traced to the development of the World Wide Web (WWW) [4], the explosive growth of the WWW triggered by the early introduction of the Mosaic WWW browser by the National Center for Supercomputing Applications (NCSA), and the more recent development of commercial WWW browsers by Netscape and other vendors.

In March 1994, the WWW ranked eleventh among the most used NSFNet backbone services [12]. At that time, WWW data accounted for less than three percent of all NSFNet backbone packets. By March 1995, WWW traffic was ranked first and accounted for almost twenty percent of the NSFNet backbone packets. This growth trend continues unabated as new WWW sites are added each minute.

Given current use of the WWW for scientific and educational information sharing and its emerging use for electronic commerce, studying access patterns is an important first step in understanding network implications and in designing future generations of WWW servers that can accommodate new media types and interaction modes. However, the large number of requesting sites, the diversity of WWW data types (text, data, images, audio, and video), and the multiplicity of server performance metrics (e.g., network packets and page faults) make data correlation and understanding difficult. Proposed HTTP protocol extensions will add demographic data, further complicating correlation and heightening the need for sophisticated analysis techniques.

To support WWW performance analysis, we expanded *Avatar*, a virtual reality system designed to analyze and display real-time performance data [17], and we applied it to the analysis of WWW traffic. One variant of *Avatar* supports real-time display of WWW server accesses by mapping them to their geographic points of origin on various projections of the Earth. By allowing users to interactively change the displayed performance metrics and to observe the real-time evolution of WWW traffic patterns in a familiar geographic context, *Avatar* provides insights that are not readily apparent via more traditional statistical analysis. Moreover, it can be extended to accommodate demographic and point of sale information for correlation of electronic commerce patterns.

The remainder of this paper is organized as follows. First, we describe the architecture of the NCSA WWW server and the performance data recorded by the server. We build on this by describing real-time data analysis software that can map WWW server requests to their geographic origin. This is followed by a description of the *Avatar* virtual reality system and its geographic representations of WWW traffic, by a discussion of our experiences, and by discussion of future directions. Finally, we summarize related work and our conclusions.

NCSA WWW Server Architecture

On an average weekday, NCSA's WWW server receives roughly 400,000 requests, each of which is recorded with ancillary data describing the transaction. At current request rates, these log files grow by over 50 megabytes per day. In addition to the standard server request logs, NCSA also records operating system and network performance metrics. Together, the access logs and the server performance metrics permit analysis of server stimuli (access patterns) and server responses.

Via statistical analysis and our virtual reality tools, we have identified server bottlenecks and typical user access patterns [10] [11]. As a context for discussion of our data analysis and visualization experiences, we first describe the architecture of the NCSA WWW server and provide a more

detailed description of the recorded performance data.

Server Architecture

Beginning with the initial release of the NCSA Mosaic WWW browser, NCSA's server site experienced explosive growth in the volume and frequency of document requests. To meet the increasing demand, NCSA adopted a scalable approach to server design [9] capable of satisfying large numbers of requests for small documents. As Figure 1 shows, the scalable server consists of a set of dedicated HP 735 workstations that service WWW requests. Document storage is provided by NCSA's Andrew (AFS) file servers via a 100 megabit/second Fiber Distribution Data Interface (FDDI) ring.

Despite the multiplicity of servers, NCSA advertises a single domain name (*www.ncsa.uiuc.edu*) as its WWW server address. To equitably distribute incoming requests across the component servers, a modified Domain Name Server (DNS) at NCSA distributes the IP address for a different component server in response to each DNS query. These IP addresses are distributed in a round-robin fashion with a recommended time to live (TTL) of 15 minutes. This results in reasonably well-balanced load unless one or more remote systems ignore the recommended TTL and continue to cache the IP address of a single server.

Under this scheme, each server operates independently of the others. As demand grows, new workstations can be added to the server pool without reconfiguring existing servers, and workstation failures need not bring down the server complex.

World Wide Web Performance Data

All the WWW servers execute NCSA's Hypertext Transfer Protocol daemon (httpd). In turn, each copy of this daemon maintains four logs (document accesses, agents, errors, and referers) that are written on the local disk of the associated

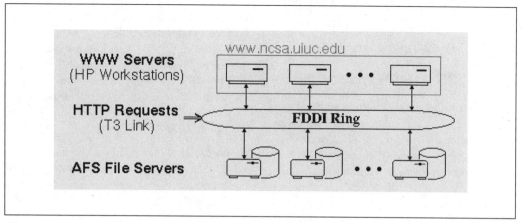

Figure 1   Real-time data collection and analysis architecture

workstation server. We focus on the document access logs, the most interesting because they record the characteristics of each request. However, the other logs provide additional data. For instance, the agent's log records the type of client requesting data (e.g., Netscape, Mosaic). The referer's log records which link a client followed to make a request (i.e., the URL whose content makes a link to the requested URL). We can easily incorporate data (e.g., demographic data) from these and other logs in the future.

Each of the access log entries consists of seven fields [13], including the IP address of the requesting client, the time of the request, the name of the requested document, and the number of bytes sent in response to the request. Despite the apparently limited information, it is possible to compute many performance metrics from the log entries and to glean several insights. For example, the extension of the file requested identifies the type of document requested and, with the number of bytes sent, suffices to compute the distribution of requests by data type and size.

Based on the file extensions, requests can be partitioned into at least six broad categories: text, images, audio, video, scientific data, and other. Within these divisions, we have classified text

files as those with extensions such as *html*, *txt*, *ps*, *doc*, and *tex*. Graphics file extensions include *gif*, *jpg*, and *rgb* as well as other formats. Audio file extensions include *au*, *aiff*, and *aifc*. Video file extensions include *mpeg*, *mov* (QuickTime), and others. The scientific file category includes *hdf*, the NCSA Hierarchical Data Format (HDF). Finally, any remaining requests are placed in the "other" category.

The IP addresses provide additional information. By converting an IP address to a domain name, one can determine the components of the domain name and, often, the location of the requester. In the United States, common domain name extensions include education (*edu*), commercial (*com*), government (*gov*), and other (*us*). Outside the United States, countries typically use the ISO 3166 (1993) two-letter country codes, or network (*net*) extension. By exploiting these two-letter country codes, one can identify the request's country of origin. As we shall see, IP addresses and domain names are the starting point for finer geographic distinctions, including mapping requests to specific latitude and longitude.

Simply put, the httpd log files provide a wealth of information about incoming WWW requests. Aggregating individual requests show larger, evolving patterns that are striking when visualized in real time.

Real-Time WWW Data Analysis

In earlier work, we characterized the NCSA WWW server access patterns statistically [10] [11]. This statistical analysis showed that request heterogeneity was growing rapidly and that data type-specific caching could dramatically reduce server access latencies. We also developed a virtual reality system for interaction and display of these dynamic statistics [18]. Although this approach provided substantial insight into WWW server performance and helped identify scalability limitations inherent in the NCSA server architecture, it did little to aid our understanding of either the origins of WWW requests or their temporal and spatial patterns. This limitation motivated our development of software capable of correlating request patterns with specific geographic locations.

Motivations

One of the major attractions of the WWW to users is that they need not know the physical location of the information they request. Mosaic, Netscape, and other browsers hide Uniform Resource Locators (URLs) behind hypertext links. In consequence, the accesses of a single user may span the globe with only a few simple mouse clicks.

Unlike users of WWW browsers, those who deploy WWW servers have a growing interest in understanding the geographic dispersion of access patterns. As digital cash makes electronic commerce via the WWW practical, providers of products can gain a competitive advantage by mining access patterns, much as large retail organizations currently mine point-of-sale information. For example, understanding which parts of the country (or world) most frequently purchase particular items from an online catalog is a major advantage—given the geographic location of an incoming IP address, one can tailor the WWW

server response by highlighting particular product types [19], and correlation of this data with geographic information systems would permit selected targeting of product information. Finally, commercial Internet service providers could exploit knowledge of user access patterns to add new services in selected geographic regions.

Geographic Location Mapping

To understand the temporal and geographic patterns of WWW server access, we developed a set of heuristics for mapping IP addresses to latitude and longitude. These heuristics rely on the domain names and the InterNIC *whois* database. The *whois* database contains information on domains, hosts, networks, and other Internet administrators. The information usually, though not always, includes a postal address.

To map IP addresses to geographic location, we first determine the domain name. For locations outside the United States, the suffix of the domain name typically is an abbreviation of the country name. For all other cases, we query the *whois* database, retrieving the textual data associated with the IP address. We then search this data for city and country names. If a city or country name is found, we then retrieve the latitude and longitude from a local database of city and country names.

Because querying the *whois* database is expensive, often requiring a second or more to retrieve the desired data, we store the latitudes and longitudes of previously matched IP addresses to avoid repeated and unnecessary *whois* queries. If the *whois* query returns information that does not contain a city or country name, we record the IP address to avoid further, fruitless queries. Offline, many of these failed queries can be identified and corrected in the database.

With our current database (35,000+ entries), about 95 percent of all requests to the NCSA WWW server can be successfully matched to latitude and longitude using only local data, 4.5 percent have undetermined latitudes and longitudes, and the remaining 0.5 percent must be found in the remote *whois* database. As our database continues to expand, the fraction of unresolvable requests continues to decline.

Despite our high success rate, network firewalls and national online services limit the accuracy of the latitudes and longitudes. For instance, an America Online (AOL) user might connect via modem from Irvine, California, and access the NCSA "What's New" page. That person's IP address (*aol.com*) would yield Vienna, Virginia, as its location because that is the site of the AOL headquarters. Similar problems arise with large, geographically disperse corporations that maintain a single Internet point of contact. Fortunately, such cases can be identified by name and can often be parsed by decomposing the domain name (e.g., *intgate.raleigh.ibm.com* is easily identified as an IBM site at Raleigh, North Carolina).

Although the primary use of our position database is to support geographic visualization of WWW request patterns in virtual environments, a WWW browser interface can be found at *http://cello.cs.uiuc.edu/cgi-bin/slamm/ip2ll/*. This interface exploits the Xerox PARC and U.S. Census Tiger map servers to display the location of the IP address on a simple, two-dimensional map.

Real-Time Processing

Our design goal was to convert IP addresses at a rate high enough to process the incoming NCSA WWW requests in real-time. At peak times, NCSA can receive 30–50 accesses per second [8]. Initially, our local database was small and translation to latitude and longitude ran more slowly than real-time due to the large number of *whois* queries needed. As our local database has grown, the processing time has decreased to a point where 24 hours of NCSA WWW access logs can be processed in ninety minutes, and we can now easily process several hundred queries per second.

To integrate the geographic mapping of WWW requests with our existing analysis software and to support real-time data reduction and interaction, we decoupled analysis of the WWW server logs from the virtual reality system. The only medium of data exchange between the virtual environment and the analysis system is the Pablo self-describing data format [2], an extensible data meta-format with embedded data descriptions. This decoupling improves system performance and increases the flexibility to adapt the system to evolving goals.

By separating data visualization from data processing, display software development and processing software development can proceed in isolation. The display software currently supports virtual reality hardware such as head-mounted displays (HMDs) and the CAVE virtual reality theater. With the isolation, new displays—such as a VRML representation—may extend display support to the 2D desktop environment. For the data processing software, the isolation simplifies the integration of analysis extensions and the integration of new analysis mechanisms such as a relational database of access pattern, performance, and demographic data.

As Figure 2 shows, data visualization and data classification execute concurrently on separate platforms. The data analysis software incrementally retrieves the WWW server logs via TCP network sockets, classifies the domains and file types, finds the geographic location of the IP address, and packages the data in the Pablo Self Defining Data Format (SDDF) [15]. The SDDF allows *Avatar* to inter-operate with performance instrumentation and analysis tools. The packaged SDDF records are sent via UDP sockets to the *Avatar* virtual reality software. *Avatar* then renders the data in the NCSA CAVE [7], an unencumbered environment for immersive data analysis. In the following section, we describe the data immersion software in detail.

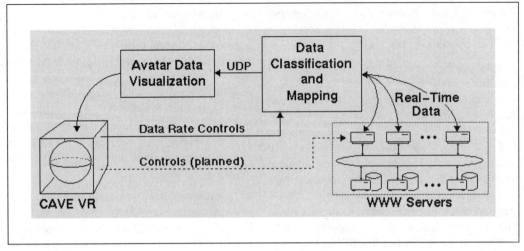

Figure 2   Real-time data collection and analysis architecture

Avatar Virtual Reality System

Avatar is a virtual reality framework, built on the Pablo performance analysis toolkit [15] that supports multiple metaphors to display dynamic data [16] [17]. By separating the metaphor display software from the data processing and interaction components, *Avatar's* software architecture has allowed us to quickly create new display metaphors.

To date, we have developed three different display metaphors for performance data: time tunnels, scattercubes, and geographic displays. Time tunnels permit analysis of time lines and event driven graphs of task interactions (e.g., parallel or distributed tasks).

Scattercubes, a three-dimensional generalization of two-dimensional scatterplots, support analysis of very high-dimensional, non-grid based, time varying data. As an example, Figure 3 shows one three-dimensional projection of the dynamic behavior of the NCSA servers [18]. In the figure, the three axes correspond to one minute sliding window averages of the number of bytes of data transferred to satisfy requests for video clips, bytes transferred for text requests, and number of requests. The colored ribbons represent the tra-

jectories of the NCSA WWW servers in the metric space. Through the translucent walls of the display, one can see three-dimensional projections of other metric triplets. In the virtual environment, one can fly through the projections to explore the data space, interactively rescale the axes, and enable or disable the history ribbons.

To complement the scattercube display of statistical WWW data and to represent the geographic dispersion of WWW requests, we developed a new display metaphor based on projections of the globe of the Earth. This metaphor is described below.

Geographic Data Metaphor

By providing true three-dimensional views, stereopsis and virtual reality allow us to avoid the distortion problems that have plagued cartographers and planar projections. Thus, although a plethora of possible projects can be integrated with the *Avatar* software, to date we have relied on a global perspective for a summary view and a simple flat projection for local views.

As Figure 4 shows, the globe consists of a texture map of the world on a sphere. The surface of the sphere includes the USGS ETOP05 database, and

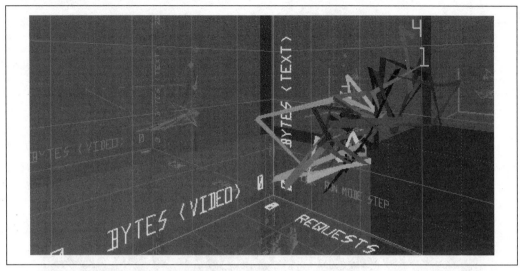

Figure 3   WWW server performance (Scattercube)

political boundaries are drawn from the CIA World Map database.

On the globe or its projection, data can be displayed either as arcs between source and destination or as stacked bars. The former can be used to display point-to-point communication traffic [3], with the thickness, height, and color of the arc representing specific data attributes.

Stacked bars convey information through three mechanisms: position, height, and color bands. For WWW traffic, each bar is placed at the geographic origin of a WWW request. As we shall see in the description of our experiences, the bar heights show location-specific attributes of the requests, typically the number of bytes or the number of requests relative to other sites. The bar color bands represent the distribution of document types, domain classes, servers, or time intervals between successive requests.

Implementation and Controls

Avatar supports both head-mounted displays (HMDs) and the CAVE virtual reality theater; see [17] for details. The CAVE is a room-sized cube of high-resolution, rear-projection displays that allows users to walk about unencumbered by a head-mounted display.

The HMD version of *Avatar* includes speech synthesis and recognition hardware for voice-directed commands, and both the HMD and the CAVE versions use six degree of freedom trackers for head and hand (three-dimensional mouse) position location. Voice commands have the benefit that they can be executed at any time, and they do not consume space in the rendered scene. However, they require the user to be familiar with the command vocabulary.

To support both the CAVE and HMDs, while providing a virtual reality interface familiar to workstation users, the majority of all *Avatar* controls are realized via a familiar menu-based interface for data analysis and display. Later, we discuss the limitations of this approach. We implemented a library of windows that have labels, buttons, pull-down menus, sliders, and scroll boxes. Users select windows and menu items by pointing the three-dimensional mouse; a cursor drawn on the window indicates where the user is pointing, and audio feedback confirms menu selections. These windows can be moved, opened, and closed via

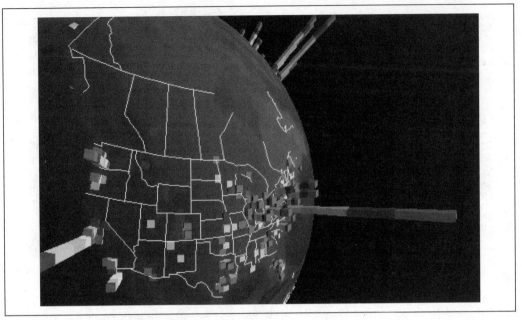

Figure 4   WWW patterns (August 22, 1995 at 6 a.m.)

the mouse and can be accessed from any location that has an unobstructed view of the desired window.

As shown in Figure 5, the menus for interaction with the geographic metaphor's display of WWW data control the scaling and position of the globe. The size of the globe and the height of the bars are controlled by sliders. The globe may be rotated by pressing buttons that increment or decrement the rotation speed, and a pull-down menu provides the option of warping to a pre-defined location (e.g., North America or Europe). Finally, one can select the characteristics of the displayed data.

In addition to providing a control mechanism, the windows convey additional information about currently displayed data. In Figure 5, they show the current time, a color code for the stacked bars, and numerical values associated with the color code. Using the mouse, one can select a particular geographic site and see the city name displayed with the legend.

Self Describing Data Format (SDDF)

Avatar builds on the Pablo (a registered trademark of the Board of Trustees of the University of Illinois) suite of performance instrumentation and analysis tools [15]. A key component of the Pablo toolkit is the Self Describing Data Format (SDDF) for performance data representation. SDDF files and data streams consist of a group of record descriptors and record instances. Much as structure declarations in the C programming language specify templates for storage allocation, SDDF descriptors define the structure for record instances. The data stream following the descriptors consists of a stream of descriptor tag and data record pairs. The descriptor tag identifies the descriptor that defines the juxtaposed data.

By separating the structure of data from its semantics, the Pablo SDDF library permits construction of tools that can extract and process SDDF records and record fields with minimal knowledge of the data's deeper semantics. *Avatar* can process WWW data, parallel system per-

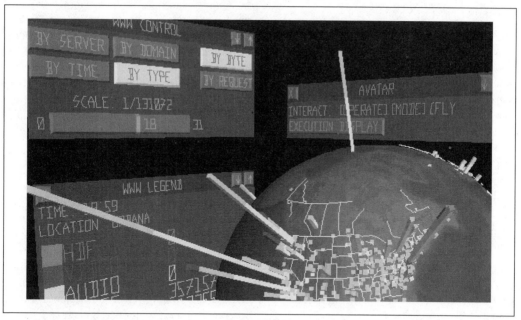

Figure 5   Avatar WWW controls

formance data, and generic statistical data with minimal software changes.

Example 1 shows one of several record descriptors used for the WWW data, and Example 2 shows one possible record instance associated with this descriptor definition. The timestamp is given in minutes past midnight, the server number is represented by an integer identifier, and the request domain types are enumerations. The possible file types are text, image, audio, video, *hdf*, and "other." The domain types differentiate the U.S. sites. The possible domain classes are *edu, com, gov, ca* (Canada), Europe, and "other." Because the *Avatar* software has no embedded knowledge of these classifications, one can add or change the classification without change to the display software. Indeed, the scattercube display of Figure 3 relies on other SDDF records that contain forty metrics on server access patterns, network performance, and processor utilization.

Example 1   SDDF record descriptor

```
SDDFA
#1:
"Mosaic_Metric" {
    int "time";
    int "server";
    int "size";
    int "file_type";
    int "domain_type";
    float "latitude";
    float "longitude";
    char "city"[];
    char "state"[];
    char "country"[];
    char "hostname"[];
};;
```

Example 2   Single SDDF record

```
"Mosaic_Metric" {
    1300, 1, 12000, 2, 3, 40.112, -88.200,
    [6] "URBANA", [2] "IL", [3] "USA",
    [8] "www-pablo.cs.uiuc.edu"
```

Analysis Experiences

Though quantitative analysis of WWW server access patterns is best conducted statistically [10] [14], understanding temporal variations and detecting patterns is simplest with dynamic graphics. The geographic representations of the WWW server logs were much more intuitive and provided the same insights with considerably less effort than the statistical methods. We have found that the most valuable aspect of the geographic display is its real-time nature—one can easily study temporal variations and see the day-by-day effects of evolving document trees, changing network topology and bandwidth, and new service providers.

The most striking attribute of Figures 4 and 6, two snapshots of a single day separated by twelve hours, is the wide variation in request frequency. Sites that act as firewalls, typically large corporations and commercial Internet service providers, appear as the originating point for the largest number of accesses. Smaller sites, typi-

cally universities, government laboratories, and small companies, constitute a large fraction of all accesses, but they are geographically distributed more uniformly. Reflecting the evolution of the Internet, visual comparison of typical days in the life of the NCSA WWW server from 1994 and 1995 shows that government and commercial access is growing much more rapidly than that of educational institutions.

Second, the distribution of the sites follows population lines—in the United States, these are the coastal areas and regions east of the Mississippi River. Because inexpensive Internet access is limited outside universities and larger urban areas, these sites originate the largest number of requests. Access to the NCSA WWW server from outside the United States is common, though far less frequent than from sites in the United States. There is little traffic from South America, Africa, or countries of the former Soviet Union, but Europe and the Pacific Rim have thriving WWW communities.

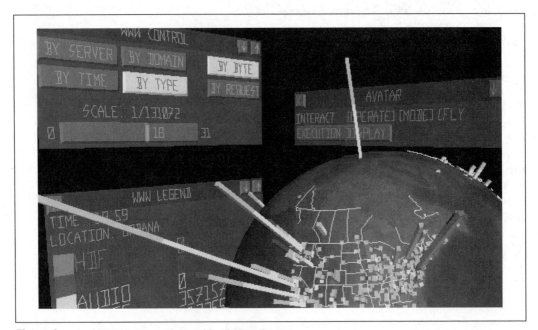

Figure 6   WWW patterns (August 22, 1995 at 6 p.m.)

As one would expect, the periods of heaviest activity and the distribution of requests by Internet domain track the normal business day. In the early morning hours (Eastern Standard Time), Europe is a major source of activity at the NCSA WWW server. As the morning progresses, the east coast of the United States becomes active. Near the middle of the day, the activity in Europe fades, while the United States requests peak. In the evening, the United States west coast has the highest level of activity.

Interestingly, the characteristics of the requested documents also change with time of day. Requests for audio and video files are much more common during the normal business day than during the evening hours. During the evening, text and image files predominate. We conjecture that this reflects both lower bandwidth links to Europe and Asia and low speed modem-based access via commercial service providers. This variation has profound implications for the design of future WWW servers and browsers—based on the capabilities of the system hosting the browser and the bandwidth of the link connecting the server and browser, the server and browser should negotiate the resolution of images to be transmitted and any guarantees for quality of service (e.g., for video).

Finally, using *Avatar* we were able to track failures of the NCSA server load balancing mechanism. Large load imbalances can result when certain locations, particularly firewall sites, cache the IP address of a single workstation server longer than the recommended fifteen minutes and repeatedly fetch data using that address. Statistically, we knew this occurred, but we had never seen its effects. With the geographic display of which servers satisfied requests from particular sites, we could see the effect in real time. Indeed, we found sites that used just one IP address for an hour or longer.

Research Directions

Although our geographic display has allowed us to understand the temporal evolution of WWW requests in ways not easily possible via other mechanisms, many issues remain unresolved, notably display of data from multiple WWW servers, variable resolution clustering of sites, and a richer set of statistics and query mechanisms.

At present, *Avatar* processes and displays data from a single WWW server. However, as the WWW continues to grow and diversify, understanding the global impact of WWW traffic becomes more difficult. Fortunately, a substantial fraction of current WWW servers export some statistics on access patterns. Combining data from these servers would provide a global view of access patterns not presently possible. In addition, in remote demonstrations *Avatar* can easily be transmitted across even heavily loaded network links, making global analysis feasible.

A second limitation of *Avatar* is the inability to adaptively cluster data based on density. High population areas (e.g., New York and Los Angeles) are major sources of WWW traffic. Variable resolution reduction and data display would allow us to zoom closer to selected regions and gain a more detailed perspective than is presently possible with fixed clustering.

Third, related to variable resolution, we would like to make finer mapping distinctions outside the United States. To date we have mapped U.S. sites to the city of origin, Canadian sites to their provincial capitals, and other sites to their country capital. The *whois* queries often return non-U.S. cities, which we cannot place on the globe due to the lack of a world-wide city databases that hold latitude and longitude information. While such databases do exist, they are often not readily available to the public. With the incorporation of new databases we plan to enhance the mapping capabilities of the globe display. We are currently in the process of adding such databases for Canada and the United Kingdom.

Fourth, geographic displays are but one way to study WWW server data. In [18] and the section "Avatar Virtual Reality System," we presented an alternate perspective, based on statistical graphics, that shows the time-evolutionary behavior of server performance metrics (e.g., page faults and context switches) and their correlation with request types. Ideally, these two displays should be coupled, allowing one to correlate multiple display views.

Fifth, a much richer set of statistics is needed. As WWW servers begin to support financial transactions, recording details of the transactions and mining that data for competitive advantage will become increasingly important. In the future, the transactions will include demographic data [19] that will add a rich set of dimensions to the geographic display. WWW users may provide profiles about their interests and other personal information to receive WWW pages tailored to their desires. Commercial sites could use the geographic display of demographics to correlate their cyber-customers with their real-world customers. Displays such as those in Figure 5 provide the metaphor for interactive query and display of data correlations.

Finally, one of the more difficult implementation problems in virtual reality is user interaction. Capitalizing on new hardware technology and the kinematic and haptic senses requires a judicious balance of new and familiar interaction techniques. *Avatar*'s use of windows and menus can obstruct the user's vision of surrounding imagery. Consequently, *Avatar* allows the user to temporarily disable the window and menu interface to provide an unobstructed view of the data display. However, a richer set of interaction techniques are needed, particularly those to specify the more complex queries that are needed to correlate demographic data.

Related Work

Our work draws on a large body of techniques for visualization of network data in the geo-

graphic domain. Notable examples include Becker *et al*'s [3] techniques for displaying communication traffic, and Cox's [6] animation of NSFNet traffic. Both show network connections by drawing links between nodes and show inbound traffic by assigning traffic volume to a range of colors. Our work is rooted in information visualization [8] and statistical graphics [5] with emphasis on interactive exploration.

User WWW access patterns and demographics have been analyzed by a large group of researchers (e.g., Pitkow *et al* [14]). Likewise, there are many studies of server behavior and caching strategies (e.g., Abrams *et al* [1]). The focus of our work is on understanding short-term trends and geographic display.

Conclusion

Given the rapid growth of WWW traffic and the emerging use of the WWW for commercial use, studying access patterns is an important first step in understanding network implications and in designing future generations of WWW servers. However, the large number of requesting sites, the diversity of WWW data types (text, data, images, audio, video), and the multiplicity of server performance metrics (e.g., network packets, context switches, and page faults) make data correlation and understanding extraordinarily difficult.

To support WWW performance analysis, we expanded *Avatar*, a virtual reality system designed to analyze and display real-time performance data, and applied it to the analysis of WWW traffic. We have found that the geographic display metaphor provides new insights into the dynamic of traffic patterns and provides a model for development of a WWW server control center, similar to that in network operations [3]. ∎

References

1. Abrams, M., C.R. Standridge, G. Abdulla, S. Williams, and E.A. Fox, "Caching Proxies: Limitations and Potentials," *Proceedings of the Fourth Interna-*

tional World Wide Web Conference, Boston, O'Reilly & Associates, December 1995.

2. Aydt, R.A., "SDDF: The Pablo Self-Describing Data Format," Tech rep., University of Illinois at Urbana-Champaign, Department of Computer Science, September 1995.

3. Becker. R.A., S.G. Eick, and A.R. Wilks, "Visualizing Network Data," *IEEE Transactions on Visualization and Computer Graphics*, 1, 1, March 1995.

4. Berners-Lee, T., R. Cailliau, A. Luotonen, H Nielsen, and A. Secret, "The World-Wide Web," *Communications of the ACM*, 37, 8, August 1994, pp. 76–82.

5. Cleveland, W.S., and M.E. MiGill, eds. *Dynamic Graphics for Statistics*, Wadsworth & Brooks/Cole, 1988.

6. Cox, D., and R. Patterson, "NSFNet Visualization," 1992, NCSA videotape.

7. Cruz-Neira, C., D.J. Sandin, and T. DeFanti, "Surround-Screen Projection-Based Virtual Reality: The Design and Implementation of the CAVE," *SIGGRAPH '93 Proceedings*, Association for Computing Machinery, August 1993.

8. Fairchild, K.M., S.E. Poltrock, and G.W. Furnas, "Three-Dimensional Graphic Representations of Large Knowledge Bases," *Cognitive Science and Its Applications for Human Computer Interactions*, 1988, pp. 201–233.

9. Katz, E.D., M. Butler, and R. McGrath, "A Scalable HTTP Server: The NCSA Prototype," *Proceedings of the First International WWW Conference*, May 1994.

10. Kwan, T.T., R.E. McGrath, and D.A. Reed, "NCSA's World Wide Web Server: Design and Performance," *IEEE Computer*, November 1995, pp. 68–74.

11. Kwan, T.T., R.E. McGrath, and D.A. Reed, "User Access Patterns to NCSA's World Wide Web Server," Tech rep., University of Illinois at Urbana-Champaign, Department of Computer Science, February 1995. *http://www-pablo.cs.uiuc.edu/Papers/WWW.ps.Z*

12. MERIT Network Information Center Services, 1995. *ftp://ftp.merit.edu/statistics/nfsnet/*

13. NCSA, "NCSA HTTPd Transfer Log," October 1995.

14. Pitkow, J.E., and C.M. Kehoe, "Results from the Third WWW User Survey," Fourth International World Wide Web Conference, Boston, O'Reilly & Associates, December 1995.

15. Reed, D.A., "Experimental Performance Analysis of Parallel Systems: Techniques and Open Problems," *Proceedings of the 7th International Conference on Modeling Techniques and Tools for Computer Performance Evaluation*, May 1994, pp. 25–51.

16. Reed, D.A., C.L. Elford, T. Madhyastha, W.H. Scullin, R.A. Aydt, and E. Smirni, "I/O Performance Analysis, and Performance Data Immersion," *Proceedings of MASCOTS '96*, February 1996.

17. Reed, D.A., K.A. Shields, L.F. Tavera, W.H. Scullin, and C.L. Elford, "Virtual Reality and Parallel Systems Performance Analysis," *IEEE Computer*, November 1995, pp. 57–67.

18. Scullin, W.H., T.T. Kwan, and D.A. Reed, "Real-Time Visualization of World Wide Web Traffic," *Symposium on Visualizing Time-Varying Data*, September 1995.

19. W3C, "Workshop on Internet Survey Methodology and Web Demographics," January 1996. *http://www.w3.org/pub/www/Demographics/960129_Workshop/*

Acknowledgments

We thank Bob McGrath for installing our daemon on NCSA's WWW servers and Bob Olson at Argonne National Laboratories for an initial script on converting IP addresses to latitude and longitude. We also thank Thomas Kwan for his work on the data retrieval system.

About the Authors

Stephen E. Lamm
Department of Computer Science
University of Illinois
Urbana, Illinois 61801
slamm@netscape.com

Stephen Lamm received an M.C.S. from the Department of Computer Science at the Unversity of Illinois, Urbana-Champaign, in 1996, where he worked on the analysis of dynamic performance data from massively parallel systems using virtual reality. Lamm received a B.S. degree (magna cum laude) in Computer Science from the University of California, Irvine in 1994. He currently works for Netscape Communications Corporation in Mountain View, California.

Daniel A. Reed
Department of Computer Science
University of Illinois
1304 West Springfield Ave.
Urbana, Illinois 61801
reed@cs.uicu.edu

Daniel A. Reed is currently professor and head of the Department of Computer Science at the University of Illinois at Urbana-Champaign, where he holds a joint appointment with the National Center for Supercomputing Applications (NCSA). Dr. Reed received his B.S. (summa cum laude) in computer science from the University of Missouri at Rolla in 1978 and his M.S. and Ph.D., also in computer science, from Purdue University in 1980 and 1983, respectively. He was a recipient of the 1987 National Science Foundation Presidential Young Investigator Award. He is the author of research papers on algorithms, architectures, resource management policies, and performance evaluation techniques for high-performance computing. Professor Reed currently serves on the editorial boards of Concurrency Practice and Experience and the International Journal of High Speed Computing. He is an affiliate member of the Center for Research on Parallel Computation and a leader of the national Scalable I/O Initiative.

Will H. Scullin
501 East Middlefield Road
Netscape Communications Corporation
Mountain View, California 94043
scullin@netscape.com

Will H. Scullin received an M.C.S. from the Department of Computer Science at the University of Illinois, Urbana-Champaign, where he studied the uses of virtual reality for the visualization of parallel and distributed systems performance. He received his B.A. (with distinction) in computer science in 1993 from the University of Minnesota at Morris. He is currently employed at Netscape Communications Corporation in Mountain View, California.

UBIQUITOUS ADVERTISING ON THE WWW

MERGING ADVERTISEMENT ON THE BROWSER

Youji Kohda, Susumu Endo

Abstract

We propose a new advertising framework on the WWW. Some popular WWW sites now provide advertising space in their Web pages. However the actual effectiveness of the advertising is questionable. In our advertising framework, an advertising agent is placed between advertisers and users. The agent's business is to deliver advertisements to users who wish to see advertisements on their Web browser. Users will see a variety of advertisements at the sites they visit, even if the sites have no advertisements on the Web servers. This will make the advertising business on the WWW really ubiquitous. **Keywords:** *World Wide Web, advertisement, advertising agent, 1:1 future, Web server, Web browser, Web page, Web site*

1. Introduction

To sell goods or services, advertisement is the first step in making them available to the public. TV and newspapers are representative media that have advertising space for commercial purposes. The operational cost of commercial TV stations and newspaper publishing companies is covered by the advertising revenue. This makes it possible for people to receive TV programs at no charge and to subscribe to newspapers very cheaply.

The World Wide Web is a new way of presenting information to the public via the Internet. Advertising on the World Wide Web has increased rapidly over the last few years. However, the mode of advertising has so far been similar to that used in TV and newspapers in essence.

Service providers on the WWW such as Yahoo! [4], a popular Internet directory service, prepare advertising space in their Web pages and sell this space to advertisers by the hour. The anchors (links to advertiser's Web servers) are placed on the sold small spaces and are displayed to users as small clickable images. When they click one of the anchors, they are then connected to that advertiser's own commercial Web server.

WWW advertising in its current state is better than nothing, but the cost benefit is questionable for the following reasons. First, the host Web server must be very popular on the Internet. If the host is not sufficiently popular, the number of the people seeing advertisements placed on the server will be small. Second, the advertising host server does not usually permit a competitor company's advertisements to be displayed. For instance, Microsoft is most unlikely to advertise IBM products in their Web server.

Therefore, the advertising host server should be very popular on the Internet and, at the same time, unbiased, to earn enough money from the advertising business. Network directory services and virtual shopping/business malls are possible candidates. However, the services offered by such servers are gateway services in essence. Users are normally busy searching for information resources through the gateway services, and there is no reason for them to waste their time reading advertisements. This creates an "advertising vacuum."

We propose a new advertising framework on the World Wide Web. It will fill this "advertising vacuum." An advertising agent is placed between the advertisers and the users. Advertisements fetched from advertisers' Web servers are merged with

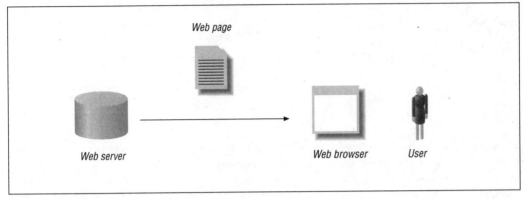

Figure 1   Ordinary WWW usage

Web pages from ordinary Web servers by the agent, and the merged pages are displayed on the users' Web browser. Thus, the users see advertisements on any server around on the Internet. Moreover, the agent has chances to deliver appropriate advertisements that suit each user's taste. This is a move away from the current state of advertising on the WWW and will make the advertising business on the WWW really ubiquitous.

2. A New Framework for Advertising on the WWW

Figure 1 illustrates the ordinary usage of the WWW. This can be compared with Figure 2, which is an overview of our new advertising framework. In Figure 2, the advertising agent company's Web server is new. It has an important role: delivering advertisements to users whenever they access ordinary Web servers.

2.1 Making Contracts with Advertising Agents

First of all, the advertising agent company makes a contract with advertiser companies. (Ordinary users can become advertisers or advertising agents if they are ready to pay for it, but we use the word, *company*, to make the explanation brief.) The agent company is responsible for

delivering advertisements to users. The advertisements are stored on the agent's Web server. Otherwise, they might be kept on the advertiser's Web servers with just the links to them stored in the agent's Web server.

Next, the advertising agent company also negotiates with users, who agree to see advertisements while browsing. This is similar to the subscription procedure for technical magazines, which are full of technical articles and advertisements that target the subscribers of the magazines. The agent company is responsible for delivering the appropriate advertisements to the users. Thus, the contract should at least allow the users to specify what categories of advertisements they wish to see. For example, a user can declare that he or she is interested in new books, new personal computers, and used cars. It would be wonderful if we could determine a user's current and long-term interests with no declaration, but the Web is not quite ripe for that use. Moreover, the contract may request a user's private information, such as sex, age, and home address. If the agent has a user's private information, it can pick up more focused advertisements for each user.

Last, the agent company should offer some clear benefit to attract the users to the business, because people do not positively want to see advertisements. The agent company could pay

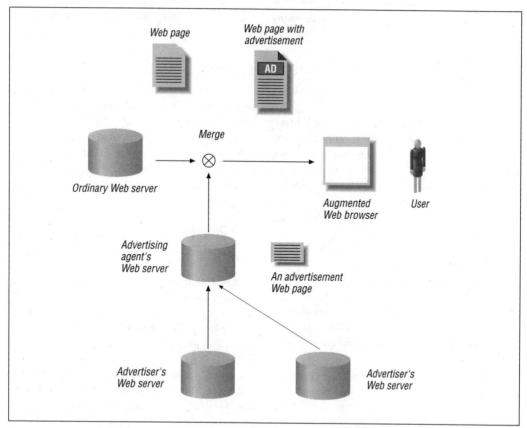

Figure 2   A new advertising framework on the WWW

for all or part of the customers' connection charges.

2.2 Delivering Advertisements to Customers

Users who have made a contract with an advertising agent are given a Web browser by the agent. The Web browser software knows how to receive advertisements from the agent. Technically, the browser merges Web pages fetched from more than one Web server and displays a composite Web page in the window. In Section 3, we will describe the browser mechanism in some detail. The modification to current browsers is very small and reasonable.

When a user clicks an anchor on a page displayed on the browser, the browser contacts the Web server and returns a Web page designated by the anchor. Simultaneously, the browser contacts the advertising agent's Web server. The agent's Web server returns a Web page of one of its advertisements. Then the browser merges those returned Web pages and displays a composite page on the screen.

Note that the agent is aware of the identity of the user and which page the user is about to read on the browser, so the advertising agent can tailor advertisements for *individuals and their current interests*. Thus, it prevents the user from having to see advertisements that are unrelated to their current interests. Unexpected advertisements would irritate users in much the same way as a magazine article that is split with intervening advertisements.

2.3 Assessing Advertising Agents

Advertisements returned from the advertising agent's Web server can have links to other pages that might, for example, be more detailed advertisements or online order forms for the advertised goods or services. When users follow these links, the advertising agent can detect these actions: who, when, to what page. The agent records the actions, and the accumulated record can be used by the agent to show the effectiveness of their services to the advertisers.

2.4 Competition Between Advertising Agents

An advertising agent must have a good strategy in order to beat the competition. The role of an advertising agent company is to offer mutual benefits to advertisers and users. If the users feel there are no benefits from using the services of one advertising agent, they will go to another. Similarly, if advertisers judge from the records that their advertisements have not been delivered to appropriate users, they will also go to another advertising agent.

There are three possible strategies for an advertising agent. First, there is no need to deliver advertisements continuously. It might be more effective and impressive to deliver advertisements at some intervals. Second, other useful information, such as the latest news and latest weather information, might be delivered instead of advertisements at the user's convenience. Third, more "intelligent" advertising is possible. Suppose that a user obtains an online order form for some goods. The advertising agent can detect this event. It then examines the order form to see what goods the user wants and the price offered. Then the advertising agent can create a special offer and deliver it to the user, which tells the user that another company (one of the agent's advertisers) would sell the same goods at a lower price than the company that has the online order form.

2.5 Privacy Issues

On the Internet, privacy is one of the major issues. Advertising agents keep their customer's private information, such as age and home address. Therefore, the contract between advertising agents and the customers should include a privacy clause that prohibits the agents from forwarding private information to advertisers without permission.

3. A Prototype of Ubiquitous Advertising on the WWW

In this section we describe a simple prototype of our new advertising framework.

3.1 Invoking Filter Programs When Opening URLs

We use a sightly augmented Web browser that can merge Web pages from different Web servers. As shown in Figure 3, a special Filter Program menu item has been added to the ordinary browser. Selecting this item, a window is opened, and the names of filter programs can be specified. Filters are programs "which have one input, one output, and perform a useful transformation on data as it passes through." [1] Those filters can be piped in order as illustrated in Figure 4.

The filters are invoked when an anchor is clicked in the browser's window. At invocation, environment information is passed to each filter program as invocation parameters. The environment information includes at least the identity of the user and information about the selected anchor. The contents of a Web page designated by the anchor are input into the pipe of filters, and the output from the pipe is displayed on the browser's window as an HTML document.

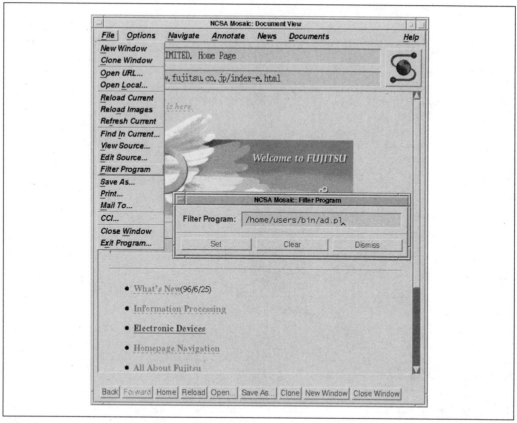

Figure 3   The Filter Program menu item is added

3.2 A Filter Program that Weaves Advertisements

A special filter program is shipped from the advertising agent to a user, once the user has made contract with the agent, and the user puts the filter program in his/her browser. The filter keeps in memory the contact path (URL) to the agent's Web server. When it is invoked, it forwards the invocation parameters passed from the browser to the agent's Web server, and waits for a reply. Then, the agent's Web server returns one of its advertisements or other useful information. The filter merges the reply from the agent's Web server before the input from the pipe, i.e., Web pages from other Web servers.

Figure 5 is an example of a Web page with an advertisement; a new product advertisement and a home page. The strategy on how to weave advertisements in this example is quite easy; the advertisement is inserted before. Note that the advertisement in Figure 5 has an anchor (labeled as "For More Information") in it. When a user clicks this anchor, a more detailed advertisement would be displayed. At the same time, the click action is recorded at the advertising agent. The advertising agent can show a summary of the record whenever the advertisers request it.

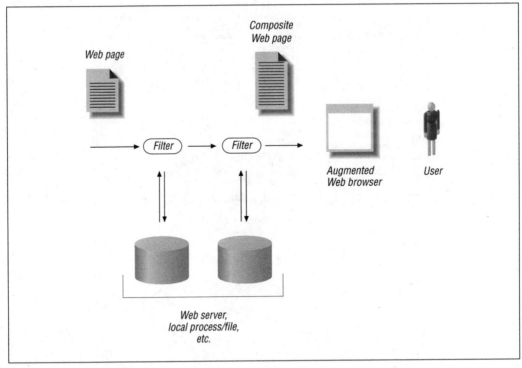

Figure 4   A pipeline of filter programs

3.3 Comments on the Current Implementation

We have already implemented a working prototype of this ubiquitous advertising on the WWW. Figures 3 and 5 are snapshots taken from the computer screen.

We have made a very small improvement to NCSA Mosaic. We have added a new menu item, Filter Program, just after the Edit Source menu item. Edit Source in NCSA Mosaic invokes an editor whose initial content is the HTML document of the currently displayed Web page. When exiting the editor, the edited HTML document is displayed as a new Web page. Filter programs set by the Filter Program menu item do almost the same work without user intervention. For example, if we apply a capitalize filter (though it should remain intact between <A> and </A>), the characters displayed on the browser are all capi-

talized. We believe that this additional feature is simple and powerful, and therefore it is reasonable to add this feature to ordinary browsers as a standard facility. A specially tailored proxy server could realize the same functionality, but authentication of users should be incorporated in the proxy server at the same time to distinguish individuals.

A sample filter program, which inserts advertisements before the original Web contents, has been coded in Perl, which includes access to remote Web servers. This advertisement-insertion needs extra time and might make users irritated, but we believe this performance degradation will soon become smaller.

A sample Web server for advertising agents has been implemented as a set of Perl programs that are invoked through CGI. The programs include a program for advertisement delivery that

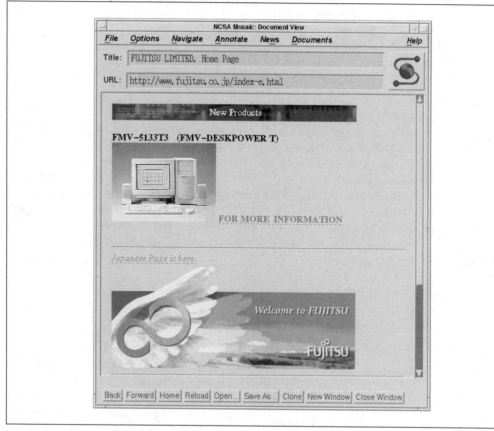

Figure 5　　A Web page with an inserted advertisement

searches an appropriate advertisement and delivers it to the browser, when the advertisement-insertion filter program set in the browser invokes the program via CGI. The call address to the delivery program will be coded in the filter program at the shipping time. The programs also include two programs for contracts, one for agent-to-user, the other for agent-to-advertiser. This means that users and advertisers can make a contract with an advertising agent on the Internet just with their Web browsers.

In this paper, we have proposed and prototyped the ubiquitous advertising on the WWW. However, further research effort (e.g., a test for advertiser/consumer acceptance) is still necessary before putting this idea on the market.

One more comment on privacy issues. You can take off the advertisement-insertion filter program temporarily from your browser anytime you want, when you want to escape from the "supervision" of your advertising agent. This guarantees your freedom of exploration on the Internet, though you might miss some useful and important advertisements.

4. Conclusion

We have proposed a new advertising framework, in which an advertising agent plays a central role. It delivers advertisements to users under contract, and the advertisements are woven into ordinary Web pages on the browser. This differs from the current advertising technology in the WWW; advertisements are woven in the servers that users contact. The PostCast Network is a typical example, which delivers personalized news, weather, and other information, possibly including advertisements, through a special browser [3].

Our proposed framework can be seen as one feasible step toward 1:1 advertising on the WWW [2]. First, the advertisement is merged into an ordinary Web page on the Web browser, instead of on the Web servers. Hence, users could encounter a variety of advertisements on any server in the world. Second, the advertisement delivered is chosen, according to the user and the Web page he or she is about to read. Therefore, it focuses advertisements on the interests of the user. Third, the actions of users in relation to a particular advertisement (i.e., reading its details or buying the goods or services) are recorded by the advertising agent. This record can be used to prove the effectiveness of the advertising agent to the advertisers. ■

References

1. Kernighan, B.W., and P.J. Plauger, *Software Tools*, Reading, Addison-Wesley, 1976.

2. Peppers, D., and M. Rogers, *The 1:1 Future: Building Relationships One Customer at a Time*, New York, Doubleday, 1993. ISBN 0-385-42528-7.

3. PointCast Internet News Network, *http://www.pointcast.com/*

4. Yahoo!: Internet Directory, *http://www.yahoo.com/*

About the Authors

Youji Kohda
Institute for Social Information Science
Fujitsu Laboratories Ltd.
1-9-3 Nakase, Mihama-ku, Chiba-shi, Chiba 261, Japan
kohda@iias.flab.fujitsu.co.jp

Youji Kohda received a B.S. degree in Information Science and an M.E and Dr. Eng. degrees in Information Engineering from the University of Tokyo, Tokyo, Japan, in 1981, 1983, and 1986, respectively. In 1986, he joined Fujitsu Limited, and in 1990 he joined Fujitsu Laboratories Ltd. His research interests include advanced user interface, groupware, and socialware.

Susumu Endo
Institute for Social Information Science
Fujitsu Laboratories Ltd.
1-9-3 Nakase, Mihama-ku, Chiba-shi, Chiba 261, Japan
susumu@iias.flab.fujitsu.co.jp

Susumu Endo received a B.E. degree in Information Engineering and an M.S. degree in Information Science from Tohoku University, Sendai, Japan, in 1992 and 1994, respectively. In 1994, he joined Fujitsu Laboratories Ltd. He has been engaged in research on socialware.

INTERNET
Programming Books from O'Reilly & Associates, Inc.
SUMMER 1996

Internet Programming

HTML: The Definitive Guide

By Chuck Musciano & Bill Kennedy
1st Edition April 1996
410 pages, ISBN 1-56592-175-5

HTML: The Definitive Guide is a complete guide to creating documents on the World Wide Web. To become a true master of HTML, you need to develop your own style. That means knowing not only what's appropriate, but what's effective. This book describes basic syntax and semantics and goes on to show you how to create beautiful, informative Web documents you'll be proud to display.

HTML: The Definitive Guide helps you become fluent in HTML, fully versed in the language's syntax, semantics, and elements of style. It covers the most up-to-date version of the HTML standard, plus all the common extensions, especially Netscape extensions. The authors cover each and every element of the currently accepted version of the language in detail, explaining how each element works and how it interacts with all the other elements. They've also included a style guide that helps you decide how to best use HTML to accomplish a variety of tasks, from simple online documentation to complex marketing and sales presentations.

Designing for the Web: Getting Started in a New Medium

By Jennifer Niederst with Edie Freedman
1st Edition April 1996
180 pages, ISBN 1-56592-165-8

Designing for the Web introduces you to the unique considerations of Web design and gives you the basics you need to hit the ground running. Although geared toward designers, this book covers information and techniques useful to anyone who wants to put graphics online. It explains how to work with HTML documents from a designer's point of view, outlines special problems with presenting information online, and walks through incorporating images into Web pages, with emphasis on resolution and improving efficiency.

You'll find a step-by-step tutorial on putting together a Web page from scratch, pointers on creating graphics that are optimized for the Web, tips on using background images and colors in Web pages, recommendations for reducing download times of images, and instructions for transparency and interlacing to Web graphics. This book also discusses the impact of different browsers and platforms on your design, explains how HTML tags are used for design, and offers guidelines on navigational and orientation aids, as well as on conceptualizing your Web site as a whole.

CGI Programming on the World Wide Web

By Shishir Gundavaram
1st Edition March 1996
450 pages, ISBN 1-56592-168-2

The World Wide Web is more than a place to put up clever documents and pretty pictures. With a little study and practice, you can offer interactive queries and serve instant information from databases, worked up into colorful graphics. That is what the Common Gateway Interface (CGI) offers.

This book offers a comprehensive explanation of CGI and related techniques for people who hold on to the dream of providing their own information servers on the Web. Gundarvaram starts at the beginning, explaining the value of CGI and how it works, then moves swiftly into the subtle details of programming. For most of the examples, the book uses the most common platform (UNIX) and the most popular language (Perl) used for CGI programming today. However, it also introduces the essentials of making CGI work with other platforms and languages.

Programming Perl 5

By Larry Wall, Randal L. Schwartz, et al.
2nd Edition Fall 1996
700 pages (est.), ISBN 1-56592-149-6

Programming Perl, second edition, is the authoritative guide to Perl version 5, the scripting utility that has established itself as the programming tool of choice for the World Wide Web, UNIX system administration, and a vast range of other applications. Version 5 of Perl includes object-oriented programming facilities. The book is coauthored by Larry Wall, the creator of Perl.

Perl is a language for easily manipulating text, files, and processes. It provides a more concise and readable way to do many jobs that were formerly accomplished (with difficulty) by programming with C or one of the shells. Perl is likely to be available wherever you choose to work. And if it isn't, you can get it and install it easily and free of charge.

This heavily revised second edition of *Programming Perl* contains a full explanation of the features in Perl version 5.002. It covers version 5.002 Perl syntax, functions, library modules, references, debugging, and object-oriented programming. Also includes a Perl cookbook.

Learning Perl

By Randal L. Schwartz, Foreword by Larry Wall
1st Edition November 1993
274 pages, ISBN 1-56592-042-2

Learning Perl is ideal for system administrators, programmers, and anyone else wanting a down-to-earth introduction to this useful language. Written by a Perl trainer, its aim is to make a competent, hands-on Perl programmer out of the reader as quickly as possible. The book takes a tutorial approach and includes hundreds of short code examples, along with some lengthy ones. The relatively inexperienced programmer will find *Learning Perl* easily accessible.

Each chapter of the book includes practical programming exercises. Solutions are presented for all exercises.

For a comprehensive and detailed guide to advanced programming with Perl, read O'Reilly's companion book, *Programming Perl*.

Perl 5 Desktop Reference

By Johan Vromans
1st Edition February 1996
39 pages, ISBN 1-56592-187-9

This is the standard quick-reference guide for the Perl programming language. It provides a complete overview of the language, from variables to input and output, from flow control to regular expressions, from functions to document formats—all packed into a convenient, carry-around booklet.

Java Series

Exploring Java

By Pat Niemeyer & Josh Peck
1st Edition May 1996 (est.)
426 pages, ISBN 1-56592-184-4

Exploring Java introduces the basics of Java, the hot new object-oriented programming language for networked applications. The ability to create animated World Wide Web pages has sparked the rush to Java. But what has also made this new language so important is that it's truly portable. The code runs on any machine that provides a Java interpreter, whether Windows 95, Windows NT, the Macintosh, or any flavor of UNIX.

With a practical, hands-on approach characteristic of O'Reilly's Nutshell Handbooks®, *Exploring Java* shows you how to write dynamic Web pages. But that's only the beginning. This book shows you how to quickly get up to speed writing Java applets (programs executed within Web browsers) and other applications, including networking programs, content and protocol handlers, and security managers. *Exploring Java* is the first book in a new Java documentation series from O'Reilly that will keep pace with the rapid Java developments. Covers Java's latest Beta release.

Java Virtual Machine

By Troy Downing & Jon Meyer
1st Edition Fall 1996
300 pages (est.), ISBN 1-56592-194-1,

The Java Virtual Machine is the software implementation of a "CPU" designed to run compiled Java code. Using the Java Virtual Machine (JVM) unleashes the true power of Java—making it possible to develop additional syntaxes for expressing the problems you want to solve and giving you the ultimate control over the performance of your application. This book is a comprehensive programming guide for the Java Virtual Machine. It'll give you a strong overview and reference of the JVM so that you can create your own implementations of the JVM or write your own compilers that create Java object code.

The book is divided into two sections: the first includes information on the semantics and structure of the JVM; the second is a reference of the JVM instructions, or "opcodes." The programming guide includes numerous examples written in Java assembly language. A Java assembler is provided with the book, so the examples can all be compiled and executed. The reference section offers a complete description of the instruction set of the VM, and the class file format including a description of the byte-code verifier.

Java in a Nutshell: A Desktop Quick Reference for Java Programmers

By David Flanagan
1st Edition February 1996
460 pages , ISBN 1-56592-183-6

Java in a Nutshell is a complete quick-reference guide to Java, the hot new programming language from Sun Microsystems. This comprehensive volume contains descriptions of all of the classes in the Java 1.0 API, with a definitive listing of all methods and variables. It also contains an accelerated introduction to Java for C and C++ programmers who want to learn the language fast.

Java in a Nutshell introduces the Java programming language and contains many practical examples that show programmers how to write Java applications and applets. It is also an indispensable quick reference designed to wait faithfully by the side of every Java programmer's keyboard. It puts all the information Java programmers need right at their fingertips.

JavaScript Reference Manual

By David Flanagan
1st Edition Summer 1996
500 pages (est.), ISBN 1-56592-193-3

From the bestselling author of *Java in a Nutshell* comes the definitive reference manual for JavaScript, the HTML extension that allows programs to be embedded in Web pages, making them more active than ever before. In this book, David Flanagan describes how JavaScript really works (and when it doesn't).

The first eight chapters document the core JavaScript language, and the next six describe how JavaScript works on the client-side to interact with the Web browser and with the Web page. Following this detailed explanation of JavaScript features is a complete reference section that documents every object, property, method, event handler, function, and constructor used by client-side JavaScript.

This book documents the version of JavaScript shipped with Navigator 2.0, 2.0.1, and 2.0.2, and also the much-changed version of JavaScript shipped with beta versions of Navigator 3.0. The 3.0 information is current as of the 3.0b4 release. Lists known bugs and documents commonly encountered bugs on reference pages of JavaScript objects.

Internet Security

PGP: Pretty Good Privacy

By Simson Garfinkel
1st Edition December 1994
430 pages, ISBN 1-56592-098-8

PGP is a freely available encryption program that protects the privacy of files and electronic mail. It uses powerful public key cryptography and works on virtually every platform. This book is both a readable technical user's guide and a fascinating behind-the-scenes look at cryptography and privacy. It describes how to use PGP and provides background on cryptography, PGP's history, battles over public key cryptography patents and U.S. government export restrictions, and public debates about privacy and free speech.

"I even learned a few things about PGP from Simson's informative book."—Phil Zimmermann, Author of PGP

"Since the release of PGP 2.0 from Europe in the fall of 1992, PGP's popularity and usage has grown to make it the de-facto standard for email encyrption. Simson's book is an excellent overview of PGP and the history of cryptography in general. It should prove a useful addition to the resource library for any computer user, from the UNIX wizard to the PC novice."
—Derek Atkins, PGP Development Team, MIT

Building Internet Firewalls

By D. Brent Chapman & Elizabeth D. Zwicky
1st Edition September 1995
544 pages, ISBN 1-56592-124-0

Everyone is jumping on the Internet bandwagon, despite the fact that the security risks associated with connecting to the Net have never been greater. This book is a practical guide to building firewalls on the Internet. It describes a variety of firewall approaches and architectures and discusses how you can build packet filtering and proxying solutions at your site. It also contains a full discussion of how to configure Internet services (e.g., FTP, SMTP, Telnet) to work with a firewall, as well as a complete list of resources, including the location of many publicly available firewall construction tools.

Practical UNIX &Internet Security

By Simson Garfinkel & Gene Spafford
2nd Edition April 1996
1004 pages (est.), ISBN 1-56592-148-8

This second edition of the classic *Practical UNIX Security* is a complete rewrite of the original book. It's packed with twice the pages and offers even more practical information for UNIX users and administrators. In it you'll find coverage of features of many types of UNIX systems, including SunOS, Solaris, BSDI, AIX, HP-UX, Digital UNIX, Linux, and others. Contents include UNIX and security basics, system administrator tasks, network security, and appendices containing checklists and helpful summaries.

Computer Crime

By David Icove, Karl Seger & William VonStorch
1st Edition August 1995
464 pages, ISBN 1-56592-086-4

Terrorist attacks on computer centers, electronic fraud on international funds transfer networks, viruses and worms in our software, corporate espionage on business networks, and crackers breaking into systems on the Internet...Computer criminals are becoming ever more technically sophisticated, and it's an increasing challenge to keep up with their methods.

Computer Crime: A Crimefighter's Handbook is for anyone who needs to know what today's computer crimes look like, how to prevent them, and how to detect, investigate, and prosecute them if they do occur. It contains basic computer security information as well as guidelines for investigators, law enforcement, and computer system managers and administrators. The book also contains a compendium of computer-related U.S. federal statutes, the statutes of individual states, representative international laws, a resource summary, detailed papers on computer crime, and a sample search warrant for a computer crime.

Internet Administration

DNS and BIND

By Paul Albitz & Cricket Liu
1st Edition October 1992
418 pages, ISBN 1-56592-010-4

DNS and BIND contains all you need to know about the Internet's Domain Name System (DNS) and the Berkeley Internet Name Domain (BIND), its UNIX implementation. The Domain Name System is the Internet's "phone book"; it's a database that tracks important information (in particular, names and addresses) for every computer on the Internet. If you're a system administrator, this book will show you how to set up and maintain the DNS software on your network.

sendmail

By Bryan Costales, with Eric Allman & Neil Rickert
1st Edition November 1993
830 pages, ISBN 1-56592-056-2

This Nutshell Handbook® is far and away the most comprehensive book ever written on sendmail, the program that acts like a traffic cop in routing and delivering mail on UNIX-based networks. Although sendmail is used on almost every UNIX system, it's one of the last great uncharted territories—and most difficult utilities to learn—in UNIX system administration. This book provides a complete sendmail tutorial, plus extensive reference material on every aspect of the program. It covers IDA sendmail, the latest version (V8) from Berkeley, and the standard versions available on most systems.

Managing Internet Information Services

By Cricket Liu, Jerry Peek, Russ Jones, Bryan Buus & Adrian Nye
1st Edition December 1994
668 pages, ISBN 1-56592-062-7

This comprehensive guide describes how to set up information services and make them available over the Internet. It discusses why a company would want to offer Internet services, provides complete coverage of all popular services, and tells how to select which ones to provide. Most of the book describes how to set up Gopher, World Wide Web, FTP, and WAIS servers and email services.

Networking Personal Computers with TCP/IP

By Craig Hunt
1st Edition July 1995
408 pages, ISBN 1-56592-123-2

This book offers practical information as well as detailed instructions for attaching PCs to a TCP/IP network and its UNIX servers. It discusses the challenges you'll face and offers general advice on how to deal with them, provides basic TCP/IP configuration information for some of the popular PC operating systems, covers advanced configuration topics and configuration of specific applications such as email, and includes a chapter on NetWare, the most popular PC LAN system software.

TCP/IP Network Administration

By Craig Hunt
1st Edition August 1992
502 pages, ISBN 0-937175-82-X

A complete guide to setting up and running a TCP/IP network for practicing system administrators. *TCP/IP Network Administration* covers setting up your network, configuring important network applications including sendmail, and issues in troubleshooting and security. It covers both BSD and System V TCP/IP implementations.

Getting Connected: The Internet at 56K and Up

By Kevin Dowd
1st Edition June 1996
424 pages, ISBN 1-56592-154-2

A complete guide for businesses, schools, and other organizations who want to connect their computers to the Internet. This book covers everything you need to know to make informed decisions, from helping you figure out which services you really need to providing down-to-earth explanations of telecommunication options, such as frame relay, ISDN, and leased lines. Once you're online, it shows you how to set up basic Internet services, such as a World Wide Web server. Tackles issues for PC, Macintosh, and UNIX platforms.

Stay in touch with O'REILLY™

Visit Our Award-Winning World Wide Web Site

http://www.ora.com

VOTED
> "Top 100 Sites on the Web" —*PC Magazine*
> "Top 5% Web sites" —*Point Communications*
> "3-Star site" —*The McKinley Group*

*O*ur Web site contains a library of comprehensive product information (including book excerpts and tables of contents), downloadable software, background articles, interviews with technology leaders, links to relevant sites, book cover art, and more. File us in your Bookmarks or Hotlist!

Join Our Two Email Mailing Lists

LIST #1   **NEW PRODUCT RELEASES:** To receive automatic email with brief descriptions of all new O'Reilly products as they are released, send email to: **listproc@online.ora.com** and put the following information in the first line of your message (NOT in the *Subject:* field, which is ignored):
`subscribe ora-news "Your Name"`
`of "Your Organization"`
(for example: `subscribe ora-news`
`Kris Webber of Fine Enterprises`)

LIST #2   **O'REILLY EVENTS:** If you'd also like us to send information about trade show events, special promotions, and other O'Reilly events, send email to: **listproc@online.ora.com** and put the following information in the first line of your message (NOT in the *Subject:* field, which is ignored): `subscribe ora-events` `"Your Name" of "Your Organization"`

Visit Our Gopher Site

- Connect your Gopher to **gopher.ora.com**, or
- Point your Web browser to **gopher://gopher.ora.com/**, or
- telnet to **gopher.ora.com** (login: **gopher**)

Get Example Files from Our Books Via FTP

There are two ways to access an archive of example files from our books:

REGULAR FTP — ftp to: **ftp.ora.com** (login: **anonymous**—use your email address as the password) or point your Web browser to: **ftp://ftp.ora.com/**

FTPMAIL — Send an email message to: **ftpmail@online.ora.com** (write "help" in the message body)

Contact Us Via Email

order@ora.com — To place a book or software order online. Good for North American and international customers.

subscriptions@ora.com — To place an order for any of our newsletters or periodicals.

software@ora.com — For general questions and product information about our software.
- Check out O'Reilly Software Online at **http://software.ora.com** for software and technical support information.
- Registered O'Reilly software users send your questions to **website-support@ora.com**

books@ora.com — General questions about any of our books.

cs@ora.com — For answers to problems regarding your order or our product.

booktech@ora.com — For book content technical questions or corrections.

proposals@ora.com — To submit new book or software proposals to our editors and product managers.

international@ora.com — For information about our international distributors or translation queries
- For a list of our distributors outside of North America check out: http://www.ora.com/www/order/country.html

O'Reilly & Associates, Inc.

101 Morris Street, Sebastopol, CA 95472 USA
TEL 707-829-0515 or 800-998-9938 (6 A.M. to 5 P.M. PST)
FAX 707-829-0104

O'REILLY™
Listing of Titles

INTERNET PROGRAMMING

CGI Programming on the World Wide Web
Designing for the Web
Exploring Java
HTML: The Definitive Guide
HTTP Programming with Perl
Learning Perl
Java Reference Manual
JavaScript Reference Manual
Java Virtual Machine
Programming Perl, 2nd. ed.
 (Fall '96 est.)
Webmaster in a Nutshell
The World Wide Web Journal

USING THE INTERNET

Smileys
The Whole Internet User's Guide
 and Catalog
The Whole Internet for Windows 95
What You Need to Know:
 Using Email Effectively
What You Need to Know: Marketing
 on the Internet (Summer 96)
What You Need to Know: Bandits on the
 Information Superhighway

JAVA SERIES

Exploring Java
Java in a Nutshell
Java Language Reference
 (Summer '96 est.)
JavaScript Reference Manual
 (Summer '96 est.)
Java Virtual Machine

WINDOWS

Inside the Windows Registry

SOFTWARE

WebSite™ 1.1
WebSite Professional™
WebBoard™
Poly Form™

SYSTEM ADMINISTRATION

Building Internet Firewalls
Computer Crime:
 A Crimefighter's Handbook
Computer Security Basics
DNS and BIND
Essential System Administration,
 2nd ed.
Getting connected:
 The Internet at 56K and up
Linux Network Administrator's Guide
Managing Internet Information Services
Managing Netnews (Fall '96)
Managing NFS and NIS
Networking Personal Computers
 with TCP/IP
Practical UNIX & Internet Security
PGP: Pretty Good Privacy
sendmail
System Performance Tuning
TCP/IP Network Administration
termcap & terminfo
Using & Managing UUCP (Summer '96)
Volume 8 : X Window System
 Administrator's Guide

UNIX

Exploring Expect
Learning GNU Emacs, 2nd Edition
 (Summer '96)
Learning the bash Shell
Learning the Korn Shell
Learning the UNIX Operating System
Learning the vi Editor
Linux in a Nutshell (Summer '96)
Making TeX Work
Multimedia on Linux (Fall '96)
Running Linux, 2nd Edition
 (Summer '96)
Running Linux Companion CD-ROM,
 2nd Edition (Summer '96)
SCO UNIX in a Nutshell
sed & awk
Unix in a Nutshell: System V Edition
UNIX Power Tools
UNIX Systems Programming
 (Summer '96)
Using csh and tsch
What You Need to Know:
 When You Can't Find your
 System Administrator

PROGRAMMING

Applying RCS and SCCS
C++: The Core Language
Checking C Programs with lint
DCE Security Programming
Distributing Applications Across
 DCE and Windows NT
Encyclopedia of Graphics File
 Formats, 2nd ed.
Guide to Writing DCE Applications
lex & yacc
Managing Projects with make
ORACLE Performance Tuning
ORACLE PL/SQL Programming
Porting UNIX Software
POSIX Programmer's Guide
POSIX.4: Programming for
 the Real World
Power Programming with RPC
Practical C Programming
Practical C++ Programming
Programming Python (Fall '96)
Programming with curses
Programming with GNU Software
 (Summer '96 est.)
Programming with Pthreads
 (Fall '96 est.)
Software Portability with imake
Understanding DCE
Understanding Japanese Information
 Processing
UNIX Systems Programming for SVR4

BERKELEY 4.4 SOFTWARE DISTRIBUTION

4.4BSD System Manager's Manual
4.4BSD User's Reference Manual
4.4BSD User's Supplementary Docs.
4.4BSD Programmer's Reference Man.
4.4BSD Programmer's Supp. Docs.

X PROGRAMMING
THE X WINDOW SYSTEM

Volume 0: X Protocol Reference Manual
Volume 1: Xlib Programming Manual
Volume 2: Xlib Reference Manual
Volume. 3M: X Window System
 User's Guide, Motif Ed.
Volume. 4: X Toolkit Intrinsics
 Programming Manual
Volume 4M: X Toolkit Intrinsics
 Programming Manual, Motif Ed.
Volume 5: X Toolkit Intrinsics
 Reference Manual
Volume 6A: Motif Programming Man.
Volume 6B: Motif Reference Manual
Volume 6C: Motif Tools
Volume 8 : X Window System
 Administrator's Guide
Programmer's Supplement for Release 6
X User Tools (with CD-ROM)
The X Window System in a Nutshell

HEALTH, CAREER & BUSINESS

Building a Successful Software Business
The Computer User's Survival Guide
Dictionary of Computer Terms
The Future Does Not Compute
Love Your Job!
Publishing with CD-Rom (Summer '96)

TRAVEL

Travelers' Tales: Brazil (Summer '96 est.)
Travelers' Tales: Food (Summer '96)
Travelers' Tales France
Travelers' Tales Hong Kong
Travelers' Tales India
Travelers' Tales Mexico
Travelers' Tales: San Francisco
Travelers' Tales Spain
Travelers' Tales Thailand
Travelers' Tales: A Woman's World

SONGLINE GUIDES

NetLearning
Political Activism Online (Fall '96)

TO ORDER: **800-889-8969** (CREDIT CARD ORDERS ONLY); **order@ora.com**; http://www.ora.com
OUR PRODUCTS ARE AVAILABLE AT A BOOKSTORE OR SOFTWARE STORE NEAR YOU.

International Distributors

Customers outside North America can now order O'Reilly & Associates books through the following distributors. They offer our international customers faster order processing, more bookstores, increased representation at tradeshows worldwide, and the high-quality, responsive service our customers have come to expect.

EUROPE, MIDDLE EAST, AND NORTHERN AFRICA
(except Germany, Switzerland, and Austria)

INQUIRIES
International Thomson Publishing Europe
Berkshire House
168-173 High Holborn
London WC1V 7AA, United Kingdom
Telephone: 44-171-497-1422
Fax: 44-171-497-1426
Email: itpint@itps.co.uk

ORDERS
International Thomson Publishing
Services, Ltd.
Cheriton House, North Way
Andover, Hampshire SP10 5BE,
United Kingdom
Telephone: 44-264-342-832 (UK orders)
Telephone: 44-264-342-806 (outside UK)
Fax: 44-264-364418 (UK orders)
Fax: 44-264-342761 (outside UK)

GERMANY, SWITZERLAND, AND AUSTRIA

International Thomson Publishing GmbH
O'Reilly-International Thomson Verlag
Königswinterer Straße 418
53227 Bonn, Germany
Telephone: 49-228-97024 0
Fax: 49-228-441342
Email: anfragen@arade.ora.de

ASIA *(except Japan)*

INQUIRIES
International Thomson Publishing Asia
Block 211 Henderson Road
#08-03 Henderson Industrial Park
Singapore 159552
Telephone: 65-272-6496
Fax: 65-272-6498

ORDERS
Telephone: 65-268-7867
Fax: 65-268-6727

JAPAN

O'Reilly Japan, Inc.
Kiyoshige Building 2F
12-Banchi, Sanei-cho
Shinjuku-Ku
Tokyo 160 Japan
Telephone: 8-3-3356-55227
Fax: 81-3-3356-5261
Email: kenj@ora.com

AUSTRALIA

WoodsLane Pty. Ltd.
7/5 Vuko Place, Warriewood NSW 2102
P.O. Box 935, Mona Vale NSW 2103
Australia
Telephone: 61-2-9970-5111
Fax: 61-2-9970-5002
Email: woods@tmx.mhs.oz.au

NEW ZEALAND

WoodsLane New Zealand Ltd.
21 Cooks Street (P.O. Box 575)
Wanganui, New Zealand
Telephone: 64-6-347-6543
Fax: 64-6-345-4840
Email: woods@tmx.mhs.oz.au

THE AMERICAS

O'Reilly & Associates, Inc.
101 Morris Street
Sebastopol, CA 95472 U.S.A.
Telephone: 707-829-0515
Telephone: 800-998-9938 (U.S. & Canada)
Fax: 707-829-0104
Email: order@ora.com

SOUTHERN AFRICA

International Thomson Publishing Southern Africa
Building 18, Constantia Park
240 Old Pretoria Road
P.O. Box 2459
Halfway House, 1685 South Africa
Telephone: 27-11-805-4819
Fax: 27-11-805-3648

O'REILLY™